RISE

RISE

Life Lessons in Speaking Out,
Standing Tall & Leading the Way

Gina Miller

Written with Elizabeth Day

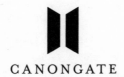

CANONGATE

First published in Great Britain in 2018 by Canongate Books Ltd,
14 High Street, Edinburgh EH1 1TE

canongate.co.uk

1

British Library Cataloguing-in-Publication Data
A catalogue record for this book is available on
request from the British Library

ISBN 978 1 78689 290 4
Export ISBN 978 1 78689 292 8

Typeset in Sabon by Biblichor Ltd, Edinburgh

Printed and bound in Great Britain by Clays Ltd, Elcograf S.p.A.

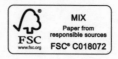

'You may write me down in history
With your bitter, twisted lies,
You may trod me in the very dirt
But still, like dust, I'll rise.'

– Maya Angelou, 'Still I Rise'

Contents

Prologue

Before I'd even started this book, there was a petition against it. After it emerged in the press that I was writing a memoir, a man felt aggrieved enough to take to the internet to demand that the publisher cancel my contract. His reasoning was, 'She has had quite enough publicity already, and doesn't deserve to profit from causing our country such deliberate harm!' He ended his plea for support with the rallying cry (borrowed from the *Express*), 'Who voted for Gina Miller? Nobody!'

At the time of writing, the petition on Change.org had garnered more than 3,000 signatures.

If I hadn't already realised I was a divisive figure, this made it crystal clear. There aren't many memoirs which have prompted petitions against their very existence before they were published, let alone written. I suppose I could see it as a badge of honour. Besides, I've become used to people I've never met forming strong and sometimes highly critical opinions of me.

It does strike me as bizarre that these opinions are formed solely because I stood up for something I thought was right – for asking a perfectly legitimate question about our democracy and possible political abuse of power.

The bad news for the author of the petition is that I don't have a history of backing down. Quite the opposite: I firmly believe that if you see things going wrong it's important to raise your voice, even when others seek to drown it out. In fact, it's *especially* important on those occasions. So, with all due respect to the petitioner and his fellow signatories, I have written my story.

Introduction

Over the past two years I've been the target of extreme bullying and racist abuse. Ever since I took the UK government to court for attempting to force through Article 50, the mechanism for starting Brexit, which would have led to the nation leaving the European Union (EU) without Parliamentary consent, I live in fear of attacks; I receive anonymous death threats almost every day. Strangers have informed me graphically that they want to gang-rape me and slit the throats of my children, and how the colour of my skin means I'm nothing more than an ape, a whore, a piece of shit that deserves to be trodden into the gutter.

I have had to install various security measures around my family home. I rarely go out to social events, and when I do there is always the thought process of 'Who will be there?', 'How safe will I be?', 'Do they have enough security, or do I need to arrange my own?' I am not deemed a 'public figure', so the police cannot provide enough security for high-risk events. I'm scared of dying and leaving my beloved three children without their mother. In my darkest moments, that terror keeps me awake at night.

At every juncture, the bullies hoped to undermine my integrity and my values. The media called me a 'shameless self-publicist' and drew attention to the fact that I was 'foreign-born' (I was actually born in the British Commonwealth and have lived in the UK since the age of eleven). There was, in every grubby little sentence, the implicit message that I had no right to raise my head above the parapet. When I did so, I was swiftly dubbed a traitor.

At the height of it, I received repeated threats that told me I would be 'the next Jo Cox', the Labour MP slaughtered in broad daylight by an unhinged man, who later proclaimed at his first court appearance, 'Death to traitors, freedom for Britain'. That was not me being a shameless self-publicist. That was real.

A lot of people questioned why I wanted to pursue the case in such a poisonous climate. Why would I want to tackle this when it was causing me so much aggravation, when it was putting my family in danger?

To this my answer has always been: what was the alternative? Let the bullies and the haters win? Not follow my conscience and my heart? Let someone else fight my battles? Drop the baton when life passed it to me because I was too worried about myself? I am simply not that person.

Whenever I have stumbled and fallen, I have never blamed anyone else but picked myself up and found a way to survive, happy in the knowledge that it is my choice to do what I do and how I live my life. I did this when I was sent to boarding school in England as a child, even though I'd never stayed away from home; I did it when the other girls teased me for looking and sounding different, and being too geeky.

I did it when I gave birth to a child with special needs at the age of twenty-three.

I did it when I left my damaging second marriage.

I did it when I took on rip-offs in the financial services sector.

And, yes, I did it when, in the aftermath of the Referendum results, I feared the government was pursuing a back-door Brexit, at any cost, and without putting it through the necessary democratic Parliamentary process.

I did it time and again, and will continue to do so.

It wasn't an easy decision. It cost me money, energy and precious time I could have been spending with my family. It made me, in the eyes of some, a national hate figure.

Examining why this has happened – why the state of our public discourse has become so toxic – is partly what motivated me to write this book. I also wanted to share my personal back story of how I got to this place at this time, in the hope that it might help other people to see that there is a way through whatever difficulties they are experiencing.

In an increasingly divided society, our only hope for progress is to seek to understand each other, to find the common ground rather than that which sets us apart. I hope that this book will help you understand me better, even if you are one of the signatories to that petition – perhaps especially if you *are* one of them. Help people to be empathetic, not apathetic.

Let's be honest: there are a lot of people out there who don't like women like me. They don't like the fact that I challenge power or position where I see it being abused. They don't like that I use my voice to defend values I hold dear – inherently British values of fair play, tolerance, justice, civility and the rule of law. They can't understand why I don't simply put up and shut up and accept that oft-quoted 'will of the British people'.

In the context of Brexit, what matters more than the 52 per cent of the 72 per cent that turned out to vote in the 2016 EU Referendum is the future for all citizens. That means not ignoring or bullying the 48 per cent who voted to remain, as this was also an expression of the will of the British people, or indeed those who did not vote on this occasion: everyone is equally entitled to have their say in the shaping of the future of their country. I accept that the majority voted to leave the EU, of course I do. But it's *how* we leave, what leave really means, the detail, the reality and the pros and cons that we need to understand.

The irresponsibility of politicians for holding such a binary Referendum should plague their consciences for years to come. Having been on the Referendum debate trail up and down the country alongside those arguing for Leave against my stance of 'Remain and Reform', I was 100 per cent certain that this was a huge political miscalculation, that neither side had considered leaving as the outcome, that it would not be win/win, but lose/lose for all involved.

On the Friday morning after the vote, 24th June 2016, Prime Minister David Cameron stepped down. He said: 'I will do everything I can as prime minister to steady the ship over the coming weeks and months, but I don't think it would be right for me to try to be the captain that steers our country to its next destination.'

Like a rat jumping off a sinking ship, he slunk away to write his memoirs.

Every morning over the next few weeks we awoke to British political chaos, with the Conservatives trying to find a new leader and Labour leader Jeremy Corbyn facing calls to resign. Boris Johnson then ruled out running for leader after being stabbed in the back by his Brexit pal Michael Gove, who then decided to stand himself. So began the descent of British politics into farce.

When Theresa May won the Tory leadership contest, I learned the government was planning to trigger Article 50 without the consent of Parliament, using an ancient Royal Prerogative. This surely was the last straw in the madness of those few weeks. But instead of outrage at the mere suggestion that Theresa May could put herself above the law in this manner, there was silence. In that void I became the lead claimant in a successful legal challenge that would confirm Parliament's sovereignty.

My case was not whether Brexit was right or wrong. My point was that the rule of law had to be properly observed. Parliament is sovereign. You could not have a government rolling back our constitution and behaving in an authoritarian manner. I could not keep silent over something I passionately believe in, even if the consequences appeared frightening. I told myself that those with the loudest voices are not necessarily those with the wisest heads. Surely if I spoke up, others would join the chorus, and emotion would abate in the face of reason and common sense? I could not have been more wrong.

Leaving the EU without a Parliamentary vote would have been profoundly unconstitutional. In truth, I was seeking to defend our democratic process – which is ironic, given that I'm so often accused of being anti-democratic.

My legal challenge was not funded by shadowy, as-yet-never-identified 'paymasters' – the implications being these alleged paymasters were powerful men operating as my puppet masters and, as a mere woman – let alone a woman of colour – that I couldn't possibly have the brains or money to be leading such a charge.

Rest assured: I know my own mind, and I don't need other people's permission – or money – to stand up. Yet, no matter how much I can convince myself that I'm standing up for what I believe is right, I know there will always be people who close their ears and their minds to what I have to say. These individuals will be angered by whatever I do or say.

*

I have become the person I am today because of both the successes and failures in my life. There have been challenges along the way, but these challenges taught me more about what it is to be strong than any amount of triumph or happiness. They also taught me how important it is to fight for what you believe in, for the kind of world you want to live in. If you don't – if you allow your voice to be silenced by those who don't agree with you – you are in danger of living the life other people want you to live, rather than your own. I've always believed in refusing to be cowed by those who shout over me, who want me to simply go away, who think that just by dragging me through the mud they will break me.

If you fail to make your own voice count, it will be drowned out by those who shout the loudest. They will be the ones to shape what happens next, and you might not like what the future becomes. You might not be welcome there. You might find it is a place where ignorance, fear and loathing flourishes, where you are marginalised and undermined at every turn because your face doesn't fit. And if that thought scares you, those are precisely the times to act. Those are the times to rise.

And you will not be alone. Many people will be with you, even if they cannot vocalise that support. You know in your heart they are with you.

I hope this book acts as a rallying call to anyone who might be worried about speaking up and standing tall in the face of oppression. You need to stay true to your own conviction, your own self-belief and your own truth. Instead of retreating, we must take an even more strident step forward. Because if you run away when things are at their least stable, who knows what you'll find when you come back? If you put your head in the sand, what will be there when you re-emerge? Who will have fixed it for you? No one. That is why we've got to roll up our sleeves and build on values we're proud of. Together, we can be stronger, we can be compassionate, we can right wrongs.

This is only the beginning. The wounds opened up by Brexit have been festering for years and will not be easy to heal. At the time of writing, there is no legally binding deal on the table for our exit from Europe. We are being pitched into uncertainty and it feels as if there is a lockdown on public discussion. Fear has taken hold: fear of backlash, fear of abuse, fear of what will happen to our families, friends, businesses . . . People are feeling lost. We must get to a different place. Where we are now, and where we appear to be heading, is too destructive, too painful and too heartbreaking.

I wanted to write this book so that my children could live in the Britain that we all love: the Britain that is tolerant, inclusive and cherishes free speech. All of that could be in danger. I liken Brexit to the adage of Pandora's box: the box contained the evils of the world, but at the bottom of the box there was a butterfly of hope. But how do we get to hope? We get to it by talking, by exposing, by having a sense of community, by shaming the abusers and the bullies; by calling out and shaming people who do bad things.

This book is not a manifesto, nor is it a dry political history; rather it's a thematic memoir, which I hope shows how any individual, from whatever background, can stand tall, speak up and win in the face of unbelievable odds.

Lots of women I meet say it's difficult to find their voice: they don't complain; they don't speak out when somebody says something offensive or they think they're being discriminated against. I believe this is partly because sexism today is far more nuanced than it used to be. But it's also because women have been put down or kept in their place for centuries. They are fearful of being seen as weak, complaining too much, being a nuisance. Fearful of what might come next.

This is a book about how I found *my* voice. It's a book about the lessons I've learned and the changes I've made. It's a book about empowerment in adversity and strength in the face of battle. It's for *anyone* who wants to tell their own stories, to forge their own paths: it's for people who believe in doing what's right, while constantly questioning themselves; it's especially for all women who balance families and careers, relationships and marriages, friendships and fallings-out, and those who need to let go of the past to live a more fulfilled future.

It's for all those who want to rise.
Because *everyone* can make a difference.
Every single person can speak up.
Every one of us can rise.

1

How on Earth Did I Get Here?

On the morning of 13th October 2016, I was picked up by a taxi. From the outside it looked like any normal London cab: glossy black paint, hooded headlights and a winking orange sign. But appearances can be deceptive.

The driver was trained in high-speed manoeuvres and knew the shortcut routes of London like the back of his hand. The door was opened by Michael, the six-foot-five owner of a private security company I had been recommended. His clients ranged from Hollywood stars to singers and CEOs. His career in the armed forces and his relaxed but alert air filled me with confidence.

'Morning!' Michael said cheerily, holding the door open and ushering me inside.

I slid into the back seat, feeling the squeak of leather against my clothes. Michael got in next to me. There was an umbrella lying on the floor of the cab. It was a clear day, with no rain forecast, so I was puzzled.

'What's that doing there?'

He rolled the umbrella across to me. When I tried to lift it, the umbrella was so heavy I could barely get it off the ground. According to Michael, it could be used to fend off anyone intent on attacking me.

'Great,' I thought, my heart thumping as I imagined angry-faced protesters running at me from every direction.

'Does it open up?' I asked.

Michael nodded. 'Yes,' he said matter-of-factly. 'Because if someone throws something at you, it acts like as a shield as well.'

'Clever,' I thought. I tried to stay calm and composed. We probably wouldn't need to use the umbrella . . . would we?

On that strange, topsy-turvy morning, everything looked like something it wasn't – myself included. I had dressed carefully for the occasion: a black trouser suit with a crisp, feminine but business-like white shirt and a pair of comfortable high heels. I always wear high heels because they make me feel as if I'm stepping up; they are part of my armoury as I get ready for battle. But inside I was so jittery that I hadn't managed to eat anything for breakfast. I hadn't even drunk a cup of coffee, which would have been a must on any other morning.

The special taxi pulled out into the morning traffic, with my husband Alan in a second taxi following behind. We were on our way to attend the first day of a High Court hearing into whether the government was legally obliged to put the plans for leaving the EU to a Parliamentary vote. I was the lead claimant in the case.

Alan and I were both dropped off at the back entrance of the offices of the law firm representing me, Mishcon de Reya. My legal team had gathered as pre-arranged for the short walk to the High Court. There was the super-organised Emily Nicholson, a managing associate litigator who has not only worked in politics in the UK and US but who I'm sure is destined to have a hugely successful career. The ever-smiling, approachable Rob Murray, who is a partner in the firm's Dispute Resolution Department, who always took copious notes and never missed any details from a conversation or meeting. Lisa Tremble, who was the head of communications and who, along with her colleague Hayley Geffin, brilliantly managed the overwhelming amount of media requests that were coming from all over the world, as I had no team of my own. Lurking at the back of the group was the most senior Mishcon member, James Libson, partner and head of Mishcon Private, with his glasses on his forehead and his attention on the email he was writing. James exuded seniority, but in a calm, collected and confidence-inspiring manner. We were ready to set off.

I chose to be flanked by the two women, followed by Michael and his fellow security officer, then Rob, Alan, James and the rest of my Mishcon team. As we turned the corner and walked towards the iron railings of the Royal Courts of Justice, there was already a daunting crowd of media and protesters gathered outside. Some of them wore nooses around their necks and tabards with my name printed on their chests. Others had placards denouncing what I was doing.

This was the first time reality struck – I realised that people actually wanted me dead. It took all my strength to stay calm and carry on walking past. I wanted to stop, I wanted to talk to them, I wanted to explain, but my team hurried me on.

I wondered what Michael could possibly be making of it all. On the journey, to lighten the mood, he'd told me his team's previous job had been looking after Lady Gaga at the Victoria's Secret fashion show. This was quite a change in pace: there were to be no beautiful supermodels parading down a catwalk in glitzy underwear on that cool October morning in London.

On the walk towards the entrance, I heard photographers screaming my name. One angry voice rose above the fray and shouted, 'Traitor!'

It was the strangest feeling. I knew I was doing this because I loved my country, not because I wished to betray it. I was doing this because I wanted to protect the freedoms that made Britain great, not destroy them. I was doing this because I believed it was right. And here I was, accused of being a traitor by someone I'd never met. It was hurtful and bewildering, but there was no time to dwell on it. The case was about to start. Michael bundled me past the protesters towards a back entrance and down a series of corridors until we got to the appointed courtroom.

The High Court is housed in an imposing Victorian Gothic building, built in the 1870s, and inside the courtroom it felt as though not much had changed since then. It had that old library smell – the kind of dusty, bookish fragrance you associate with many centuries of learning. I sat on a wooden bench, flanked by two senior members from my legal team. I've got a short torso and one of my lawyers joked that, from behind, I resembled a child sitting between two big men. I certainly felt dwarfed by the sense of occasion.

In front of me was a row of QCs, including my barrister, the brilliant and unmistakable Lord Pannick. They were all wearing their wigs, and I remember thinking that, from my vantage point, the silhouette of the wigs looked like waves in the sea drawn by a toddler's hand. As a girl I attended a convent and was taught by strict English nuns who made us recite pages of proverbs and collective nouns. I thought a fitting one for the sight before me might be 'a sea of silks'.

The juniors were finishing bringing in boxes full of files containing the arguments and precedents they would use during the case, wheeled in on trolleys, twelve to fifteen boxes in each. Amidst the pomp and regalia of the court, the trolleys struck a duff note: like the wheels of a trolley you'd put your groceries in.

The courtroom was bursting at the seams. The press was sitting in a special boxed area towards the front of the court, all staring at me. I was permanently aware of the movements I was making and how they might be perceived – a glimmer of a smile in the wrong place could be misinterpreted; as for yawning (it had been impossible to sleep the night before), forget it! I kept wondering what these assorted members of the media were thinking. It was a constant pressure being under their gaze.

Above me, the public gallery was full. I didn't feel particularly safe. There were so many people up there – what would happen if someone threw something at me?

The whole situation was surreal. There I was, flanked by men used to being bodyguards for American pop stars, sitting a few benches away from the Lord Chief Justice of England and Wales and having every tiny movement on my face scrutinised by dozens of people I'd never met. Inside the courtroom, the attention was intense. But outside the courtroom, the entire country – and beyond that, even nations as diverse as Australia and China – was watching. And I thought to myself: 'How on earth did I get here?'

2

The Promised Land

Four months earlier, on the evening of 23rd June 2016, I'd been lying in bed at home, glued to the television, watching the results of the Referendum roll in. On one side of the bed was my husband, Alan. On the other was our eleven-year-old son, Luca, who had asked to stay up late because he was so interested in the result. In the weeks leading up to the Referendum, Luca had taken part in a series of school debates about Brexit.

I was so anxious about the result and what it would mean for the country that I couldn't switch off. I know I barely slept that night because Alan, who is always paranoid I don't get enough rest, had some weeks earlier given me a watch which tracked my sleep. On the night of 23rd June, it registered thirty-six minutes.

I remember seeing the UKIP leader Nigel Farage's speech just after 10 p.m., within minutes of the ballot closing, when he effectively said he expected defeat for Leave, despite a secret poll by the Leave.EU campaign website putting Leave four points ahead. I relaxed a little, but, like the pollsters, was nervous it would be a very close vote. I eventually drifted off to sleep around 11.45 p.m., but woke little more than half an hour later to the noise of cheering on the screen – the result for Sunderland's whopping 61 per cent vote to Leave versus 39 per cent to Remain was just in. It was a far larger margin than pollsters had predicted, and from there things seemed to take a turn: suddenly we were on course to leave the EU. My first reaction was one of total disbelief. I felt a dreadful pain in my stomach. I just couldn't get my head around what was happening.

I woke my son at about 6 a.m. to break the news. He started crying. 'What's going to happen to me and all my friends?' he asked me, the tears rolling down his cheeks.

I held Luca close, but there was nothing I could say to make it go away. Although I felt completely helpless, I said, 'Don't worry, people will be sensible, the people who can make sure everything is done right will make sure it's all right.' As a mother, it's the worst feeling to know your child is upset and that you can't do anything to alleviate their sadness.

Over the following days, the country fell into a state of disarray. The margin of victory had been so narrow – 51.9 per cent in favour of Brexit; 48.1 per cent voting to remain – that debate became increasingly toxic, with both sides claiming the moral high ground. Remainers were disillusioned and exhausted. Even the most hardened Leavers were unsure about what would happen next. We knew we were leaving. But no one seemed to know *how* exactly. After all, we didn't even have a prime minister.

Once my disbelief at the result had passed, I reflected and realised I wasn't entirely shocked by what had happened. Since the previous October I'd been a spokesperson for the Remain campaign. I had been invited to speak by forums, think-tanks, the media and at various other events in all parts of the country. On my travels around the UK I had started to understand how so many people had felt ignored, futureless, angry and hopeless. I realised that when people feel rock bottom they also feel they might as well roll the dice and hope for a better life rather than putting their faith in a political system that had let them and their families down.

It was summed up in a report I read in August 2016 by the Joseph Rowntree Foundation (JRF)[1], which examined specific data on the roles of poverty, place and individual characteristics driving the Leave vote. As I had seen first-hand, their report showed how Britain was divided along economic, educational and social lines. They found that the poorest households, with incomes of less than £20,000 per year, were much more likely to support leaving the EU than wealthier households; in other words, people who were unemployed, in low-skilled[2] and manual jobs, people who felt that their financial situation had worsened, had all voted Leave. The vulnerable, feeling voiceless, had found a way to shatter the complacency of the politicians, the liberal elites, the experts and academics who seemed so out of touch and ignorant of their daily lives.

The JRF concluded that age, income and education mattered, though it was educational inequality that was the strongest driver. They found that, other things being equal, support for Leave was thirty percentage points higher among those with GCSE qualifications or below than it was for people with a degree. In contrast, support for Leave was just ten points higher among those on less than £20,000 per year than it was among those with incomes of more than £60,000 per year, and twenty points higher among those aged sixty-five than those aged twenty-five.

There were also strong regional differences: in areas with a high percentage of low-skilled workers, the proportion of A-level holders voting Leave was closer to that of people

1 'Brexit vote explained: poverty, low skills and lack of opportunity' – Matthew Goodwin, Oliver Heath, jrf.org.uk, 31st August 2016.
2 'Low-skilled' being defined as not having or needing a high level of skill or education.

with low skills; in high-skilled areas, the vote of A-level holders was much more similar to graduates. Groups in Britain that the politicians like to class as 'left behind' (as if their situation had nothing to do with successive governments' failed policies) felt that they had been cut adrift and forgotten. As the JRF clearly articulates, these voters face a 'double whammy':

> While their lack of qualifications put them at a significant disadvantage in the modern economy, they are also being further marginalised in society by the lack of opportunities . . . in their low-skilled communities. This will make it extremely difficult for the left behind to adapt and prosper in future.

Quite early on, I started to ask myself whether the Referendum vote was really going to be about the EU. From the work I had been doing since 2009 through my True and Fair Foundation, aimed at supporting small, dynamic grassroots charities, I had seen first-hand the pathways to deprivation in Britain and met some of the most marginalised people in our society. At numerous Referendum events I had expressed my fear that people might vote Leave as a means of improving their families' lives, to take a chance. They needed to do something dramatic to alter their own futures.

The problem was that this was not the question Conservative politicians were asking. The question *they* wanted an answer to was how to heal their own party, not the country.

As I travelled around the UK, I realised people I spoke to didn't want to hear facts and figures or any explanations about the consequences of staying or leaving the EU; they weren't being reasoned into a decision, they were just following their instinct to do *something*. That's when I started to ask myself, 'What happens if we lose and have to leave? Where do we even begin . . . ?'

I was becoming so alarmed that after a trip to Wales I tried to relay my concerns to the Remain team, who sent out to all their spokespeople a list of facts, figures and talking points each morning. All I got back was a condescending pat on the back. 'Don't worry, Gina. We know what we're doing. We've got a lot of experienced politicians[3] on our side.'

I felt patronised, angry and frustrated. I started straying from their script and talking about 'Remaining and reforming – being the leaders of change from the top table. Not throwing the baby out with the bath water.' Suddenly the requests to speak or for media appearances from their team stopped. I was replaced by more 'obedient' women.

I started conducting my own research, looking into the history of Europe and the EU, beyond that which I already knew. I have always liked to read, to know why things are the way they are. As a girl, my other love was archaeology and I would spend hours reading about who we were, where we came from; about ancient civilisations, ancient mythologies, history. I have carried this habit and curiosity throughout my life, and now I applied it as I started reading Article 50. In fact, I memorised Article 50 (1) and (2) – all 118 words. Sad, I know.

In March 2017 when I read the draft Article 50 Bill, which was designed to do nothing more than start the negotiating process on leaving the EU, it struck me that only a few words of legalese could create such momentous change.

*

3 Code for older, out-of-touch, arrogant men with egos the size of mountains.

On the Monday after the Referendum results, I was speaking at an event organised by Mishcon de Reya. It was a panel debate about the lack of diversity in the City, in front of an audience comprised of clients, Mishcon employees and other interested parties.

It was held in a smart conference room in their offices, with a stage set with four chairs on a platform just like a TV debate. I had thought it was going to be an informal gathering and was surprised to see the room full to capacity, with about 120 people waiting to hear what we had to say.

I'm never short of an opinion or six, so I said some typically politically incorrect things about how certain women held out as heroines of diversity are more like men in skirts, coming from the same small pool of universities, public schools and social backgrounds; with the same unconscious biases. That real diversity should be about much more than gender; that real diversity is about psyche as well as outward diversity (but that's probably a whole other book).

As the event concluded, I was approached by a man wearing a light grey suit. He had an air of authority and he introduced himself as a senior partner at Mishcon. After some polite small-talk, he said, 'Gina, you were really passionate and don't seem afraid to speak your mind. Is there anything else you feel passionate about?'

Immediately, I thought of everything that had happened over the preceding days. The feelings of the previous Friday night came flooding back to me: the sense of shock and confusion; the sleepless night; my son's tears. I couldn't help myself. I started rattling off my fears that I thought nobody knew what they were doing with Brexit; that the politicians who campaigned for us to leave didn't seem to have a clue about the detail – it was all about ideology. That it was an arrogant political miscalculation and I was worried about the Article 50 process – I was warming to my theme. Would MPs finally have the debate they hadn't had to date? Would they really deliver the advisory result as binding? Finally, would there be serious debate about what Brexit would really mean to our country?

I explained my concern was that Cameron might be replaced by a more right-wing prime minister who might just trigger Article 50 without a plan. Whether I had voted to leave or remain was nothing to do with it. There were much bigger, more important issues at stake now. How could we minimise the damage that appeared to be upon us? What could we do!

At the end of my rant, he just looked at me and said, 'I have a letter we've drafted that I need to send you. Once you've read it, call me, and if you are in agreement you must come to a meeting here, as there is an urgency in terms of filing.'

Overnight the draft letter was sent to me, and a few days later I met with the Mishcon team, who were already planning a legal action. They said they had been thinking along the same lines as I was, and they were hoping to put together a case with two existing clients: would I be interested in coming on board? At that point, it felt as if everything had come together. There was something fatalistic about it. Instinctively, it felt right.

When they asked if I would do it, I immediately said, 'Absolutely, I'll join the other two.'

Later that week, Mishcon sent out a letter revealing that they had been instructed to pursue a case against Her Majesty's Government. At that stage, the three clients – myself included – were not named. But it didn't stop the trolls. Mishcon de Reya were taunted online with horrific anti-Semitic slurs for issuing the letter. Their offices were attacked.

I watched it unfold with mounting horror. But instead of making me scared for my own safety, it made me angry, because we weren't doing anything wrong. These respected, expert legal individuals were putting their necks on the line. They were asking the court's permission to clarify a matter of constitutional law and it was a perfectly legitimate but urgent question. To attack them with such foul language and with such venom seemed to me to be out of all proportion. It was bullying – and I hate bullies.

As the complexity of the legal arguments unfolded, I realised how fortunate I was that my team at Mishcon was being led by the legendary James Libson, with his intellectual agility.

Months after we won in the Supreme Court, Alan and I watched a film called *Denial* in which there is a lawyer character called James Libson, played by the actor Jack Lowden. James had never mentioned it to me, but he is the same James Libson who, in 2000, had been instrumental in successfully defending Deborah Lipstadt when the Holocaust denier David Irving sued her for libel in the UK Supreme Court. As James himself put it, this was 'a world pre 9/11, pre the ubiquity of social media and, for Jews, pre the emergence of much-debated new forms of anti-Semitism'.

It was therefore bitterly ironic that his firm and his offices should be subject to anti-Semitic attacks. It is extremely distressing that so little appeared to have changed over nearly twenty years.

When my name emerged as a claimant in the administrative hearing on 19th July and Lord Leveson named me as the Lead Claimant, I too was the target of racist and sexist abuse. The other two claimants in my case, both men, ultimately decided to withdraw from the action when they saw the level of hate directed towards me. And that's how I came to be the sole Lead Claimant.

I understood the other two claimants' reticence: the case would have had a huge effect on their businesses and families. They were far more high-profile than me. They had so much more to lose. That said, I'm a mother to an adult daughter with special needs and to two young children, who were then eleven and nine, and I jointly run an investment business. I was also keen to protect my family and our privacy, so it was a very tough decision. But, when it came down to it, this was just too important. The rule of law, British values, these are worth fighting to protect. It was a battle worth pursuing for my children, their future, and the country's future. There was something almost inevitable about these events – fate seemed to conspire to hand me this baton. Of course I would pick it up and run with it.

It was exhausting. As the only client I had to read every single bit of communication in preparation for the case. Not just from my team but from the other parties who also wanted to question the government's legal position. Rather than have a series of cases clogging up the courts, it was decided that several other cases, dealing with different legal angles, such as expats' rights and the rights of minors, would be heard at the same time as my case.

I didn't feel alone, but I suppose I *was* disappointed that no academics, politicians, business or high-profile people decided to come out in support of me or the action. They seemed quite happy to let me take the full heat.

I consoled myself by saying they would support me, that they were with me in spirit but were fearful of the backlash I was experiencing. In the aftermath of the Referendum results, it was hard not to feel there was a lock-down on public debate. Fear had taken hold. And then fear turned into a sort of apathy, as people felt confused and lost. It was as if Brexit had polluted the British consciousness.

That was how I found myself in the High Court, facing three eminent judges who were about to decide on a fundamental principle of the British constitution. As I sat there on that autumn morning, surrounded by the sounds of shuffling papers and dry coughs and the tap-tap-tapping of the stenographers as they got ready to transcribe the opening arguments, I thought back to my childhood. I felt this day had all been set in motion many, many years before.

3

The Things I Was Going To Do

I was born in Guyana when it was still a British colony, then called British Guiana. When I was a year old, Guyana became independent and part of the Commonwealth. My childhood home had pictures of the Queen hanging on the wall. My mum collected Wedgwood china with royal-themed photographs printed on plates and every evening when my father was home he would tune the radio into the BBC World Service and we'd listen to it as a family.

My siblings and I grew up thinking Britain was the highest pinnacle of all that was best in the world. It stood for everything to which we most aspired. At school, I learned about Queen Victoria, Dickens and Shakespeare. I was taught to speak English with perfect grammar by British nuns: no 'couldn't' or 'wouldn't', it was always 'could not' or 'would not'. Guyana is supposedly where Eldorado existed, but for me Britain was the Eldorado: a promised land of civility, culture, greatness and great people.

My father was a barrister, with an overwhelming sense of social justice, who would later go on to become Attorney General of Guyana. My mother had been a schoolteacher but became dedicated to her children when we were born. She was also respected as a botanist who loved orchids and flowers: she once entered – and won – a competition to grow a black rose. Our brick house was designed by her, comfortable but not lavish. Downstairs, there was a sitting room, study and a lovely wooden spiral staircase leading up to our bedrooms. At the top of the stairs stood my father's desk and a piano, which was my mother's pride and joy – we all took piano lessons. There was a veranda that stretched the entire length of the house, which kept it cool when it became very humid.

I spent most of my time outdoors in the beautiful garden my mother had created. I have one older brother, two younger brothers and a much younger sister, so it's little surprise I was a complete tomboy. We had dens and a tree-house, and we used to camp outside, playing cowboys, which often ended with me being tied up by my brothers and left until someone took pity on me and loosened the knots. We grew up with an incredible amount of freedom and used our imaginations a lot. There was no television, so we had to invent our own worlds.

We could cause as much chaos as we liked in the garden, but my parents were disciplined when it came to academia. Their view – which I still hold – is that one of the most precious things you can ever give a child is education. We were taught never to waste it. When we weren't studying, we were expected to do chores: watering the garden, mowing the lawn, deadheading the flowers, walking to the dairy for milk.

When I was around seven or eight years old, my father bought a brand-new car. He had been doing well at work and his legal practice was becoming more successful. One day he returned from the office at the wheel of a Holden automobile. It was olive green and so shiny you could almost see your face in the paintwork, and my siblings and I were all really excited by this new apparition. We opened the passenger door and scampered inside, giggling as we inhaled the expensive smell of new leather.

The next day our father drove us around so that we could experience the Holden for ourselves. I sat in the back with my older brother in the front, and my father turned on the air-conditioning. It was a real treat, sitting there having our faces fanned with a cool breeze when it was so hot outside.

The car became indelibly associated with my father. Everyone around Georgetown knew when they saw the Holden that it was my father driving and that he was doing well for himself. I was so proud of him.

That was the first time I remember being made acutely aware of what money could bring you. I realised that if you worked hard, like my father, you could potentially earn enough to buy yourself and your family nice things. Even so, my mother was always modest and hardworking. She would always remind us that life can change in an instant, so we shouldn't take things for granted or be frivolous. I supposed she was speaking from experience, as everything did change for her when her father was murdered, when she was just ten years old. Men broke into the house, tied up my grandmother and murdered my grandfather amidst a burglary as he would not tell them where the safe was. My grandmother was a loving, compassionate woman, but as she could not read or write, my mother had to help with the paperwork associated with my grandfather's business and land ownership. She had to grow up fast and become responsible overnight. The echoes of how fate conspired to rob her of her childhood resounded with my situation as I sat in Eastbourne so far away from her. She was an eco-warrior, even before the term was invented. Every bit of packaging, plastic bag, string and ribbon was neatly folded or rolled and put away into its assigned cupboard or drawer. Every bottle, tub or tin was made useful – habits that are imprinted on my siblings and me. I can hear her words – 'You never know when you might need it'.

In the neighbourhood our house was in, there were also lots of families who didn't have smart cars or the trappings of a comfortable life, or the luxury of going to good schools. There were wrought-iron gates at the end of our driveway and in the street outside there would usually be children playing in torn clothes and bare feet. I would look through these gates and wonder what their lives were like.

My mother scolded me for being a daydreamer. She thought I was away with the fairies half the time. But I wasn't daydreaming – I was just curious about what made other people tick. I loved people-watching, wondering about their lives. (This has stayed with me: my husband Alan likes to joke that if ants could talk, I'd be lying down on the floor with them and asking them questions.)

I got into trouble as a child because I would give away my things to these children. It didn't seem fair that I had so much and they had so little. My mum used to have our clothes made for us by an old-fashioned English dressmaker. As a tomboy I hated them. On one occasion, when I was about eight, my mother had a dress made for me which I instantly disliked because it had puffed sleeves and was far too girly. But my mother was very proud of it, as the material had come from Britain and was the best quality cotton.

The dress was red and blue, and had a pattern of robins all over it. She also bought me some red sandals from Clarks (it was always Clarks). One day when my mother was busy in the garden, I ran down the drive as fast as my legs would carry me. There were children on the other side of the iron gates, laughing and playing games. I caught the eye of one little girl I had got to know. She was playing barefoot, so I beckoned her over and gave her the dress and the sandals.

'You mustn't tell anyone,' I said, whispering. 'This has to be our secret.'

The little girl smiled and nodded and gleefully ran up the road to the fire hydrant, where her friends were waiting. I turned and ran back up the driveway, feeling happy that she was happy. The dress and the sandals were only for best, so I knew my mother wouldn't discover they were missing for a while.

Later I started giving the little girl delicious biscuits and cakes my mother had baked, chocolate, too. The political situation in Guyana became very difficult and our President Forbes Burnham had banned the importation of many goods. But on several occasions, visitors from England would bring my parents presents and chocolates for us children; Cadbury's chocolate that came from England, and because it was from England it was like gold. It was so hot in Guyana that the chocolate used to melt, my mother kept it in a special fridge. I would tell the girl to hide behind the gatepost for the handover and then I'd run to the fridge, get the chocolate and run all the way down our drive to give it to her. I made her promise never to tell anyone. My mother would be furious at the disappearance of the chocolate, since it was so hard to lay hands on, but I was much happier eating Mum's plantain chips or my grandmother's bittersweet tamarind balls instead of the chocolate that was meant to be such a luxury.

I didn't speak a word about our transactions.

Then, one day, my mother wanted me to wear the dress for a special event. In a panic, I told her I'd packed it with the sandals to stay over at my best friend Sharon Chung's house, and had forgotten it. She didn't believe me.

'Go and get the cane,' she told me, and I knew at once that I was going to be punished for what I'd done.

My mother was the disciplinarian in our family and in those days it was quite normal for children to be caned for their misdemeanours. The cane was made of bamboo and kept in the hat-stand in the hallway, along with the umbrellas and coats. I went to retrieve it as my mother had ordered, and because I knew what was coming I rapidly stuffed one of my comic books down my pants so that it wouldn't hurt as much. If my mother knew I did this, she never said anything.

I went back to my mother and handed her the cane. She made me bend over and then – thwack! – brought the cane down sharply on my bottom and the back of my legs. It was like a lash: an instant stinging pain that burned immediately. She caned me a few more times, and I winced with each blow but refused to cry. The next day there were long, vivid bruises criss-crossing my skin.

Although the caning hurt, it didn't bother me as much as it should have because I'd done something I thought was right. I just kept thinking of the happy smile on the girl's face at handovers. I just couldn't see the point in having a new dress when I already had so many clothes. The pain was trumped by the happiness I felt that I had done something good, and the smile that shone on the girl's face.

It wasn't until I was a grown-up, with a child of my own, that I finally confessed to my mother in my small bungalow in Yate, north-east of Bristol. She was amazed. She said, 'You let me cane you and still never told me the truth!' Then paused and added, 'But I would still have caned you for lying.'

*

At night, when I was meant to be in bed, I'd sometimes stay up and sneak to the top of the spiral staircase, listening in to the adults' conversation below when people came over. My father was heavily involved in Guyanese politics and he would have meetings at our home in the evenings or on weekends, which I knew were extremely important.

The meetings were predominantly attended by men, who smoked cigars, drank rum or Johnnie Walker whisky, and talked about big things like politics, justice and socialism and how to improve people's lives. My mother would make sure she baked delicious snacks and cut lots of coconuts for their water, which would be mixed with rum. The men would agree and disagree with passion and intensity, but always with respect for each other. Even though I didn't understand all the words, I knew what they were saying was important. I remember the conviction in their voices and the smell of their cigar smoke, and I remember thinking, from my position at the top of the stairs, 'These men are like the heroes in my books, they care, and I want to be part of their world.'

Even as a young girl I felt I could change things. I never really felt that as a girl I was weak or limited. I knew I wasn't like other girls my age: I was not a pretty girl in any way, shape or form. I had knotty, wild, long dark hair that went far below my waist, and I was very skinny, tiny and quite awkward-looking. I realised I wasn't going to be treated in a special way for being pretty or as dainty as some other girls, or as clever as my siblings were, but it never really bothered me. I was just happy being me – playing make-believe in our idyllic garden. I decided when I was quite young that I would be a brilliant lawyer, or archaeologist, or historian – that I would do important things.

I don't know if it's nature or nurture, probably a combination of both, but my childhood taught me to stand up for what I believed was right, no matter the personal cost. It also left me with an abiding sense of wanting to be involved in important discussions about the things that really mattered. Even though I was a girl I wanted to be included in those male-dominated conversations. I didn't want to be the woman on the sidelines, serving the snacks and drinks; I would be just like my father.

4

Going Public

The court case was over in three weeks. On 3rd November 2016, shortly after ten in the morning, the judges ruled that the government did not have the power to trigger Article 50 without first putting it to a Parliamentary vote. It would take some weeks for the win to actually sink in.

Soon after that, I stood on the steps of the High Court with a crumpled piece of paper in my hand plucking up the courage to speak. I should have been elated. Instead, I was terrified. On either side of me stood the lawyers, and the 'Superstar of the Bar'[4] Lord David Pannick, who had made legal history. Beyond them was a noisy rabble of photographers and news reporters from around the world all shouting out my name.

It was daylight, the sky was gloomy grey, and my eyes were dazzled by the irregular pop-popping of the camera flashes. I felt like a small animal being hunted by wolves. The last thing I wanted to do was speak. But the press was waiting.

I'd hastily scribbled some words down in the courtroom as the judgment was passed down. We hadn't been given any warning of what to expect from the verdict, and I hadn't wanted to tempt fate by writing something in advance. In

---

4 *Chambers UK*, 2016.

fact, I'd been apprehensive right up until the last minute that the ruling might not go our way. It wasn't that I doubted the strength of our case, but I wondered, would the court be brave enough to make the correct decision in the febrile landscape that erupted after the Referendum vote?

When the verdict was read out, my team said I needed to make a statement to the waiting press. I cobbled together some semi-coherent thoughts for the journalists gathered outside, and fished out a piece of paper from a notepad I had pushed into my handbag after an event at which I had recently spoken. It was from a financial services company called Morningstar, which coincidentally shares its name with a newspaper of Communist origins. It was the lovely Lisa who headed up Mishcon's PR department who said, 'Gina, you can't hold up a piece of paper that says Morningstar!' She carefully ripped the logo off, which made me look even less professional.

There I was, holding up my ragged, torn piece of paper, looking down the lens of dozens of television cameras and trembling inside from the nerves and the stress. I put on my glasses and, hands shaking, read out a brief statement.

'It's about our United Kingdom and all our futures,' I said, feeling my heart beating wildly in my chest. 'It's not about how anyone voted.'

I have no clue whether anything else I said made any sense. I honestly couldn't have told you what I said.

As soon as I finished the statement I was whisked off for a debriefing from the lawyers. We had two hours to read a thirty-two-page judgment filled with sophisticated legal argument. I wanted to know everything about it, but there wasn't time to digest it all because our email inboxes were already filling up with interview requests.

I kept thinking, 'I can't do all of this,' but somehow I got through it. I did the round of the television studios, blinking with tiredness with each new question fired at me. I felt so sick I couldn't eat or drink anything and was operating mainly on adrenaline. I spoke to journalists all through the night, from countries from all continents, as far afield as Colombia, Nigeria, Japan, China and India.

When I woke up the next day, I was on the front cover of twenty-two newspapers around the world: I was infamous, whether I liked it or not.

*

In the weeks and months that followed I became a public figure. It's odd to think of myself in those terms, because I'd always lived a private life, despite my years of campaigning. I hadn't fully anticipated the level of interest in the case – or the level of vitriol it would provoke. It can be hard for women to find their voice at the best of times, but I was catapulted into a situation where I was not only expected to have a voice, but also expected to be able to defend my opinions like the most seasoned politician at a time when debate between the Brexiteers and the Remainers had acquired a poisonous intensity.

Quite early on I decided not to publicly display emotion or be too soft; to be professional because I felt it was important to show grit and determination. I realise now that when I'm in front of a television camera I do not come across as particularly warm. Even my own husband has commented that I should smile more, and be the Gina he knows and loves. 'It's such a shame they don't see the you that I see,' he says. 'You're so much softer at home; so much funnier.'

The truth is, it's incredibly intimidating to have to make a public statement on the steps of the High Court with a pack of media in front of you. It's equally nerve-wracking to have to defend yourself under the gleaming lights of a TV studio when you're not an experienced or professional politician. What you can't see when you watch me is that my heart is pounding so hard I sometimes think it's going to leap out of my chest entirely.

Different people deal with nerves in different ways. In order to function without dissolving into a gibbering wreck on air, I developed a hard outer shell. It's a harder exterior than I'd like, and it isn't an accurate representation of who I am as a person because, obviously, it's only one side of me. I've had countless offers from publicists and 'image experts' to help me work on my 'warmth problem', but I've always felt there'd be something dishonest about that. I am who I am. I'm not in the business of trying to deceive anyone. I have always found it hard to speak other people's words.

I don't think the same criticism would have been levelled at a man. I'm not sure why women in a public role are expected to emote or show their softer side to be liked, while men can be as bullish and uncompromising as they wish without being accused of coldness.

The 'lack of warmth' was one thing. Even worse was the outpouring of hatred that subsequently came my way. The court case propelled me into the limelight in ways I could never have imagined.

I have had little training for being on a public or political platform. I had no PR consultants or speech writers or strategists, just my belief that truth and right would win out. And sometimes, as I was to discover, that simply wasn't enough.

5

Speak Up

In early 2017, I was approached by the producers of *This Week*, a late-night political discussion programme on BBC1. They wanted me to come on air and talk about my tactical voting campaign for the forthcoming June 2017 General Election. Brexit would be one of the most historic and important decisions to change the course of our history since 6 June 1944, when we, along with our Western allies, invaded France – and so began the end of the Second World War. The country would need MPs who would act with integrity – putting country before party, people before political ideology. My idea was that every voter would be able to use a tactical voting website to inform themselves on which local candidates would act with such integrity; as well as back a call for a meaningful vote in Parliament at the end of the Brexit negotiation process.

I realised that by agreeing to appear on television I was potentially walking into a situation that would stoke up further controversy. But I did it because I always think it is worth engaging with people who might not agree with you: it's worth walking into the lion's den and stating your case if there's a hope of reaching some sort of understanding between different points of view. If I were just to spend my time talking to people who agree with me, then I'd never get anywhere; debates would never progress.

The producers of *This Week* wanted me to film a two-minute segment about Brexit for the beginning of the show, then come in later that day for a live discussion in the studio. That afternoon I was sent the script at the very last minute, as I was walking into the venue to be filmed – a strange games arcade with stage sets, including an old pub and graveyard. I literally had five minutes to go through the entire script while leaning on an old beer barrel. The producer and cameraman were impatient, saying we needed to get this done as soon as possible so it could be sent back for editing. I changed it as much as I could in order to more accurately reflect my views, but I didn't have time to check it properly, which I later regretted. Still, I did my piece to camera and thought nothing more of it.

That evening I sat under the warm lights of the television studio on a velvety red sofa with a microphone pinned to my top. Opposite me were the Labour MP Chuka Umunna and the former Conservative politician Ann Widdecombe. The presenter of the show was Andrew Neil, a seasoned broadcaster of some twenty years' experience who used to edit the *Sunday Times*. As soon as the pre-recorded film came to an end, he launched into me.

'You said at the end there, talking about voting for people who'll do their best for Britain, but that's just code for voting for people who want to stop Brexit, isn't it?' he asked.

I spluttered. That was the script his team had written for me to say. It seemed unnecessarily aggressive for him to have a go at me for it.

'But everything you do is calculated to thwart Brexit, that's what you're about,' he continued from behind his desk, his chest puffing out. 'Why not just admit it instead of having this kind of carapace of other motives?'

'I love that you know what's in my mind because it's not,' I replied, trying to stay calm. 'I'm interested in the facts.'

Neil kept verbally prodding and poking, trying to get a rise out of me. But I knew my position. I got to the end of the first part of the discussion in one piece. Umunna and Widdecombe then came in with their thoughts. After about ten minutes, Neil turned to me and asked, 'Have you turned tinkering in the democratic process into a rich woman's hobby?'

That's when I got really annoyed.

Let's be clear: I know I'm privileged, but I've worked very hard and earned the life I have today. I'm extremely grateful to be in a position where I can use my money to pursue the causes that are important to me. I never take any kind of wealth for granted and I realise that, for the clear majority of people in this country, my way of life looks cosseted and comfortable at a time when many are struggling.

I too have struggled to make a living at various points in my life. During those times, I took every job I could to make ends meet. Ultimately, I ended up working in the financial sector and have been rewarded along the way. I worked hard. I agree that it's not fair that bankers and irresponsible executives get paid millions of pounds in bonuses, while a nurse or a teacher must survive on a pittance. For what it's worth, I give back to the society that affords my success by donating time and money to good causes and doing a lot of charity work through my Foundation, and as a benefactor.

The point is, both my husband and I have earned our money and, as I told Andrew Neil that night, it was perfectly acceptable for me to use that money to carry out what I believed was my civic duty: it certainly wasn't a hobby for me. But if by 'hobby' Neil meant using most of my spare time speaking up against dishonesty and being passionate about causes, I'm happy to agree that my activism is my hobby.

There were two presumptions in Neil's question that I take serious issue with. One is that I can't possibly have made any money independently ('hobby' implying I had a lot of leisure time on my hands), so it must be that I'm rich because of my husband or my marriage. Wrapped up in that is this idea that I can't have acted as a claimant on my own. I would continue to hear these unoriginal accusations so many times.

The second implication of the word 'hobby' is that I'm bored and have nothing else to do, so I've chosen to have a little dabble in our country's constitutional history and politics just for fun. Was he seriously saying that taking the government to court could be a *hobby*? That makes it sound like I'm baking cupcakes or knitting tea-cosies! I hadn't done it to while away the time. Nor had I done it for my own self-gratification. I did it because I thought it was the right thing.

It took me aback because I'd just had a decent enough conversation with him about the salient issues, yet Neil had attacked me with a cheap, low jibe. Sitting there on the sofa, listening to him dismiss me with such casual disregard, I thought: 'You callous man. What is it you're trying to do? Is this just to get better viewing figures for the programme, or do you really mean this? Is that what you think?'

I believe that he meant it. And in a way that makes it easier to deal with. If someone shows you they are a misogynist who has little respect for women, as I felt Neil did that night, then you must ignore them. Because they're wrong. They're ignorant. And you'll never change their mind unless they listen to what you're *actually* saying rather than what they think you *should* be saying. That conscious decision has to be theirs.

Ironically, shortly after filming finished Neil told me he was about to jet off to his house in Grasse, in the south of France. Knowing it would be a luxurious pad, I thought, 'you utter hypocrite!'

*

Andrew Neil wasn't the first man who seemed intent on making me feel I had no right to speak up and I'm sure he won't be the last. Luckily, though, I've had lots of practice at dealing with ingrained, often unconscious, sexist attitudes in the world of finance and the City. In 2012, my husband and I set up the True and Fair Campaign, which I spearhead, to clean up the UK investment and pension industry's excesses, in the aftermath of the global economic crisis. For years, financial services operated as a sort of closed shop, run by men for men who seemed to take delight in baffling the rest of us by employing the most opaque, jargon-heavy language they could and by recruiting from the 'boys' club' and filling their pockets at the expense of ordinary, hardworking people.

We were campaigning for 100 per cent transparency in pensions and investments, and for 100 per cent transparency of holdings, giving people the basic consumer rights of knowing what they are really buying and what they are really paying. We lobbied for the introduction of a transparency Code of Ethics and campaigned for significantly increased consumer protection. We've called out numerous dubious practices. This hasn't made us popular. Men come up to me at parties and tell me I have no right to speak out about things that don't concern me. They have endlessly tried to belittle me. It's worth noting that these angry men rarely approach my husband. He would just be ignored, given the silent treatment, while they actively went out of their way to insult me. I've lost count of the number of times over my career that I've had my opinions dismissed or been told that the top table in the business world is 'no place for a woman like you'.

Then there are the nicknames. I've been given a plethora of unflattering monikers. I was once speaking on a panel about the future of financial services and one of the male panellists, a man who was very high up in the City, looked me up and down, then looked at the name plate in front of where I would sit and said, laughing, 'Should we just call you Director of Lipstick?'

During another round-table discussion, I was the only woman on a panel of five. We were going around introducing ourselves. The last person to do so was a senior director of a major American bank, who said his name, then added: 'And I can tell you everything Gina Miller is about to say is wrong.'

'Woah,' I thought. 'We haven't even started yet!'

I am only human so that kind of thing really used to bother me. But I've developed strategies for dealing with arrogance – from both men and women. I've learned that if someone is attacking you from the off, without having listened to what you have to say, it means they're feeling defensive. Often they realise they don't have a leg to stand on, so, like a dog backed into a corner, they lash out; they bark and bite. If they attack you on a personal level, it's probably because they're unable to attack what you're saying. Now when someone dismisses me like that I remind myself that if they're targeting *me* and not my arguments, then I've already won. Their aggression is simply a sign that they've lost control. The best way to counter it is to stay composed, take a deep breath and continue calmly making your points.

Most women will have had some experience of this. We are frequently made to feel we should shut up; that we don't have a right to a voice; that we shouldn't speak out when we believe something is wrong. In our professional life, we often go into meetings only to have the men talk over us. Or we go to a dinner, make a joke but no one laughs, and then a man sitting nearby will make the same joke in a louder voice to be greeted by a rousing chorus of appreciative hilarity. Or a colleague steals our idea because we didn't claim it firmly enough, or vocally enough, as our own.

Women tend to believe they have to be collegiate, but the problem with that is that you can be stepped over by glory-hunters. When we have ideas, all too often we express them too quietly or nervously because we're worried about sounding stupid. By and large, men don't have that same worry. It's the peacock versus the peahen analogy.

Internal research conducted by Hewlett Packard in 2008[5] found that their female employees applied for a promotion only when they believed they met 100 per cent of the qualifications listed for the job. Men, on the other hand, were happy to apply when they thought they could meet 60 per cent of the required criteria. Perfectionism can be women's enemy. Because without having the courage to step up, speak up, put ourselves forwards and take risks we may never get to where we want to be.

There's a bigger cultural problem at school and work in terms of failing to teach young women the practical tools of confidence. All too often we fall into gender stereotypes and teach boys to be assertive and bold and risk-taking, while girls are encouraged to be kind, good, feminine, not 'shriek' – all laced with controlling undertones. The result is that, as women, we often gain our sense of self from other people, from pleasing others, rather than ourselves. We care about being liked by others – and that can hold you back. It's quite a disabling emotion to want people to like you because you're always going to be hesitant while you second-guess what someone else might or might not want from you or think of you. It's a rein that's holding you back, a burden that can weigh you down. And, in my experience, it's bad for

5 'The Confidence Gap' – Katty Kay and Claire Shipman, *The Atlantic*, May 2014 issue.

business, too – the need to please is linked to lower wages, lack of innovation and poorer negotiation skills.

Fairly early on in my career I made a conscious decision that I would try not to worry what other people thought about me. At university, there seemed to be an attitude that I would never succeed as a barrister because my face didn't fit with their image of what someone at the legal bar should look like. I realised quite quickly that how I felt about myself had to exist separately from someone else's prejudice, and that not being liked by everyone was not the same thing as being 'unlikeable'. To this day, I keep a very close circle of friends and family, and I share with them: my husband, my children, my siblings and a few friends. That's it. They are my cornerstone relationships. They are steadfast and solid and will always be there for me. It doesn't matter how frequently or infrequently we're in touch: we love each other, we trust each other, we are not jealous of each other; we lift each other up when we are down. These cornerstone relationships are where I go when I need reassurance or understanding, or an honest appraisal of events. I care what these people think. The rest of it? I don't let them get to me.

It wasn't easy. In fact, it took me several years to come to this place – emotionally and mentally. But once I got the hang of it, I couldn't believe how liberating it was.

*

When I moved from my loving family home in Guyana to a boarding school in Eastbourne, it took me a while to settle in; however, once I had, I felt part of a small, supportive community. Then I moved to London to study law at the University of East London and I felt swamped by the intimidating hustle and bustle of the city. It was the first time I had lived in a big city, or even used the underground on my own, and every morning I found the crush of rush-hour over-whelming. I was suddenly an outsider. On campus, I stood out. Even though there were many nationalities, I was in an identity limbo. Having been in the south of England since the age of eleven, my accent was English, my attire was more conservative than many other girls there and I did not join any groups apart from debating or sporting ones. I felt vulnerable walking around, as if everyone was looking at me, silently criticising my appearance, wondering which tribe I belonged to. I simply didn't fit into any box. I remember application forms at the Freshers' Fair that had tick-boxes of ethnic categories I didn't identify with, so I drew my own box 'Other' and ticked that.

The lecturers looked as if they'd walked out of a 1975 edition of *University Challenge*: they had crusty beards, corduroy trousers and tweed jackets with leather patches at the elbow. In lectures, they were remote and condescending to the female law students. In the first term, one professor went around the class asking us each what our ambitions were. And I felt bold and said that I wanted to become a criminal barrister like my father.

Straight away he said, 'That's not likely to happen. You need to be more realistic, being an ethnic woman from this university – maybe think about employment law or immigration.'

There were also hints from another lecturer that I wouldn't be taken seriously because I was too glamorous: he often stood too close to me, 'accidentally' touched me too much, and offered extra help at his place if I was struggling. They told me that law was a tough profession for anyone, and that for 'a woman like you' my dreams were unrealistic. Limits and expectations were set in place very early.

It was heartbreaking to think that my childhood dream of being a barrister like my father was pie-in-the-sky. My parents suggested I study at a university in the West Indies, but I could not contemplate leaving Britain: it was my home, which I loved so very much. I realised that, to avoid falling into a heap of despair, I had to find a way of supporting myself mentally through my degree. It was clear no one else was going to do it for me. I had to back myself.

One day I sat at a desk in one of the lecture halls when everyone had left and made a list of my strengths and weaknesses on a piece of paper. I was very honest. In the strengths column, I included: common sense, hardworking, determined, eager to learn and ability to communicate. In the weaknesses, I put: not as academically bright as my siblings, impatient, not good at the detail and I could be stubborn. No point lying as I would just be lying to myself. It was important to me that this was an unflinching, truthful account. I assessed myself and when I re-read the sheet of paper I realised I wasn't that bad after all.

Every morning after that, whilst brushing my teeth, I would look at my reflection in the mirror above the sink and remind myself of my good points. I told myself I didn't care what people thought because I knew who I was. I would not let anyone make me feel bad. The only person I could really rely on was myself.

After a few weeks of this Robert De Niro from *Taxi Driver* routine, I really started to believe in myself again. Having my childhood dream of becoming a barrister like my father dashed so brutally did take me to a dark place for a while, but I had to be courageous, I had to fight and find a way to be the best I could be. Over the next few years I learned that when you're courageous once, it becomes easier to be courageous a second time, a third time. You learn strategies to deal with hurt, disappointment and failure. That there is always a choice in the point of view you adopt and move forwards with; how to listen to yourself and how to project a sense of your own self-worth.

Over the years, I have spoken to young women who work in male-dominated industries who have excellent qualifications, who've worked harder to be better than their male peers, but by the time they're in their thirties, with some juggling the demands of babies, childcare, careers and partners, they're bone tired. They're in mid-management and they wake up one day thinking, 'Do I really want to go further? Is it all too much?' A lot of them end up leaving because the support and infrastructure simply isn't there. That's a problem, not only for the women, who feel pushed out of a job they worked so hard for, but also for the business, which loses out on dedicated and talented female employees.

During one of these conversations recently, I was speaking to a woman who works for a financial regulator. She's in her mid-thirties and she said to me, 'Gina, I find it so difficult because people won't let me speak. They speak across me. It's really frustrating. No one listens to me. If I must leave a little early to collect my toddler, colleagues look down their noses at me. As if I'm failing to work out my life properly. But when my daughter is in bed, I often work for hours.'

I asked her where she sat when she goes into a meeting room. She looked a little surprised.

'Well,' she replied, 'normally I'm early so I'll go into the room first and sit at the back to let the others come in easier.'

I said, 'No. You mustn't do that. When you go into that room, you sit right in the middle. Don't let them miss your presence: it's good if some of them have to walk around you.'

When we speak up as women, we must own the space we are in and not let others encroach on it. We must exude confidence in our stature, in the way we sit, in the way we project. Even before we utter a word, we need to make our presence felt. We must fight a constant battle against being unnecessarily apologetic.

One of the strategies I've learned over the years in meetings is to let everyone else talk over each other and discuss the issues first. Show their hands, if you like, whilst I sit and listen. Often the others in the room, especially the peacocks, will at some point expose any gaps in their thinking, any weaknesses or contradictions, and then you can step in, speak up, be the voice of reason and creativity.

But if you decide to have a strong voice, you may also have to accept it might be a lonely voice. Sometimes people are frightened of unsettling the group-think, as well as those who rock the boat. They keep their heads down; keep their distance from you in case they get tarred by the same brush, believing safety lies in silence or anonymity or status quo. But all that does is to allow discrimination, ignorance, unconscious bias, prejudice and weak decision-making to flourish. If you believe in what you are saying, that what you're doing is right, let your voice ring out.

If a provocative broadcaster wants to call me a rich woman with a hobby, that's his prerogative. But I'll keep speaking up for what I believe in. That's not a hobby: that's a mission.

*

It might sound obvious, but to speak up you first need to know what you want to say.

Sometimes sifting through your own mind and heart to come to what you believe is right takes time, effort and honesty with yourself. Especially for women, as we don't tend to have an overwhelming belief in our own point of view. We tend to ask others for their opinions and take on board their feelings and their outlook before forming our own: we accommodate more than we articulate. It's social conditioning, going back centuries.

A study of 470,000 people carried out over thirty years by the University of Buffalo[6] found that men feel more entitled to power than women and are more likely to exploit it. Researchers found that men consistently scored higher in narcissism across multiple generations and regardless of age.

Narcissism can be a seriously damaging affliction, wreaking havoc in personal relationships and contributing to excess aggression but, according to the report's lead author, Emily Grijalva, there were also other side effects: 'at the same time, narcissism is shown to boost self-esteem, emotional stability and the tendency to emerge as a leader'.

Now, I'm not for one minute saying all men are narcissists or that all women are shrinking violets, riven with anxiety and constantly passing the smelling salts. Far from it. I suppose what I'm saying is that – broadly speaking, and judging from my own lived experience – women are more likely to question their own beliefs about what's right and what's wrong, the strength of their abilities and contributions, while men are more likely to back their own opinions and beliefs to the hilt.

This goes beyond gender: if we don't have enough self-belief, it can be impossible to work out what one thinks about anything because everyone seems to have a point, even if they're talking from opposite sides of the debate! How many times have you sat around a dinner table and been asked what you think about an important political issue of the day? And how many times have you ventured a few thoughts, only to have someone else put forward the

---

6 'Gender differences in narcissism: A meta-analytic review' – Emily Grijalva et al, *Psychological Bulletin 141*, 2015.

contradictory perspective and then lost confidence in your original ideas? In my earlier days, it certainly happened to me a lot.

Of course, I'm not talking about the clear rights and wrongs in society. No one is ever going to convince me that murder is right or that racism is acceptable; just as I'll never believe that giving women the vote was wrong. For me, there are certain topics that are beyond moral relativism.

I'm often asked why I took the government on over Brexit, when it has come at such a high personal cost. And my answer is always, 'Because it was the right thing to do.' For months, it struck me as self-evident. If a government dares to put itself above the law, attempts to break the law, then that government should be held to account.

As time went on I realised that many people found that an unsatisfying answer. I can see why: if you don't know me, it can sound trite. As a society, we've grown suspicious of people doing the right thing for no personal gain. It's so much easier to take the simple road and not disrupt your life, not deplete your bank balance on an injustice that does not appear to affect you, and not be vilified by the national media for taking a stand over a seemingly esoteric matter of historical protocol. During the court case, I began thinking about where my sense of right and wrong comes from, and what gives me the motivation to stand up for what I believe in. Once again, I found the roots of my identity in my childhood – in my father's shadow.

6

My Father's Daughter

My father was called Doodnauth Singh. He had short curly hair, with just the right number of waves. As a young man he was tall, slim and stately-looking. When he started out as a barrister, he gained a reputation in Guyana for being the most handsome man in court.

He took care of his appearance and always prided himself on being beautifully turned out. He would brush his hair with an old wooden hairbrush and splash on Old Spice. Despite the heat and humidity in Guyana, he would go into court wearing the full wig and gown, with a stiffly ironed and starched white collar that my mother took great pride in preparing. Whatever the temperature, he entered the court-room as if it were the Crown Court in London because he believed that by dressing impeccably, he was showing respect for not just his clients and the occasion but the institution of law and justice.

My mother, Savitri, was famed for her beauty. Before they were married, she was viewed as an extremely eligible young woman, with a tiny waist and a fair complexion – if a little too feisty and independent.

In our household, my father was the gentler one and my mother the stricter. I remember he was sometimes criticised by his work colleagues for being too soft, for letting too many of his clients off their fees, allowing them to pay with a goat or rice or whatever they could afford. My mother was often worried he didn't pay enough attention to the financial security of his own family. Money never really bothered him: if we had enough to survive on, he was content. He was a humble man.

Like so many little girls, I loved my father and looked up to him. My favourite time of each day was when he came home from work. I would hear the engine of his Holden car and run up the driveway to meet him. He would gather me up in his arms and I would bury my head in his chest.

This was when I was about six or seven and I had very long hair. It hung down past my bottom so that I could sit on it. A routine developed where I would sit next to my father on the white concrete bench outside the front door every evening after he got back from work and he would brush my hair from the top, all the way down to the ends, in long, smooth motions.

It was the nicest part of the evening, before dusk fell and the mosquitoes descended. There was a light breeze in the air. As he brushed my hair, I could smell the tang of his after-shave. Sometimes we would sit on another bench at the top of the garden under an umbrella-shaped grand mango tree, where he would tell me about his cases as the sweet aroma of ripening mangoes filled the air, crickets chirruping in the background. We had a parrot called Polly and we could hear her squawking away, too.

It was an idyllic time, and it always felt very special to me because it was just the two of us: me and him; and none of my brothers. He spoke to me like an adult, which made me feel very grown up.

As I sat there, my father recounted what he'd done that day – the people who had chosen to do the right thing and those who had broken the law and needed to be punished for it; people who were not bad but did bad things; the clients who needed his help because they had been accused of crimes they hadn't committed, but were in the wrong place at the wrong time; or were of the wrong race.

He had this incredibly commanding, rich voice and I always paid attention to what he was saying. Many people who heard him in court would comment on the resonance of his voice, his command of the English language and skill as an advocate. Years later when I was studying for A-level English I read *A Voyage Round My Father* by John Mortimer. So many of the descriptions brought back images and memories of my own father. There was one particular sentence about his father using words in court like they were soldiers being sent into battle: I read it and thought, 'that's my father!' He taught me the importance of working out what lay beneath people's words, and how sometimes it was a matter of following one's instinct rather than the prevailing opinion or narrative. Because Guyana has the death penalty, he would tell me how he had to stay unemotional amidst hysteria, desperation, discrimination and distortion.

I remember one evening he came back up the driveway with a frown on his face. We sat down on the bench, he picked up the brush and started to brush my hair, and I asked him what was wrong.

'A husband and wife came to see me today,' he said. 'They are poor, and have little money. They are manual labourers in the sugar-cane fields and their seventeen-year-old son has got into a fight with a cutlass [a kind of machete] and now he's being held for murder. But he didn't do it. He didn't kill anyone. He's been wrongly charged.'

The son had drunk cheap rum with his friends and passed out, so couldn't remember where he had been. My father said the medical evidence proved the young man innocent but the police weren't interested: they just wanted a quick conviction. Besides, his life was cheap to them.

'What are you going to do, Daddy?' I asked.

'They said to me they had no money and could not afford to pay me any fees. But I told them, "It doesn't matter. The only payment I need is to save your son." The important thing to know, Gina, is that no matter how little people have, you still have to fight for them. Do you understand?'

I nodded.

A few months later, my father came home carrying a bundle of sugar cane. He had got the son off and the boy's parents had come to his office, crying: they were so grateful. They had paid my father the only way they could.

'I didn't want payment but I had to take the sugar cane,' he explained to me. 'Because you must accept when people give you something. It is part of their pride; part of their dignity.'

We had a sugar-cane mill at the back of our garden, where you put in the cane, turned a wheel that crushed it and squeezed out a dark, yellowy liquid that tasted of pure demerara sugar. I was thrilled my father had been paid in this way because it meant we all got to drink this delicious, incredibly sweet juice, which we normally only had as a treat. That's why I remember this story so vividly: the idea of doing something without any hope of a reward just because you knew it was the right thing to do made a great impression on me. And the taste of the nectar-like sugar-cane juice.

I had a lucky childhood: a beautiful home and, for a while at least, no money worries. But it was always made clear to me by both my mother and father that this should never be taken for granted. We had a good life, but there was always an undercurrent of 'don't take anything for granted'. I grew up with a strong sense of how important it was to work and to help get things done. When I was five or six, one of my chores was to go around the garden with a basket and pick the yellow leaves off the hibiscus plants. It was often quite boring under the heat of the tropical sun, but luckily I had an active imagination and I used to tell imaginary friends stories and make up songs to pass the time. I also had to wash the car and collect heavy bottles of milk from the dairy, which was a long walk away.

All of this meant that, from an early age, I was raised with a very strong notion of worth and value. My father instilled me with core values of equality, justice and fair play. Looking back, I realise these formative years were of crucial importance to me. They explain why I firmly believe in doing what's right, no matter the personal cost. Repeatedly, those talks with my father have enabled me to stand tall in the face of pressure. Because I have an ingrained sense of right and wrong it has never once crossed my mind not to stand up for what I believe in.

I limit my children's screen-time, so they're only allowed it at weekends, because when so much of our life is lived online it can be hard to remember that your actions can have a direct effect on an actual human being, not just a screen avatar. Looking at the daily litany of bile and abuse I get on social media reminds me of that. What my father gave me was a very real idea of how one individual's actions affect another's life. I try to teach my children these same lessons.

And I think that's why, when I saw public debate becoming so infected by the Leave versus Remain vitriol, I knew I had to do something. As a child of the Commonwealth, I had been brought up to believe Great Britain was the promised land: a culture where the rule of law was observed and decency was embedded in the national fabric. In the aftermath of the Referendum results, it felt as if those values I cherished – the values of civility, fair play and tolerance – were in danger of getting lost altogether.

If you decide to have a strong voice and use it to defend the causes you believe in, it can also be an isolated voice.

When I raised my head over the parapet on the issue of Brexit, I think a lot of onlookers saw the abuse I attracted and – quite understandably – felt it was safer to stay silent.

But it's when I come under attack that I need to believe, even more firmly, that I am on the right side of the debate. This was brought home to me by the disturbing actions of an aristocrat called Rhodri Philipps.

*

Four days after I won my Brexit legal challenge, Viscount Philipps offered via Facebook a bounty of £5,000 'for the first person to "accidentally" run over this bloody trouble-some first-generation immigrant'. Describing me as a 'boat jumper', he added: 'If this is what we should expect from immigrants, send them back to their stinking jungles.'

Pretty shocking. Not the kind of thing you'd want anyone to think, let alone write down in a public forum. But Viscount Philipps apparently had no such qualms in widely sharing his racist views with his network of friends online.

When I became aware of the Facebook post, I felt violated and scared. It chilled me to my core. How could Facebook allow this post? Why wasn't it moderated? Why hadn't Facebook reported Philipps to the police? I have lived in Britain for more than forty years: I'm British, my children and husband are British; this is my home. I have every right to ask legitimate questions.

This man was inciting someone to run me over, to kill me because he didn't like my questions, my actions or the colour of my skin. It was worse than the sacks full of abusive mail I received daily because it was quite deliberately encouraging people to kill me for a cash reward.

This threat was more frightening than the many others I received, as Philipps appeared to have the means, resources and connections to carry it out. He lived near my office; he knew people who knew me. He or any one of his acquaintances could run me down as I was crossing the road. I began to think about what would happen if he carried out the threat. Would I be killed or crippled? Who would look after my children? How would my husband cope?

That's a terrifying place to be, and I was extremely worried for the safety of myself and my family.

There was no question in my mind that what Viscount Philipps had done was wrong. But was I prepared to engage in a potentially long, complex and emotional court case over it? I thought long and hard about this and the conclusion I came to was that there had to be an aim to what I was doing to make it worthwhile. For me to stand up for what was right, I needed to know I would be making a positive change. In the end, I agreed to be a witness because I thought it was important the Crown Prosecution Service (CPS) looked at their policy on online abuse and began to treat it as seriously as threats made face-to-face.

I reasoned that putting myself out there and facing down my abuser was worth it because if I was successful the change in policy would have important ramifications for others. For me, it's not just about making a noise, it's about creating change. I'll use my voice to speak up, take risks, be the target of abuse, but only if I know the rewards will be impactful and far-reaching and change the outcomes for others.

Entering public life as a woman – be it as a politician, journalist, expert or activist – makes you the target of the most sinister threats, abuse and language. A 2017 report[7]

---

7 'All-Party Parliamentary Inquiry into Electoral Conduct, Final Update' – July 2017, researched and funded by the Anti-Semitism Policy Trust.

by the All-Party Parliamentary Group on anti-Semitism revealed the full extent of the abuse received by general election candidates, particularly ethnic minority candidates and women of all ethnicities. When I've asked Parliamentary candidates why they have not spoken out more, their reply is often: 'It's normal, so we just have to accept it.' But we must not normalise hatred and intimidation. Lines of decency are being violated and, as the old saying goes, bad things happen when good people do nothing, so we must all stand up and push back. It is not an acceptable price to pay for having a public face; for doing your public duty.

Social media, email and other online platforms create breeding grounds for hate that are terrifying. I've watched as perpetrators have discovered a new boldness. They no longer hide under anonymity but openly sign their names. They no longer linger alone in their rooms, or at the end of some bar in a pub. Social media has amplified their destructive voices and created echo chambers that reinforce their views.

That's why someone had to take a stand, and that's why I took on the racist aristocrat.

Viscount Philipps decided to represent himself in the court case. He turned up to court in July 2017 wearing a tweed suit. He refused to stand when the court officials referred to him as 'Mr St Davids'.

'I'm not Mr St Davids, I'm afraid,' he replied. 'It's Lord St Davids.'

It struck me as slightly odd that Rhodri Philipps should be so hung up on social niceties after the names he'd called me, but he clearly wasn't a reasoned individual acting on logic. One thing I have learned is that the vitriol I receive crosses all socio-economic groups, classes and professions. It's not just a small minority who hate my guts, and that's something I still struggle to understand. People from all walks of life seem genuinely to believe that if you are not born in the UK you have no rights and should just be grateful to be in Britain – in some sort of servitude.

I was dreading facing Viscount Philipps in court. As he'd declined the services of a lawyer, there was a moment when I was worried I would have to be cross-examined by him in the flesh and answer his questions, which I felt would lay me open to further abuse from him. But at the last minute, he dropped his request to cross-examine me. He'd tried to maintain that what he said was 'satire', but the law saw through his act and he was found guilty of two of three charges of sending menacing and racially aggravated communications under the Communications Act 2003 and sentenced to twelve weeks in prison. At first, he said he was going to appeal, but then he abandoned that too.

The senior district judge at Westminster magistrates' court, Emma Arbuthnot, told him: 'Why public figures deserve this warped behaviour is beyond me ... You showed this hatred by publicly directing abuse at others, which is a criminal offence in this multicultural society we are fortunate to live in.'

A month after the court case was concluded, Alison Saunders, the director of the CPS, announced that prosecutors will now be ordered to treat online hate crime as seriously as offences carried out face-to-face. There will be stiffer penalties for abuse on Twitter, Facebook and other social media platforms. Saunders rightly said that the crackdown was needed because online abuse can lead to extremist hate crimes. She cited my case as one of the reasons such action was necessary.

Viscount Philipps was a bully – a mean, dangerous, racist bully – but, as I was finding out, he was by no means the only one.

What I've often found in the past is that if you stand up to bullies, they crumble. They don't expect you to fight back. They're never as strong as you think they are, and that applies whether they're a Lord, a Lady or a plain old Mr or Mrs.

7

Bursting the Bully Bubble

I remember the letter vividly.

The envelope felt thick to the touch. It was off-white, high-quality paper, and when I opened it and slid out the folded letter I saw that it was written in the most beautiful calligraphic style. The ink was a sort of faded brown, as if what I had in my hands was an old-fashioned document, written with superior penmanship to record some important event.

And then I started to read.

Sentence after sentence was filled with the most unimaginable hatred and rage. Every single word was so poisonous and vile that I was shocked beyond my expectations. The writer compared me to an ape and a monkey, said I wasn't human and used the n-word repeatedly to describe me. 'You're only good for sex,' he wrote. 'You should go back to being a whore, which must be how you earned your money, but your days are done. You're too old now. You should be taken out and shot and put out of your misery.'

I was shocked that anyone could think those things. And it was terrifying to know he was thinking them about me.

In the months after the court case, I'd become used to receiving a steady stream of death threats and abusive letters. The day after my High Court win, the switchboard at my office was jammed full of abusive callers. My assistant was

51

being inundated with vitriolic emails, to the extent that I once walked in and saw her in tears because she was so disturbed by what she'd had to read. After that, I insisted no one but me was going to open my personal mail or any suspicious-looking emails. I didn't want to put my staff through that. None of this was their fault.

I received hundreds of threatening communications, filled with the most horrifying bile: that I'm not even human, I'm a primate, that I should be hunted and beheaded, that the only thing I'm good for is to be a slave or a cleaner, or worse, that my children would have their throats cut and I should watch and then be burned alive. My head should be put on Traitor's Gate.

People had written these letters, put them in an envelope, bought a first-class stamp and gone to all the effort of finding a postbox to send them to me. One of them was a cartoon strip made from cut-out newspaper photographs of my face, which showed me being gang-raped. Another said they'd throw acid in my face. Occasionally I'd come across a London postmark, which would really unsettle me because it was so geographically close.

The police acted quickly. They also gave us a stack of clear evidence bags, and showed us how to get the IP address from emails. They gave my assistant, my husband and me a talk about white powder, which they reassuringly said would most likely be a hoax. Letters filled with anthrax spores killed five people in the United States in the autumn of 2001. But the police explained that there had never been an anthrax attack in the UK – only anonymous threats from people using white powder to evoke fear in the recipients.

Eventually, I stopped showing my husband the letters too. He got very upset – more upset than me because he loves me and wanted to be able to protect me. Wading through the post was a solitary, and often scary, task. Once I spotted an abusive letter, I had to put it into an evidence bag and forward it to the police, who would then send it for forensic analysis to the laboratory. This was how I tried to keep myself safe. It became an unemotional routine.

But my tormentors were resourceful. When they couldn't find my home address, they sent the letters to my work instead, and many of them arrived addressed to my charitable True and Fair Foundation. I got used to spotting the worst ones – they were often written in illegible scrawls – but I soon realised I could never tell the contents by looking just at the envelope. Some letters were sent on beautiful station- ery with first-class stamps, and I had to steel myself to open all the mail I received.

After opening this particular letter, I sat there for several seconds, puzzled at the idea that I could inspire such a depth of hatred in another person I'd never met, for speaking up for our sovereignty.

After a while these kinds of threats have a cumulative effect. No matter how much I tell myself they won't get me down and no matter how much I believe in what I'm doing, I wouldn't be human if I wasn't upset from time to time. I have become wary of walking down the street, of using public transport, of going out to public places.

These days, Alan and I live a far quieter life. We have two or three trusted restaurants where we can occasionally go for meals. I often go out wearing my running gear and a baseball cap pulled low over my face, with sunglasses. The family laugh that instead of 'work Gina', I look like 'gym Gina'. That 'you still look like you, Mum!' Laughter helps to keep us sane.

Outside my home, I feel I'm walking on eggshells. I have developed a sixth sense for possible conflict. I've had people hissing 'black bitch' at me as I go past. That happens quite a lot. Alan and I used to love going to theatre or concerts, but we don't go as often any more. Generally, we'll go to friends' houses or we'll just stay at home, have dinner, play board games with the kids. There's very little spontaneity left. We can no longer say, 'Let's just go here.'

I miss the freedom to be invisible. I used to love people-watching; it was one of my pleasures, to watch the world go by. It brought me such comfort to know that everyone is essentially the same.

I'm not saying this to complain about it, or to indulge in any sort of self-pity. I say it to state the facts and to ask why it has come to this: where did this hatred spring from? How can we tackle it? What can it teach us about bursting the bully bubble?

I call it a 'bubble' because bullies tend to stick together and get justification for their behaviour from those inside the same distorted space.

The truth is the tide of hate is rising. We live a comfortable life, and although the police can't give me the highest level of protection afforded to politicians or public figures they have been brilliant and taken many precautions, for which I'm immensely grateful.

People have to deal with bullies in all walks of life – particularly women: relationship bullies, workplace bullies, even friends who bully us into doing them favours. In 2014, a survey of 25,000 people in the workplace[8] found that 52 per cent of women said they had experienced bullying or harassment over the past three years, while another 12 per cent had been sexually harassed. There are no comparable figures for men.

I believe the key to withstanding bullies is realising they can only win if we let them. The power is ours. By not

---

8 'Project 28–40: The Project' – Kathryn Nawrockyi et al, 2014, survey by Opportunity Now and PWC.

standing up to bullies, we allow their terror to flourish and fear can lead to silence. If that happens, the world becomes shaped by those with the loudest voices and the darkest hearts. We need to have the strength to confront the people who want us to stay silent, who want to discourage us from our convictions. We must raise our voices to drown out theirs.

Which is why, when I folded that letter up and placed it back in its beautifully addressed envelope before dropping it into the police evidence bag, I didn't allow myself to feel cowed. I remembered a time, many years before, when I'd also had to confront a bully. It was when I was eleven years old, as a homesick schoolgirl who found herself very far from home.

8

A Homesick Schoolgirl

When I had just turned eleven, my parents sent me to board at Moira House, an all-girls school in Eastbourne, East Sussex.

My father was one of the most senior people helping to organise a new opposition party, the Working People's Alliance, to fight the Guyanese dictator Forbes Burnham and his corrupt government. There was a young, charismatic leader called Walter Rodney, who was causing our dictator problems by attempting to overthrow him, and the country was becoming volatile. (Rodney was killed in 1980 by a car bomb in his brother's car. It was later confirmed the bomb had been planted by the government; as my father always contended). My parents had already been thinking of sending my elder brother and me to the UK for 'the best education in the world', but in this febrile political situation they were convinced it would be best for us to leave.

At school, I looked different from everyone else, I dressed differently and I spoke differently too. My parents were strict, and back in Guyana I'd attended a very strict convent and was taught English with a precision that came from terrifying nuns. We had to learn pages of proverbs and compete in spelling bees. Even though I was so excited to be in England, I felt very much like the outsider.

My mother knew that I might get homesick, so she packed me off with a bottle of her perfume, Nina Ricci's L'Air du Temps, to remind me of her. The bottle was oval, with curved lines shaped into the glass, and the stopper was a white dove with its wings spread outwards. Every time I undid the stopper and inhaled the scent of bergamot and gardenia, I was transported in a swirl of memories straight back to my home: the sweet smell of the garden roses, my mother's face, my father brushing my hair, the chirruping of crickets and the smell of the ripening mango tree. It was one of my most prized possessions.

On nights when I felt particularly homesick I would put a tiny bit on my pillow to help me sleep. Every Sunday, before going to church, the school allowed us to wear perfume as a special treat, and I would dab a spot on each of my wrists and feel all grown-up. This was in the days long before mobile phones or the internet, so that perfume bottle was a strong link I had to my mother and everyone back home.

My other most precious possession was a red pocket-sized photo album my mother had given me before they left me at school. On the first page was a picture of my mother and father standing in our garden. The next page was of all my siblings smiling, wearing ridiculous T-shirts my mum had specially ordered from England with our names on them; the next was a photo of all of us – including me. Every night before going to sleep I would kiss each person in the photos and whisper, 'I love you, I miss you.' Then I would carefully tuck the album under my pillow. I did this ritual well into my teens.

My mother's perfume got me through the first weeks of my first term in this new and unfamiliar place. I was slow to make friends, with some girls ostracising me. They couldn't always understand my odd accent, and my awkward beanpole frame and ridiculously long black hair only made me stand out more. I retreated into myself and tried not to draw attention to anything I was doing. I just got on with my work, and at nights I'd escape to the relative safety of my dormitory bed and whichever book I was reading.

But one weekend things came to a head. A group of girls ganged together and, when I was out of the dormitory, stole the bottle of perfume from my chest of drawers and decided it would be funny to tip it down the basin in the shared bathroom. They then refilled it with water. When, later that night, I opened the bottle to dab it on my pillow, I knew instantly something was wrong. The perfume didn't smell like my mother any more. I sniffed it again. Then the realisation dawned. My throat constricted. I could feel tears pricking against my eyes. The other girls were looking at me, scanning my features for a reaction, but I knew that if I showed them I was upset they would have won.

I tried to hold myself together. As calmly as I could, I put the bottle back on the chest of drawers and walked to the toilets. I locked the door of the cubicle, sat down and cried into a towel so that no one would hear. I cried and cried and cried. I got all the tears out of my system, and then I dried my eyes, splashed my face with water and walked back into the dormitory. No one said anything. When they saw I wasn't going to break down in front of them, the girls lost interest and returned to their chatter, choosing whoever else they were going to pick on next.

There was one girl who I knew was the ringleader. I suspected that she had been the one to orchestrate the whole thing. As I drifted off to sleep, I thought about what I should do. I didn't want to tell a teacher and be accused of snitching. I didn't want to show I was hurt and risk being seen as weak. Then I remembered something else my mother had packed into my suitcase before I left for school: it was a necklace with a Virgin Mary pendant (I was raised a Catholic) and a little rope-chain gold bracelet. The bracelet came in a red velvet bag.

The next morning I put the bracelet into its bag, drew the strings tightly and I gave it to the ringleader, saying, 'This is so we can be friends.' The girl stared at me, then looked inside the bag and took the bracelet out, holding it up to the light to examine it. She seemed nonplussed and didn't know what to say. She just took the bracelet, then turned and walked away.

She didn't speak to me for a couple of days, but I sensed a slight thawing in the atmosphere. And then, gradually, she started suggesting things. She'd invite me to join in a game or ask me to be part of her hockey team, and by the end of that week we were friends. I eventually realised that her parents were diplomats whom she hardly ever saw, and who rarely sent her letters or presents. The bracelet became one of her most treasured possessions.

I never had a problem with bullies at school again.

All of this taught me an important lesson. It was that bullies can sometimes be complex, that they may be acting from a place of weakness, not strength – from a lack of love. They can feel threatened and backed into a corner by something – or someone – they don't understand. Bullying is the way they lash out. But underneath all the bravado there's often a fragile individual riven with insecurities and weakness who doesn't know how to express him or herself when confronted by the unknown.

As soon as I reached out to the girl who was bullying me, her defences crumbled. I didn't counter anger with anger. Nor did I show I was upset. Instead I tried to disarm her with kindness, so that we could engage with each other. Once a bully sees you as being more like themselves, that's half the battle.

I teach the same lesson to my eleven-year-old daughter. At the same age I had experienced bullying, she started being left out by her best girlfriends. And, similarly to me, there was one specific girl who she thought was being mean. My solution was to sit my daughter down and say, 'Why don't you invite this girl over for a play date, and find out from her what her favourite things are to eat and what she most likes to do, and then do that when she comes over?' It's exactly what she did and the two of them are now firm friends. It's not always that easy, but walking in other people's shoes can change both your and their hearts and minds.

Of course, when you're an adult, things get more complicated. I'm not suggesting everything can be settled with a play date (if only they could, things would be a whole lot simpler!). But that early experience has stayed with me throughout some of the toughest periods of my life.

*

There were times, after the Brexit court case, when I was repeatedly told I was the most hated woman in Britain. There seemed to be such a level of fury directed towards me and I was puzzled as to where it came from. It's not that I was surprised exactly – as a woman of colour, I've become used to discrimination in all its varied forms – but I was taken aback by how relentless the backlash seemed and how many people felt so violent towards me over what was essentially a political, rather than a personal, issue.

Perhaps I was naive, but I had this innate certainty of the rectitude of standing up for what I believed in. I didn't think I was harming anyone by doing what I did. Far from it: I was using my own money to safeguard some important constitutional and civil liberties I thought were at risk in the

Britain I knew and loved. Of course, I expect people to disagree with me – freedom of speech and differing opinions make us a stronger society, not a weaker one. What I didn't expect was the irrational loathing my very existence seemed to trigger.

It wasn't just the social media or personal bullying, I was also being bullied via ceaseless personal attacks in some of the right-wing press. There was one paper that repeatedly sought to undermine me. They would write profile pieces on me that were riddled with inaccuracies and which tried to diminish my every accomplishment by falsely claiming I wasn't using my money to fund the court case, and that it was my rich husband's fortune or some male moneybags pulling my strings. I wasn't a businesswoman any more, I was a 'former model'. They attacked everything: my achievements, my standing, my integrity and my principles, even questioning if I am British.

One female journalist from the *Daily Mail* wrote an extraordinarily venomous article making out I was wearing a real fur coat and sapphire and diamond earrings as I left court – it was an old sheepskin and a pair of £25 diamante earrings. This same journalist had, just a few days before Christmas, sent me a list of ten intrusive questions on my husband's and my personal finances and our investment business, giving us just twenty-four hours to respond. It was clear from some of the questions that they were aiming to portray me and my husband as non-tax-paying non-doms with offshore investments. No doubt if I didn't answer their questions they would print saying I refused to comment, which is designed to make the person appear guilty. Even though we have never been non-doms, and told the journalist this plainly, she still wrote, 'Despite her wealth and overseas parentage, she says she has not claimed non-domicile status in order to save on her tax bill.'

The thread that ran through all of it was the idea that I, an immigrant, a woman of colour, had no right to speak up, and that if I did I was a traitor.

I once spoke to a journalist from this paper and asked, 'Why are you doing this to me?'

He said, 'Gina, you're an enigma.'

'What do you mean?' I asked.

'Well,' he replied, 'nobody does anything for the right reason.'

That said more about them than it did about me, and it was difficult and shocking to hear; it meant that these tabloid journalists wouldn't stop until they'd found some dirt on me. And if they couldn't find any dirt, I discovered they'd simply make it up, or slant the commentary to inflame passions against me. It was bullying on a scale I'd never previously experienced, and one that was difficult to know how to fight against. The pieces written made many errors – some of them, such as the fact I went to Roedean School (I didn't), were relatively harmless; others were less so.

I was constantly referred to as 'foreign-born' and it seemed maliciously intended, as if the colour of my skin excluded me from having any say in the future of a country I had lived in, and paid taxes in, for over thirty years and had always considered my home. I believe it came from a place of misogynist bigotry and racism. They were seeking to shut me down; to break my spirit.

The *Daily Mail* and the *Daily Express* were particularly vicious. It got to the stage where it felt like if I sneezed they would run a double-page spread on it. Both papers implied that I couldn't possibly be bright enough to be acting on my own as a mere woman – there must be lots of powerful, rich men controlling me. Alan joked that he did not need to ever call to see where I was, as the *Daily Express* seemed to always have my movements and my words, albeit with a very strong editorial slant, available on their website within hours.

The second suggestion was always that I couldn't have made my own money and must be getting it from somewhere else. The idea that I could have been successful in my own right was anathema to these blinkered media barons. I couldn't possibly have achieved anything on my own. I mean, who exactly did I think I was?

And behind it all there was the insistent drumbeat of racism, as if I wasn't allowed to speak up because of the colour of my skin, because supposedly I didn't 'belong'. My face didn't fit. I should shut up and be grateful to Britain, and my gratitude should result in my silence. One paper went as far as darkening my skin colour in a photo in yet another article maligning me.

The irony is that, prior to the court case, I do know and have helped the very same journalist at the *Daily Mail* who decided to write a hatchet job on me. Although I've never met its then editor, Paul Dacre, I was a regular contributor to articles in the *Money Mail* about rip-offs in the City, thanks to the work of my True and Fair Campaign for greater transparency and a Code of Ethics in the UK investment and pension industry. In fact, I would go further and say they were very supportive and saw what I was doing as a fight that would benefit their readers.

But, with Brexit, the tone changed dramatically. There was one female business journalist I had known for twelve years – I'd had coffee with her, I'd helped her with stories both on investing and discrimination against women. We weren't friends, but we knew each other and, I thought, we had a level of mutual respect. Yet this woman wrote one of the most sexist articles about me I'd ever read, referring to me as 'sultry', saying I had a 'whiff of the Jackie Collins heroine' about me, before implying I'd only married Alan for money. It then went on to say I was 'the Remainers' answer to Joan of Arc'.

'But of course,' this woman wrote, 'Joan was burnt at the stake – a fate some Brexiteers might view as too kind for this heroine.'

It's astonishing to me that a respected business journalist on a national newspaper can blithely write about another woman being burnt at the stake and get away with it.

At points, it went beyond bullying into pure hatred, directed more broadly at other targets. When the *Daily Mail* carried a photograph of the three Supreme Court judges who had ruled in my favour that the UK government would require the consent of Parliament to give notice of Brexit underneath the banner headline 'Enemies of the People', it was like something out of 1930s Germany. It sent shivers down my spine. And what was even more despicable, in my view, was the fact that no one from the Lord Chancellor's office condemned that front page. Senior political voices should have come out immediately and said it was inciting hatred against an independent judiciary.

Yet these papers are so powerful they get away with it. I instructed lawyers to make complaints to IPSO about the *Daily Express*, the *Sun, Daily Mail* and *Mail Online*, and not one of them was upheld. They acknowledged that the *Daily Mail* article saying I should be burnt at the stake was 'offensive' but somehow not in breach of the editorial code. However, the offending line was eventually removed from online versions. You cannot appeal an IPSO decision itself, only the process by which the decision is made, which my lawyers duly challenged. We requested information, emails and minutes from meetings, but unsurprisingly none appear to exist that can be shared with us or which have not been so heavily redacted as to make them worthless.

I rarely ever watch or listen back to interviews I do on TV or radio. In print, I had to remember that most of what was being written were opinions formulated by people who didn't know me. I had to remind myself, the only people whose opinions are truly important are my husband, my children and my handful of closest friends.

Several PR professionals said my reputation was being destroyed by the press, which would hurt my business and Foundation, and that I should keep a low profile: run away and hide, in effect. But what is reputation? It is what people think of you, it is not who you are. If you bother about that – if people will like you, approve of what you do, how you act, what you say – you are playing to someone else's tune: you become trapped in a persona that constantly needs justifying. I refuse to run away, I refuse to hide; I refuse to be handicapped by how others perceive who and what I am. I do what I do because I believe we must speak up and fight against lies, injustice and conflicts of interest. So I put on my invisible armour, my high heels, and step up, striding past those who use words as weapons against me.

Not that that always feels achievable. In October 2017, a few months after the Independent Press Standards Organisation investigated my complaints, my lawyers sent me back two huge lever-arch files full of articles and online comments made about me that had formed the focus of my complaints. They suggested I shouldn't read them, as they knew I had not seen the bulk of the hatred, but there was part of me that wanted to know what had been said. Enough time had passed, I thought.

The Brexit court case had been over for nearly six months and I felt more able to tackle the abuse head-on, as it was increasingly being balanced out by supportive, kind messages. And I had this idea that if I knew what these people had written I would be closer to understanding where they were coming from. After all, you can't just listen to the people who support you; you need to understand those who don't. I thought I'd get a level of insight I hadn't had before by walking in their shoes.

I sat down at our glass kitchen table on a Sunday morning when the children were upstairs and Alan was out. I knew I had to steel myself for the task in hand. I gingerly opened the first lever-arch file. There were pages and pages of comments – sometimes as many as 3,000 under the online articles. The sheer river of hatred was extremely upsetting. 'From the colour of your skin, you're just a piece of shit,' went one comment. 'And shit should just be trodden on and I'm going to do that to your face.' 'You're nothing but a rich man's whore. You should be locked up and taken out once a day for a good banging.' 'A Jo Cox killing would be too good for you.' 'We really need indigenous British citizens as people who speak in public, not squatters from 3rd World shit holes!' 'You're not even human, just an ugly ape who needs whipping into obedience.'

I was too taken aback to cry. I couldn't move from the table. For so long during the court case I had held it together. If anything, I was criticised in the press for being too closed off, for not showing enough emotion, never smiling. But it was the only way I knew how to protect myself. Now, many months later, sitting at my kitchen table with my defences down, I wanted to cry but was too numb. Too traumatised by what I was reading. Too shocked and bewildered by the people I thought lived in my homeland. Then one thought started playing over and over in my mind: 'My children – they can't hide the colour of their skin, who they are. What if this uglier side of Britain takes over?' These thoughts struck like a dagger in my heart and I sat feeling an overwhelming sense of pain for their futures.

I sat there for an hour and a half, staring through the kitchen window into the garden beyond. When Alan came back, that's where he found me. 'Gina,' he said, 'what are you doing? Why are you reading them?' He quickly closed the files, took my hands, pulled me out of my chair and then he gave me a hug and told me: 'Remember, you're special. What you're doing is extraordinary.' Then he made me put the lever-arch files away. I haven't looked at them since.

I'm a realist. I understand that sensationalism and divisiveness sells newspapers. But I suspect there's another side to it too, and I suspect that part of the reason these newspapers were so aggravated by me is that they were frightened of losing their win. When bullies attack with vehemence, it's because they want to protect something – in this case, it was the Leave campaign's narrow sliver of victory. It's such a fragile win that they're worried they'll lose it, so they lash out. And I'm an easy target for them because I represent all the things their loyal readership most fears: they can say I'm a foreigner, an immigrant; they can wrongly allege I don't pay tax in the UK, that I'm backed by rich men; they can paint a picture that inspires hatred in others. And that's the way they keep the toxicity spinning.

But the crucial thing to remember is that it's all coming through a prism of fear. In the end that was how I managed to cope with it: I would tell myself, 'They're frightened of me and if I fall silent, then they've won.' The peddlers of hatred and vitriol ended up making me feel more powerful; made me see more clearly what needs protecting and fighting for. I decided I would thank them for stiffening my resolve. Then something changed. Mingled amongst the voices of hate, were voices of gratitude, some seeking hope, wanting to share their increasing experiences of abuse, of feeling lost and living in limbo. These positive messages made me determined to carry on, to speak up for them and their children. I was somehow invigorated and felt confirmation that I was doing the right thing because I was speaking up for others who were too scared to voice their opinions. I could channel their hopes and fears through my voice and actions, and I wasn't about to stop doing that.

Many women have experiences of bullies in all walks of life. One of the things I have taken away from my own experience is that it's important not to worry too much about being liked in the workplace. It's difficult to say that and it's difficult to live by, but you can learn to be tougher, you can build a professional persona that is separate from what you're like in private, but both must stand on principles, compassion and kindness. You're not at work to make friends – you already have friends and people who love you, who can see your softer side and who know you for who you really are. You're at work to do something well and professionally, and to be the best you can be. To earn, to look after yourself and your family, to fulfil your dreams and aspirations, to contribute to society.

I think this idea that you need a lot of friends is a modern phenomenon, encouraged by social media sites such as Facebook or Instagram, where you're judged by the number of 'likes' you accrue rather than your character or substance. It becomes an addiction that weakens who you are. As I tell my children, there's only ever going to be a handful of people who really matter, who really give unconditional love and support. These are the ones you should concentrate your time and energy on.

Standing up to bullies requires reserves of mental strength and resilience. To build resilience you need to think like an athlete and train your mind with as much application as you would train your body to perform at its best, so that when you're confronted with high-pressure moments or incidents you have those reserves to call on. We all know the physical side: in a perfect world, we'd all eat well, exercise regularly, sleep eight hours a night and exist at the peak of fitness. As simple as that sounds, it's not always practical, but we aspire to the goal. Mental strength is the same.

To build my own reserves up, I have found it incredibly important to have periods of calm when I can hear my own internal voice, reflect on the challenges of the day and allow my thoughts to meander. I spend time looking at and listening to the small wonders around me. Walking, climbing, listening to a glorious piece of music. Small pleasures that swell the heart and soul, then the mind. It has become fashionable for some to call this mindfulness. This worries me, as it can be portrayed as focusing on oneself too much, more of the 'I' culture we are adopting. I prefer mindfulness to be about the lessons I learnt as a child – to be mindful of others. Cuddling my children also helps! It's those small but important everyday moments that can help you recharge your mental batteries and make you even stronger for what lies ahead. It's important to pay it as much attention as you do your physical well-being.

I also think that if you can focus on a bigger goal – on what you will achieve by standing up to bullies – that helps power you through the difficult times. When Viscount Philipps made his racist threats towards me, I knew that online abuse had to be treated as seriously as face-to-face abuse. It's no coincidence that within weeks of his conviction the CPS announced a policy change to ensure that would be the case in the future. There are times when standing up for yourself can result in a positive impact for many other people too. You can affect real change – not just in the behaviour of the bully, but in others who might be tempted to behave that way as well.

9

Skin and Silence

I've touched on this in the previous chapter, but I want to spend some more time discussing a specific form of abuse that has been sent my way, not least because it is something that affects a considerable percentage of the population as well as myself.

Until Brexit, for more than four decades of my life in Britain, I can honestly say that whilst I had received some racial abuse, I never felt terrified.

The first time I experienced naked racism was when I was in the Lower Sixth and went on a school trip to London with a group of eight girls to see a production of a play we were studying. We were excited, as we loved escaping sleepy Eastbourne for the bright lights of the big city, and because we were sixth formers we were allowed to go accompanied by just one member of staff, in this case a teacher called Miss Wall.

We took the train to Victoria Station on the Saturday afternoon, saw the play and then quickly made our way back to Victoria at around 11 p.m. When we got there, the station was crowded and noisy and filled with rowdy groups of football fans who seemed drunk, which made us rather nervous.

One group saw us girls as we walked past to catch our train. They whistled and jeered. Then they saw me and started shouting, 'Why are you with that Paki?' and similar taunts, as I was the only ethnic minority girl in the group. I was furious. As my friends kept their heads down and quickened their pace to the ticket barrier, I broke away and strode up to the young man who appeared to be the ringleader. Miss Wall was clearly worried, and tried to call me back, but I pretended not to hear her.

'Why do you lie in the sun trying to look like me if you hate the colour of my skin?' I said. His mouth gaped open. He stared at me, lost for words. He was so shocked that it gave me time to run back to the other girls, push past the ticket barrier and board the train as the other young men tried to come after me.

I dropped into my seat, out of breath and relieved to have made it in time. Miss Wall told me I shouldn't have left the safety of the group, but I simply replied, 'If I don't stand up to bullies, they will just carry on bullying someone else.'

There have, of course, been further incidents since then. I've experienced distasteful remarks whispered under the breath, which when questioned are met with the words, 'We didn't mean you.' They were easy to brush off. I remember reading about or hearing from people who came to the UK in the 1950s from the Commonwealth who were met with signs saying, 'No Blacks, no Irish, no dogs'. That was the past – wasn't it?

Before Brexit my everyday thought processes and existence did not have to focus on whether or not I was different. However, that all changed with the vote to leave the EU. For the first time in my life, I was the target of unadulterated, blatant racism, whether it was the shaven-headed young man in the tracksuit who muttered 'black bitch' as I was getting out of my car to go into the office or the endless stream of bigoted vitriol I received both online and in my daily postbag.

Although I have become a high-profile target for a certain kind of racist rage, I'm far from alone. I get emails from people all over the country experiencing similar things and not just because they look different; for many, it's because they are not seen as indigenous. Like me, these people also feel that, in the aftermath of the EU Referendum, there's been an uptick in racist incidents and they're being singled out and bullied for their supposed 'foreignness' like never before.

It's not just anecdotal evidence. The statistics bear it out too. In 2015/16, according to the Home Office[9], there were 62,518 offences recorded by the police in which one or more hate crime strands were deemed to be a motivating factor. This was an increase of 19 per cent compared with the 52,465 recorded the previous year. Seventy-eight per cent of those were race hate crimes.

'There was a sharp increase in the number of racially or religiously aggravated offences recorded by the police following the EU Referendum,' wrote the report's authors. 'The number of racially or religiously aggravated offences recorded by the police in July 2016 was 41 per cent higher than in July 2015.'

When the *Independent* newspaper conducted a 2016 analysis of social media sites designed to report racist incidents in the month after the Referendum[10], they found a 'grim litany' of examples, including gangs prowling the streets demanding passers-by prove they could speak English; graffitied swastikas in Armagh, Sheffield, Plymouth, Leicester, London and Glasgow; assaults, arson attacks and dog excrement being thrown at doors or shoved through

9 'Hate Crime, England and Wales 2015/16' – Aoife O'Neill, Home Office Statistical Bulletin 17/17, 17th October 2017.
10 'Racism unleashed: True extent of the "explosion of blatant hate" that followed Brexit result revealed', Adam Lusher, *Independent*, 28th July 2016.

letterboxes; and toddlers being racially abused alongside their mothers. In one instance, a man in Glasgow ripped off a girl's headscarf and told her, 'Trash like you better start obeying the white man'. There were comparisons with 1930s Nazi Germany, with a crowd striding through a London street chanting, 'First we'll get the Poles out, then the gays!'

The three social media groups in question[11], who compiled their report with the support of the Institute of Race Relations, accused the prime minister and her government of paving the way for this explosion of abuse.

'If a hostile environment is embedded politically, it can't be a surprise that it takes root culturally,' they stated.

My own experience is that this is true. We live in a society that is more divided than ever. The dialogue around Brexit has been so rageful that people can now talk openly about 'cleansing Britain' and 'making it white again' by 'getting rid of the blacks who should go back to slavery'. These are all examples of statements that have been made either to or about me. It's extraordinary – and it horrifies me.

You might be able to discount one or two such cases as the product of an ignorant or unbalanced mindset, but there has been a tsunami of racist bile which, I reluctantly believe, must be indicative of something far deeper and more worrying going on beneath the surface.

I heard that the editorial team of the *Daily Mail* had gone to astonishing lengths to dig up dirt on me. One publication even sent a reporter to the tiny Guyanese village where my father was born. They asked around to find out if there was any negative spin they could put on my family or my 'foreign' upbringing, but again, they came up with nothing.

---

11 The *Independent* was allowed exclusive access to a database of accounts collected by the social media sites PostRefRacism, Worrying Signs and iStreetWatch.

My father slept on the floor for much of his teenage life, saved up his money to put himself through night school, then went on to qualify as a barrister, then QC, and ultimately became Attorney General. An incredible story in itself. But that was too positive a story for this right-wing rag. They wanted something negative, something that could be used to attack my motives and my integrity. A 'good news' story about my father didn't exactly fit the bill – so it never got printed.

Then there was the occasion I appeared on the BBC's flagship political discussion programme, *Question Time*. The other panellists included Nish Kumar, the stand-up comedian who hosts *The Mash Report* and a white, male, Oxbridge-educated cabinet minister.

I was nervous, and so my husband and my older brother kindly came with me for moral support. The three of us were sitting in the green room before the recording was due to start. I wanted to be up to date on any breaking news and check I hadn't missed any key developments, so I started scanning the newspapers in preparation.

The cabinet minister sauntered in. We'd met before, and he nodded a curt hello to me before making a beeline for my brother. He introduced himself with his first name and said, 'We're on the panel together tonight.'

My brother was puzzled.

'No,' he said. 'I don't think we are.'

I looked up from the papers and suddenly a thought hit me. Had this minister seen an Asian-looking male and assumed it was Nish Kumar, even though my brother couldn't be more physically different?

Nish has wavy hair, a thick beard and is thirty-two years old. My brother has round glasses, a number-one grade haircut, is clean shaven, and is two years older than me. They are visually polar opposites. The only thing they have in common is a similar skin colour! Did this government minister simply look at the colour of their skin and think they looked the same?

*

Why has race once again become such a focus in our seemingly civilised twenty-first-century society? I believe it's because certain power-hungry, self-aggrandising politicians know how divisive discussions can be around immigration and race, and it serves their agenda of divide and conquer to fuel the most poisonous and ill-informed of these debates.

To perpetuate division benefits the men in charge – of corporations or political pressure groups – who exploit the division to shore up their own power. They dismiss experts, academics and any people with experience. It also suits aggressive foreign powers who are seeking to destabilise Western society in a cold war that will allow them to prosper. And newspaper owners hope it will help them sell more newspapers, but I'm not sure it's a strategy that is working.

In November 2017, the share price of the parent company of the *Daily Mail* and *Mail Online* fell by more than 20 per cent after the paper reported a sharp drop in annual profits and warned of a tough year ahead. Interestingly, the staunch Brexit-waving *Daily Mail* and *Daily Express* newspapers have seen their circulations fall by 6.6 per cent and 7.6 per cent over the twelve months to the end of November 2017, in line with the overall market declines of 6.9 per cent. This suggests that the extreme Brexit messages of the *Mail* and *Express* are actually failing to win readers against their competition: their stance hasn't made much difference. It also shows more generally that the public is getting its news more and more from other sources and that the power of these publications in shaping public opinion is declining.

We've read that Marie Antoinette said of the desperation of the poor, 'Let them eat cake' – the modern equivalent is 'Let them eat chlorinated chicken'. I am deeply worried about the dangers of a collapse in the Brexit negotiations, culminating in a 'No Deal' hard Brexit, which some of the more extreme Brexiteers are seemingly trying to engineer. It is an illiberal agenda that pits social tribes against each other.

The thought of the potential for our economy to spiral downwards in such a scenario, leading to the country and industries requiring bail-outs frightens me. This doomsday scenario might require various individuals, companies or countries to step in and lend or invest at short notice to provide financial relief to Britain. No doubt these financiers will demand a steep price for coming in at our time of need, be it through inflated lending rates, or simply buying out our firms or industries on the cheap, akin to the 1970s 'asset strippers'. Some of these potential lenders with the largest cheque books may not be the most palatable names or countries, with questionable moral compasses. Will we be in a position to decline their offers? So much for 'bringing back control'. We might ultimately lose control and be a country in hock.

Undermining rational debate, or voices of concern and common sense, and silencing opposition through venomous personal attacks is now the order of the day.

'Who is heard and who is not defines the status quo,' writes the feminist author Rebecca Solnit in her essay 'A Short History of Silence'. 'By redefining whose voice is valued, we redefine our society and its values.'

The attempt to silence me, and other activists like me, should worry us all. On the one hand, our society has made considerable progress since the Second World War. We are healthier, more educated, more connected than ever before. Yet there's now an upsurge in totally ignorant behaviour, which makes me fear that the gains we've made in terms of tolerance and multiculturalism are being picked away at. Wounds are being re-opened. Racism is attaching itself like a virus to the weaknesses in our societal body.

This is partly because many of the peddlers of race hatred and division know how to play a sophisticated game, but it's also because too many people in positions of power are allowing them to win. What is happening to our social pulse, our communal conscience? People no longer fight for core values or beliefs in the way they used to. Apathy has taken hold, a sense of 'what will be, will be' or 'we just have to wait and see'. I have no idea what people who say this are waiting to see. We must actively fight all bigotry, discrimination and injustice whenever we see it, rather than say nothing and allow it to grow.

It's interesting to me that a lot of the areas in the UK that voted to leave Europe and are really scared of immigration don't actually have high immigration, or a high immigrant population. A survey conducted on behalf of the Conservative peer Lord Ashcroft shortly after Referendum votes had been cast[12] showed that 33 per cent stated their main reason for voting Leave was because it 'offered the best chance for the UK to regain control over immigration and its own borders'. In addition, 81 per cent of Leave voters regarded multiculturalism and 80 per cent regarded immigration as 'forces for ill', compared to 19 per cent and 20 per cent of Remain voters respectively.

A subsequent academic analysis of the Referendum vote published on TheConversation.com in July 2016[13] found

---

12 'How the United Kingdom voted on Thursday and why' – Lord Ashcroft Polls, 24th June 2016.
13 'Hard Evidence: how areas with low immigration voted mainly for Brexit' – Chris Lawton and Robert Ackrill, *The Conversation*, 8th July 2016.

that of the 270 districts that had a lower proportion than average of people born outside the UK in 2011, in 229 (85 per cent) the majority vote was for Leave. Of the 78 districts with a higher than average population born outside the UK, only 44 per cent voted Leave. Many of the areas that voted Leave had high unemployment and limited job prospects. The authors concluded that 'where migrants were not present, it appears they were held partly to blame for the all-too-real, but much deeper-seated, economic difficulties experienced by locals.'

Increasingly, there is a dehumanising of people who are 'not like us'. If you build a picture of people not being like you and not being human – of being more animal, not feeling and hurting like you, not having the same emotions as you, how much easier then to lash out at them and treat them as a scapegoat for your own frustrations.

I never, ever thought I'd see that in modern Britain, but here we are. It's unfolding in front of us right now and I'm shocked by the pace at which it's happening, at the quickening of it. I ask myself this perpetual question: Did it happen overnight? Or was it always there? And I think there possibly was an element of racism that was always there, lying in wait beneath the surface. For a while, it became unacceptable to express such things in public. But if you lift the lid, and you exist in a society that makes it acceptable and mainstream again, everything changes.

It is an undoing of all those decades of us getting to a place where we were more civilised, kinder, nicer, more tolerant people. Nelson Mandela once said you can judge a society by how it treats its children. I think you can judge a society by what we teach our children. And what is it we're teaching our children? What are the lessons they are seeing in our politics, media and in public debates? We're teaching them it's OK to lie, to cheat, to be irresponsible, to be misogynistic, to watch porn, to make up anything as you go along, to treat other people with disrespect, to be discriminatory.

I believe that we used to care a lot more about what was going on in the world around us. Perhaps, in this era of twenty-four-hour news and political soundbites, we're becoming too desensitised.

This goes beyond my personal experiences with race and racism, and tips into something far more endemic and insidious. We cannot afford to be complacent, or lazy. As the saying goes, 'good people need to speak out or bad things happen'. We must make sure our voices are heard amidst a louder clamour of prejudice. It's about knowing what's right and standing up for what you believe in. It's about looking to other people – the woman pushing a buggy in the street, the young boy on his way to school, the man behind the corner-shop till – and knowing that what connects us all is far more important than what sets us apart.

I dread to think what the rise in race-hate crimes means, and where it might lead. You look back at Nazi Germany and you think, 'How could people have sat in their houses and watched out of their windows as they saw old men, women, children beaten and rounded up, and not do anything to stop it?'

They stayed silent because fear set in. They stayed silent because they were scared that if they raised their voice they too would be taken away. And for a long time people didn't speak up about the small things. But the small things grew into much larger, and more dangerous, acts. That's how Adolf Hitler managed to carry out the systematic, bureaucratic, state-sponsored persecution and murder of six million Jews.

We feel safe looking at history with the twenty-twenty vision that comes with hindsight, and yet we are sleepwalking into some of the same dangerous mistakes of our forebears. That's why you have to speak up when you see your neighbour being bullied because they're not 'indigenous' to the British population. I get letters every single day from people of different ethnicities saying they are terrified of the future and want to leave. I can understand why. The thought has crossed my mind.

*

The thing I keep coming back to is I can't hide the colour of my skin. I can look after myself because I'm older, tougher, but my children can't. If the country they're going to grow up in ends up looking like an intolerant nation where they feel ashamed of who they are and get treated as second-class citizens, then my family and I would leave. Why would I want them to be here? You can change your accent, you can speak differently to fit in, but you can never change the colour of your skin. And that's what it comes down to. If that's how we're going to be judged, I want no part of it.

In my darkest moments, I have found myself crying in bed at night wanting to do something drastic to draw attention to what's happening. I even contemplated going on hunger strike. I thought it might be the only way to shine a light on what is really happening.

I'm often asked if I'd enter politics. My answer is twofold. First, being proud to be British and wanting to defend my country and its values is not a political act – I see it simply as my civic responsibility.

Second, in the current climate I think I can be more powerful operating outside the restrictions of Parliament, where you're subject to the whipping machinery of whichever party you belong to. It is difficult to act with true integrity. I could stand as an independent, but you don't really have much influence. I think politics is broken at the moment and politicians are cowering under the right-wing-appropriated notion of 'the will of the people', which is being used to silence democratic debate.

Safeguarding our country's future requires all of us to take an active part. I think we got the politicians we deserved because we became lazy: we, the people, did not fulfil our civic duty. The solution is that we, the people, must step up and get involved with our communities, whether that be at work, in schools, on boards, on social media or in the lessons we teach our children.

We can all be statespeople – indeed, we all have a right and duty to be – and that responsibility includes standing up for the law, being involved in our neighbourhoods, preserving our values, safeguarding principles and holding our government to account. In order to ensure the moral code of right and wrong, and the positive attributes of honesty, responsibility, empathy, selflessness and understanding which I've always associated with the Great Britain I love, we all need to nurture our own sense of duty and loyalty. What we signal as leaders in our own field and how we behave carries great responsibility. The signals tell others what our principles are, while the way we behave and respond to situations, people and discourse conveys what we value. This in turn inspires other people's behaviour and sets societal norms.

We did not get to the state we are in overnight and it will not be fixed overnight. There is no easy way out. This is why all of us need to put our shoulders to the mill, in order to find hope – it will be worth it to get us back to a place of healing.

Without hope, we do not have the will and determination that goals will be achieved, nor do we have the strategies in place to reach those goals. Put simply: hope involves the will to move forward, and finding different ways to get to empathy. Hope is a delicate flower that needs to be kept alive with positive energy. Because without hope, what is the point?

We all need to remember that other people matter. And, to create a change of heart, we must first change our own: if we allow ourselves to be silenced, the future for our children will be shaped not by us but by those who wish to hijack decency, tolerance and kindness.

I'm not willing to let that happen – are you?

10

The Unelected Opposition

How do you explain bullies, death threats and abuse to your children? How do you let them know that these things are being said about their own mother? And how can you equip them to deal with it, if they discover it for themselves? If you don't tell them, would they be angry in the future that you lied or hid things from them?

In many ways, it's an impossible conundrum. I want my children to be aware of the challenges we face in society. I don't want them to be unnecessarily sheltered. And yet I also have the natural maternal instinct to protect them from the evil that exists in the world.

I try to talk to them as much as possible about what is going on and, just like my father did with me, I explain to them the reason behind my actions, my day, my conversations.

I will say:

There are some people in this world – not everybody, it's a minority – but there are some people who are extreme and who believe in a bygone age where, if you had a different colour skin, you were deemed inferior. Where they judge people on what they look like, where they come from, how much money they have. But under it all there is more that makes us the same than different. Some believe that if you are not white, then you are not valued, that you're not even a human being.

But at the end of the day, we all have the same blood running through our veins and the same tears that come from our eyes. We are all the same underneath it all. And you can't let people devalue each other because that's when they'll harm each other.

It's interesting that in all these conversations I've had with my children they've never once asked why the negative people react the way they do to me. Like so many children, they have a strong sense of injustice and fairness, and a simplicity that becomes corrupted by adulthood. It means they not only understand the reasons behind why I do what I do, but give their thoughts and opinions, which are important to me – I listen to them and they listen to me. I tell them that if racist, ignorant views are allowed to flourish unchallenged, then it will have a disastrous effect on their future. They appreciate that much of what I am doing is for them and their friends. Of course, they would like me to be around more, to be less tired and not juggling so many demands. Their voices sometimes chime, 'Oh, Mum, do you have to do this? Do you have to go out again?'

It is a constant juggle, just as it is for many working mothers, and it's never perfect. There isn't some magic wand you can wave to ensure the ideal work-life balance. But I always come back to the idea that, when it comes to your children, you don't have to be with them all the time, if they know you love and care about them constantly. If they know they're in your heart and in your mind, even when you can't physically be with them they feel loved and comfortable and secure.

My chats with my family have made me think a lot about my own values. It makes me exercise my thoughts, about the ethical framework I inherited from my parents, the example and legacy I wish to leave; about what has happened in Great Britain to enable such hatred to take hold. In the aftermath of the EU Referendum, insults have been traded between the Brexiteers and the Remainers like bullets flying over a battlefield. The more extreme elements on both sides have dug into their own trenches, refusing to engage, and the rest of us are left blinking into the light of no-man's-land, trying to make sense of it all.

Like so many other observers and commentators, I don't believe this toxic nationalism surfaced overnight. It's a culmination of things that have been bubbling under the surface for well over a decade. A culture of blame has developed in tandem with needless prejudice, so that when things aren't going as you want in your own life or career, you look to blame others, to look for other groups to shoulder the responsibility for your own failures or unhappiness. People rarely own their own failures or disappointments. The cries of woe have somehow become facts: e.g. 'It's immigrants bleeding the system dry, filling our NHS wards'; 'It's the EU eating up our sovereignty, taking away our Britishness.'

That vein of dissatisfaction is being injected by some of the right-wing media, as more of the body of Great Britain becomes infected with rancour and bitterness.

Scapegoating is lazy and harmful because it puts a plaster over these festering wounds, rather than exposing the root cause of resentment. Irresponsible people at the top in all walks of life have neglected, forgotten and ignored that many pockets of silent communities are hurting, that they understandably feel marginalised by the Westminster-centric focus of our elected representatives. And when the EU Referendum came around, these communities saw an opportunity to make their voices heard. It was a cry for themselves and their families – a cry for help, a cry for attention. And they are still crying out, because the change promised is not happening quickly enough, or in a manner that was promised. The lies of the Leave politicians are coming home to roost and may well hatch into griffins instead of doves. This too keeps me up at night, worrying. How will those who have been overpromised a brighter future deal with the reality of our place in the world? There are dark echoes of so many episodes in history.

An Ernst and Young (EY) report in December 2017[14] found that the UK is becoming more geographically imbalanced, with the North–South divide set to increase over the next three years. Mark Gregory, EY's chief economist for the UK and Ireland, said, 'The UK has made little progress on regional rebalancing over the past three years, and we expect more of the same over the next three years. In fact, we expect that the fastest growing regions over the next three years will be the four most southerly ones, London, the South East, the South West and the East. This means that the economic gap between North and South could be larger in 2020 than it was in 2010.'

This goes some way to explaining the more recent 'Hate Crime, England and Wales 2016/17' Statistical Bulletin, which stated 'there were 80,393 offences recorded by the police in which one or more hate crime strands were deemed to be a motivating factor. This was an increase of 29 per cent compared with the 62,518 hate crimes recorded in 2015/16, the largest percentage increase seen since the series began in 2011/12.'

The increase over the last year is thought to reflect both a genuine rise in hate crime around the time of the EU Referendum and the ongoing improvements in crime recording by the police. The Office for National Statistics have stated

---

14 'EY UK Regional Economic Forecast: Rebalancing the economy: Time for a new push' – Mark Gregory and Debbie O'Hanlon, EY.com, 11th December 2017.

that increases in recent years in police-recorded violence against the person and public order offences have been driven by improvements in police recording. Around nine in ten hate crime offences recorded by the police are in these two offence groups. The number of hate crime offences in 2016–17 for the five centrally monitored strands were as follows[15]:

- 62,685 (78 per cent) were race hate crimes;
- 9,157 (11 per cent) were sexual orientation hate crimes;
- 5,949 (7 per cent) were religious hate crimes;
- 5,558 (7 per cent) were disability hate crimes;
- 1,248 (2 per cent) were transgender hate crimes.

It is possible for a hate crime offence to have more than one motivating factor, which is why the above numbers add up to more than 80,393 and 100 per cent. The report stated that 'There were increases in offences recorded for all five of the monitored hate crime strands between 2015/16 and 2016/17, reflecting the general improvements in crime recording.'

Another report which focused more on Brexit found that crimes involving racial and religious discrimination had soared at an unprecedented rate since the Brexit vote. Police figures obtained through Freedom of Information requests by the *Independent* newspaper in July 2017 showed that in the eleven months after the EU Referendum, compared with the year before, incidents surged by 23 per cent – from 40,741 to 49,921 – marking an unparalleled rise.

But there's another element to all this, an element typified by Viscount Philipps and his ilk. There is, in my experience, a whole cadre of well-educated, well-heeled, older individuals at

---

15 'Hate Crime, England and Wales 2016/17' – Aoife O'Neill, Home Office Statistical Bulletin 17/17, 17th October 2017.

the top of the social strata who labour under the misapprehension that things used to be better in the past. It's a nostalgic view of Britain that never really existed and it goes right back to Empire, where white men were the masters of society, and women and ethnic minorities knew their place and were easier to 'rule'. An age when there were fewer rules and regulations, so the elite could get rich quicker and more easily.

It's outrageous and offensive. That goes without saying. But I've noticed this deplorable attitude creeping back into public debate. You don't have to look hard to find it. We're lucky to live in a democracy, and I'm a firm believer in free speech, but let's not forget that the price of liberty is vigilance. We all need to be aware of when and how to speak up; we all need to be the guardians of free speech.

I teach my children the same lessons that my father taught me. That it is when things feel the most uncertain, and we are at our most tired, frustrated and worn out, that we must dig deep. That's when we need to find it within ourselves not to turn away and hide in our bunkers, but to rise up and be even more vocal. That fighting for what's right has never been easy. My son and daughters know about the Suffragettes, the great Victorian philanthropists, Martin Luther King, Gandhi, Mandela; they have met the incredible local heroes who run the charities our Foundation supports. They know the kind people who help others without fanfare or PR.

They know of great hearts and minds, of empathy, love, giving, forgiving and the power of saying sorry. We talk about the differences between being a good person and leading a good life, the danger in hiding, and injustices perpetuated by silence, division, and judging people too easily. I tell them that if we hide, when we emerge from our hiding places the world might be transformed into a hostile, alien environment in which we have no say at all and where the things we love and value no longer exist.

That's why I keep fighting, even though the *Daily Express* once ran a piece headlined: 'Who elected Gina Miller? NOBODY'. (Capitals, their own.)

On this occasion it was because I'd had the temerity to challenge the government's dodgy deal with the Democratic Unionist Party in the aftermath of Theresa May's disastrous 2017 election. Theresa May, who found herself at the helm of a minority government, had promised £1 billion to Northern Ireland in return for ten DUP votes to prop up her dwindling power. This could not only throw the Northern Ireland peace process into disarray (because how could May claim to be an impartial arbiter when she was in hock to the Unionist politicians?) but also raised serious questions about funnelling all that money into one specific area of the United Kingdom rather than sharing it equitably among the communities who really needed it. The action was to be brought by me and Jason Moyer-Lee, the activist General Secretary of the small but vocal Independent Workers Union of Great Britain. Our legal team, a small Scottish solicitor's firm called Balford Manson and a QC from Matrix Law Chambers, Aidan O'Neill, dispatched a legal letter to the Government on 17th August 2017, challenging the government's authority to make such a huge payment with our taxpayers' money without Parliamentary approval. The delayed response of the government's lawyers was that yes, they did need Parliamentary approval, but no timetable had been set. I heard that the DUP were furious, as they had expected the first payment as soon as that October.

I couldn't believe that the official Opposition wasn't doing more to stop the government trampling roughshod over our rights, bypassing Parliament, trying to use ancient mechanisms. The Labour Party talks of ordinary people, workers' rights, a fair society. This is why I have been a Labour Party supporter in the past – because of the principles the party was built on. But if I was an MP in the present Labour Party I'd be deselected for speaking my mind, for being too centrist. It's ridiculous. Increasingly, I feel it's far more powerful to be outside the system than within it, to be a wrecking ball not a ball in their game.

The establishment is broken. The old orders are failing. It makes no sense to say, 'Well, I've elected my politicians, so no one else should speak up ever.' If politicians aren't doing their duty and putting the country first, I believe we have an absolute obligation to stand up and exercise our civic duty even more. When all is well in the world, we can go about our day-to-day lives in quiet assurance, but if all is not well we must stop, think, question and speak up.

In my view, our MPs are deeply conflicted. On the one hand, they have the demands of party loyalty and tribalism, the lure of being in power and the need to keep hold of it at all costs. On the other, they have their own conscience and the fact that they became politicians to serve others. In this setting of dissonance, I think it's more useful to be independent because I don't have to pledge my allegiance to anyone. I don't have to join any club. I don't have to toe the party line. I'm free to speak where others fear to.

I hope my father would be proud of me. Not everyone is lucky enough to have had that early guidance in working out what's right from what's wrong. But what I come back to again and again is the importance of listening to your inner voice. It's one thing I've noticed in other women, too: in the past, I've worked with young girls coerced into girl gangs or prostitution and generally, when I have a conversation with them, they admit that there was a point where they knew what they were being told was wrong, when their inner voice was telling them not to do it, but they chose to ignore it and run with the pack, to satisfy someone else's (usually a man's) version of themselves.

Don't ignore that inner voice. Listening to your heart when there's doubt in your head is such an important thing to do. I believe we have an innate and impressive ability to know what's right and what's wrong: we feel it in the pit of our stomach, in our second brain.

And it is not just my experience – this is supported by recent scientific research. A 2010 study published in the journal *Psychological Science*[16] revealed how the body is able to speak intuitively to the mind. Researchers invented a card game which forced participants to rely on hunches in order to win. The ones who did best were the ones who listened and responded to the increase in their heart rate, a body change so subtle they labelled it 'intuition'.

In 2017, the Berghofer Medical Research Institute in Australia conducted their own research[17], asking 90,000 respondents to say what they thought a person's mood was, based solely on a photograph of their eyes. Women consistently outperformed men in correctly identifying how someone was feeling and they were able to do this in a single glance, suggesting greater levels of cognitive empathy.

This could be an inheritance from our long-ago ancestors. Women were historically required to evaluate situations quickly in order to protect their children. According to a 2015 article in *Medical Daily*[18]: 'Women's brains were trained with peak awareness because they were protecting a heart outside of their own bodies. Female brains therefore evolved to have a larger composition and ability to organise chunks of

16 'Listening to Your Heart: How Interoception Shapes Emotion Experience and Intuitive Decision Making' – Barnaby D. Dunn et al, Psychological Science, 2010.
17 'Genome-wide meta-analysis of cognitive empathy: heritability, and correlates with sex, neuropsychiatric conditions and cognition' – V. Warrier et al, *Molecular Psychiatry*, 2017.
18 'Your Gut Feeling Is Way More Than Just A Feeling: The Science Of Intuition' – Samantha Olson, *Medical Daily*, 12th March 2015.

environmental information at a time, giving them an edge to read people.'

Our inner voice is part of our survival mechanism. It's an instinct for knowing. And it is still there, if only we block out modern noise and listen to the ancient wisdom deep within us. If you can find it in yourself and listen to it, no matter how much external noise there is, it will guide you. And when the time is right, it will enable you to speak up and fight for what you believe in; to make better decisions for your own well-being.

11

The 'Former Model'

One of the criticisms of me I've found both irksome and perhaps most interesting – for what it says about the people who level it at me – is the reference to me as a 'former model'. I've lost count of the number of newspaper articles that have appeared in the right-wing, Brexit supporting media that label me as a 'model turned businesswoman'. I suppose the aim was to make me seem superficial or somehow ridiculous, as if a woman who had made money posing for photographs and looking pretty would be intellectually incapable of understanding the finer points of a complicated legal challenge.

I did dabble in modelling. During those years when I was single-handedly raising my daughter, Lucy-Ann, and going to university, I took on any job I could to make a little extra cash. I was walking down the street one day in London and a woman came up to me and asked whether I'd ever thought of being a model. She introduced me to an agency and I couldn't believe it when they told me how much you got paid for just standing in front of a camera and smiling (and sometimes you didn't even have to smile – how easy would that be?!). I thought, 'Hang on. If I go and do this for three hours, I can earn more than I would earn doing two weeks waitressing at Pizza Express.' I signed up with them on the spot.

It's not a route I ever expected my life to take. Although my mother was very clear about the need to dress neatly and presentably, and to show respect for people through your clothes, neither of my parents ever valued physical looks. As a girl, my mother would never allow me to wear make-up or show any hint of personal vanity. One of the most vivid memories of my teenage years is when I was at boarding school in Eastbourne and my parents came over to visit me. I was thirteen, and my older brother and I were so excited to see them that we went all the way to Heathrow so we could be there to greet them when they walked into the Arrivals hall.

I'd cut my hair so it was more manageable at school and put on a little make-up and worn one of my favourite dresses. It was a summer dress – the top part was blue, with white stripes, and the bottom half was red with a dropped waist. It looked a bit naval and had a pull-string rope belt. I wore red lipstick to match the dress and I thought I looked nice.

I was so nervous to see my parents after nearly a year apart that I kept checking the Arrivals board. When their plane landed, and the passengers started to come through, wheeling their trolleys and suitcases, I craned my neck trying to spot their familiar faces in the crowd. Finally, I saw them and, heart racing with happiness, ran up and threw my arms around them.

The first thing my father did was to step back, look at my face, and say, 'You don't need to wear that stuff, take it off at once.' Then he disappointingly said, 'And what have you done to your beautiful long hair!'

For my parents, it was always what was inside that counted the most: your integrity, your generosity, your hard work. Growing up in that household, I was taught that being beautiful didn't really mean anything. As a result, I never felt pretty and didn't particularly value my looks.

When the modelling agency signed me up, there was something absurd about it. I wasn't very tall either, although

I later learned that I was the same height as Kate Moss. I never did high-end catwalks because you need to be over 5 foot 10 for that – Moss being the exception to the rule – but I did a lot of photographic and catalogue work. I was naturally very thin back then and Iman, the supermodel who was paving the way for women of colour in fashion and who later married David Bowie, was breaking new ground at that time, so a few companies were starting to use women that looked like me. I was lucky that the world of modelling and advertising was changing.

One of my first jobs was doing a swimwear shoot for the clothing chain Monsoon. We shot in Covent Garden, in the middle of December, and it was freezing. The models all had to stand outside, posing by a flight of steps leading up to the covered part of the market, and there was this Arctic chill in the air. It was the '80s, and I'd been styled with massive *Dynasty*-style hair, pumped up with tons of hairspray and some fake blonde streaks. They gave me an animal-print swimsuit to wear (in those days I was pigeon-holed into looking 'exotic' or 'African' or 'wild') and I had to walk out into the middle of Covent Garden, half-naked, in front of all the passing tourists. I tried not to shiver and told myself I wasn't embarrassed by everyone stopping to stare and point. But I was bitterly cold and covered in goosebumps. My teeth were chattering, and I had to stand there being shouted at by the photographer because I was shaking too much for him to be able to take the picture. In the end, he got the shot. But it was a long day.

I detested modelling. You were treated like a piece of meat and it's a brutal profession: you're constantly told by bookers, designers and casting directors you're either too fat or too thin. You're told how much you can eat and your weight is constantly monitored. Or they'll take a photograph of you and pore over your features, criticising your face for not being symmetrical enough. I would literally hear them say things like, 'This half of the face doesn't match this half', as if I didn't exist. I found it the most degrading, demoralising thing to put yourself through and I couldn't understand why people want to model or why they think it's glamorous.

Some of the language used around me was so shocking. Quite often, a booker would say to me, 'We can't put you forward for this job because you're too dark; if only you were a few shades lighter we could get you so much more work.' Time and time again I felt like a thing, not a person. Prejudice was out there, front and centre. There were conversations about whether you could have a woman of colour on the cover of a magazine or fronting an advertising campaign because of worries about taking a hit in sales. I found that extraordinary.

My modelling days were horrible. I didn't enjoy them. The only way I got through them was to think of the money and get on with it. They were just about worth it for the pay cheque.

But modelling did teach me something important. It taught me how various hairstyles, make-up and clothes can make you feel entirely different. I would be given a specific brief and told what the client wanted me to embody, then I would be styled, step into the clothes and become whatever it was they wanted. It taught me that how you look can enable you to project something you don't necessarily feel inside. Inside, I was hating the work. But outside, I could pretend to be this strong, confident woman who didn't mind having her picture taken while trembling in an animal-print swimsuit in the height of winter. I learned how clothes can change you, how you could be a chameleon, and that was a very important lesson.

It was a lesson I took all the way to the steps of the High Court.

12

Looking the Part

Whether we like it or not, we are all judged on our looks.

In 2016, two sociologists, Jaclyn Wong of the University of Chicago and Andrew Penner of the University of California at Irvine, decided to analyse how physical attractiveness related to income.[19] They examined data relating to 14,000 people who were asked about income, job and education. The interviewers rated each of these participants on their physical attractiveness and grooming – which included hairstyle, clothing and, in the case of women, make-up.

Wong and Penner found that good-looking, attractive individuals earn roughly 20 per cent more than people of average attractiveness. But one of the most interesting findings was how significantly this gap narrowed when the sociologists factored in grooming.

They found that a well-groomed woman of average attractiveness made about $6,000 more annually than an average-looking, averagely groomed woman. She also made about $4,000 more than her better-looking but less put-together co-worker.

---

19 'Gender and the Returns to Attractiveness' – Jaclyn S. Wong and Andrew M. Penner, *Research in Social Stratification and Mobility*, International Sociological Association, 2016.

It was a similar story for men, although they received a comparatively smaller boost for good grooming than women.

When this 'former model' took the UK government to court over Brexit, I had to think carefully about the image I wanted to portray. I knew there was going to be a heightened level of scrutiny, with my ever-attentive critics ready to pounce if I ever put a step wrong.

I needed to look well-dressed, but not too well-dressed because I didn't want to be dismissed as a rich woman with nothing better to do with her time (as it turned out, I was called this anyway, so I suppose the joke was on me). I wanted to look presentable and to show respect for the judicial institution, just as I had been taught by my mother and father. I needed to project an outward confidence, even though I often felt riven with anxiety on the inside. I didn't want to draw unnecessary attention to myself, and yet I wanted to have presence, so that I couldn't be ignored or talked over. I also wanted to be comfortable, to look like myself.

That's not a particularly easy thing to do.

I rifled through my wardrobe the night before the first day of the court case in October 2016 with mounting panic. I'm not a keen shopper and don't buy myself that many clothes because I'm generally too busy to go shopping. I also never think it's a good idea to wear a new outfit whenever you're doing something that involves speaking in public: the first rule of thumb is to be comfortable, then you can concentrate on what you're saying rather than fidgeting in something stiff or that might not feel familiar. I didn't want to be tugging at a hemline when I was trying to listen to barristers discussing the finer points of our constitutional law.

So, in the end, I settled on an old favourite: a dark blue trouser suit, cut with feminine tailoring, which I teamed with a plain white shirt and black heels. High heels have always made me feel empowered, as if I'm stepping up to the plate. I knew this pair was comfortable enough that I'd be able to do the long walk to the courthouse from where the special taxi dropped me off each morning.

The heels not only made me feel emotionally resilient, but physically taller and stronger. During the court case, I experienced some agonising bouts of recurring back pain and needed to strap myself up with various braces and back belts, and dose myself with strong painkillers to get through the day. Oddly, wearing heels helped: one particular pair tilted at exactly the right angle to relieve my spine.

Over the following days, I wore a version of the same outfit, always in black or dark blue. I wanted to look professional and neat and to convey the message that I was taking this seriously and that I respected both the environment and the legal process.

Anyway, I must have been doing something right because at the end of the hearing one of the women from my legal team came up to me and said, 'We've voted you the client with the "best court dress sense".'

I was so surprised, because my legal team was comprised of clever, really strong, fantastic women who had been dressing like this for years and who I thought wouldn't have notice something so minor.

'Really?' I asked, unable to suppress a smile.

'Yes,' she said. 'We thought, maybe because of all the publicity, you'd want to be in the limelight and you'd dress up for that.'

That made me laugh. I could have done with a lot less of the limelight, to be honest. That simply wasn't me.

But dressing the way I did had another important function. Every morning, when I got dressed, I felt as if I was putting on armour, in readiness for battle. It was like being a model again: I decided to be this 'other Gina'. On the inside, I would be quivering with nerves. On the outside, however, I wanted to look calm and poised; ready for whatever the day would throw at me. And when I got home, crucially, I could take that armour off and be with my children and become plain old Mummy again. By shedding the skin of battle, the act of taking off my professional layers allowed me to take off my professional persona. I was also shedding some of the toughness I'd had to acquire to get through the day.

Of course, sometimes it wasn't as easy as that. Sometimes, I'd come back from court totally drained. I tried not to read the newspapers or watch the news too much to protect myself from some of the more aggressive commentary, but it seeped through regardless. Well-meaning friends would email to say I shouldn't pay any attention to what such-and-such had said, and then I'd find out anyway. It was hard to keep my public self separate from my private self in those moments. My son Luca once said to me, 'Mum, you're being tougher with us; you don't have to be.' It took him saying that for me to realise I was not handling things as well as I'd thought. I made a more concerted effort to leave the exhaustion and the stress of the day behind me, hanging up in the wardrobe along with my trouser suit. There was something about the physical action of taking those clothes off that helped: I could allow myself to be vulnerable again around the people who loved me. I would put on my soft comfortable lounging clothes and Mum was back.

It is a paradox that while women are the most heavily judged for how they look, they are also made to feel stupid for caring about clothes, as if it undermines their seriousness. On the contrary, I've learnt that finding the armour that works for you can enable you to face any challenge. Far from being superficial, the way a woman dresses can be an act of self-worth, and be both defining and an act of defiance.

Scientific studies have shown that the clothes you choose can affect your mood, health and overall confidence. In a 2012 study published in the *Journal of Experimental Social Psychology*[20], professors Hajo Adam and Adam D. Galinsky coined the term 'enclothed cognition' to define both 'the symbolic meaning of clothes and the physical experience of wearing them'.

Their research at the Kellogg School of Management at Northwestern University asked participants to perform tests of observation wearing a lab coat or a painter's coat or no coat at all. Those wearing the lab coat were found to have the greatest improvement in attention.

It has long been suspected, as Dr Galinsky put it, that 'clothing affects how other people perceive us as well as how we think about ourselves', but this experiment demonstrated that the clothing you wear can alter your psychological processes. If you wear something you feel confident in, your choice of outfit can have a positive impact on your interactions with the world.

I have found other experiments fascinating. One found that a teaching assistant who wears formal clothes is perceived as more intelligent than one who dresses more casually. In 2014, Professor Karen Pine from the University of Hertfordshire[21] also found that what you wear can boost or lower your self-esteem. When she asked a group of students to wear a Superman T-shirt and answer a series of questions, she discovered that they felt more confident and physically stronger. Wearing the T-shirt made the students 'rate themselves as more likeable and superior to other students', said Professor Pine. 'When asked to estimate

20 'Enclothed Cognition' – Hajo Adam and Adam D. Galinsky, *Journal of Experimental Social Psychology*, 2012.
21 *Mind What You Wear: The Psychology of Fashion* by Professor Karen J. Pine, 2014.

how much they could physically lift, those in a Superman T-shirt thought they were stronger than students in a plain T-shirt or in their own clothing.'

Another test involved women completing a maths test while wearing a swimsuit or a sweater, with the latter group performing better.

I didn't wear a Superman T-shirt or a Superwoman outfit to court, although perhaps I should have done.

Since we are judged for what we look like, no matter what we do, dressing in a way that conveys what we wish to say about ourselves can be a crucial tool for women. Although we might suffer from a lack of confidence about taking up a big promotion or having to speak in public, if we dress a certain way it can give us the tools we need to fake it. And faking it eventually helps you make it: confidence is a muscle you must flex. It's a habit as much as anything else.

To me, part of your dress confidence is being honest to yourself about your body – your good bits and the not-so-good bits. You've got to feel comfortable in your clothes and remember, it's more about your personality and how best to reflect that.

As women, we're so often made to feel guilty for things. I'm sure I'm supposed to exercise far more than I do, and I always have the best of intentions, but when it comes to it I don't really have the time. We should be getting up at 5 or 6 a.m. for an hour-long cardio workout before a full day of work, fuelled by green juice and quinoa salads, and then winding down with a yoga session at the end of the day and perhaps another hour of guided meditation. I mean, there's no way I could do that. It's completely unrealistic.

Instead I give myself permission to do what I can do and not to feel bad about it. What I can do is ten minutes on the floor doing some back-strengthening exercises because I know my back is my weakness; it's where I hold my stress.

Or I take the stairs rather than the lift, for example. I rarely sit still or put things off for tomorrow, I am a real fidget, so I suppose that nervous energy keeps me fit, too.

Looking the part is about having an innate sense of self, which clothes can add to and emphasise. It's not about having the skinniest waist or the longest legs. It's about knowing who you are. Standing tall, owning your space. When I started out in business the trend was for women to dress as men in pinstriped suits with big shoulder pads and zero jewellery. That didn't feel comfortable to me. But nor did it feel comfortable when my second husband pushed me to the opposite extreme and wanted me to wear super-feminine, floaty dresses. I needed to find a happy medium, and that only came with age.

My rule now is that I want people to be able to engage with me, rather than my clothes. I want them to see me as a person, rather than being scared to approach me or intimidated by what I'm wearing. As Coco Chanel once said: 'Dress shabbily and they remember the dress; dress impeccably and they remember the woman.'

Looking the part has been an issue for me as a woman of colour. When I started campaigning for more transparency in financial services, I understood I stood out. There aren't many women in that world, let alone feisty, troublesome ones originally from South America, who didn't go to the right university or private school, and who refuse to play by the accepted, normal rules.

A few years ago I was at a summer drinks party at a huge law firm that works with big-name investment clients. I was with my husband and a couple of friends when I noticed a group of chaps staring in my direction. Being me, I walked over to them and confronted them. I just couldn't let it slide. I said, 'Hi guys. Couldn't help noticing you staring. Can I help?'

The response was immediately aggressive.

'You are an utter disgrace,' one of them said. 'Just because you think you're good-looking black woman, you think you can get away with anything.'

I was appalled. But another in the group carried on the abuse.

'We have a nickname for you. We call you the "Black Widow Spider".'

That term was wrong on so many levels. It took me back twenty-five years, to my modelling agency telling me 'coloured girls' couldn't sell magazines. I couldn't believe these narrow-minded fools were saying these things in what was a supposedly civilised professional setting.

But, to my surprise, I found that I wasn't angry. If anything, it seemed absurd they were getting so het up. It confirmed that I was absolutely on the right track. I took it as a compliment that such senior men were upset by me and my actions.

'It's good to know you're all so riled,' I calmly replied. 'I must be doing something right!' Then I turned and walked away.

Looking the part doesn't always have to be about clothes. It can also be about other people's ignorance when they're confronted with someone who doesn't seem to 'fit'. As a woman of colour, I am aware of unconscious biases, prejudice and discrimination. When I say I wear clothes as an armour, I mean that literally. If I look smart and feel confident, other people's bigoted assumptions have less power to harm me.

13

'Tough Softness'

On the subject of clothes and appearances, as I mentioned briefly before, when I first started out in business in the early '90s I found myself surrounded by women wearing huge shoulder pads, pinstripe trouser suits, and dark, sombre colours. It was a uniform that deliberately stripped us of our individuality and femininity. There was an unspoken rule that you weren't allowed to wear accessories or too much make-up. Acceptable accessories to the uniform were tiny pearl earrings and a discreet pearl necklace.

It felt as though we women were being made to be 'masculine' to fit in. In the office, any sign of so-called 'female' emotion – crying, tiredness or frustration, for instance – was seen as a weakness. Being androgynous meant you being strong.

I hated this. I never understood why I had to wear pinstriped trousers or why I wasn't allowed to wear the jewellery that expressed who I was. It might sound superficial, but to me it highlighted something more fundamental and deeply troubling: instead of celebrating women, the workplace culture was diminishing us, with the none-too-subtle message that to get ahead – to be valued – you had to be shoe-horned into being more like a man.

A lot has changed since then. Laws have been passed to make overt sexual discrimination illegal. But sexism still exists: it's just become more insidious. As women, we still feel the need to compensate for this misogynist notion that we're somehow 'the weaker sex'. We need to resist thinking we must act 'like a man' – to be more aggressive, more bullish than the next person and not be entirely ourselves.

The good news is things have moved on, but the question is if it's for the better? Recent scientific research has thrown up some confusion about what is 'male' and what is 'female'. The notion of gender is more fluid than ever before, and there's no doubt that we are a product of nurture just as much as nature. The glorious Grayson Perry made a three-part documentary on modern-day masculinity, *All Man*, which questioned how men see their place in society and how they deal with emotions in a world where the sexes are said to be forgetting what makes them unique, invaluable and interlinked.

Having said that, certain biological factors cannot be denied. One influential 2001 study into the differing characteristics between the sexes involved over 23,000 men and women from twenty-six cultures filling out personality questionnaires. Women consistently rated themselves as being warmer, friendlier, more anxious and more sensitive to their feelings than men. The men, meanwhile, consistently rated themselves as being more assertive and open to new ideas.[22]

More recently, testosterone has been shown to inhibit crying, while the hormone prolactin (seen in higher levels in women) may promote it. A 2013 study conducted by the University of Pennsylvania[23] analysed nearly 1,000 brain

---

22 'Gender differences in personality traits across cultures: robust and surprising findings' – Paul T. Costa Jr., Antonio Terracciano and Robert R. MacCrae, *Journal of Personality and Social Psychology*, 2001.

23 'Sex differences in the structural connectome of the human brain' – Madhura Ingalhalikar, Alex Smith, Drew Parker, Theodore D. Satterthwaite, Mark A. Elliott, Kosha Ruparel, Hakon Hakonarson, Raquel E. Gur, Ruben C. Gur and Ragini Verma, *PNAS*, 2013.

scans and found that stark differences exist in the wiring of male and female brains. Maps of neural circuitry showed that on average women's brains were highly connected across the left and right hemispheres, and wired more for social skills, memory and multi-tasking. Men's brains, by contrast, had typically stronger connections between the front and back regions and were apparently better wired for perception and coordination.

These findings support the notion of evolutionary psychologists, who believe our modern personalities still reflect the impact of survival demands experienced by our distant ancestors. Women with more nurturing personalities were more likely to be able to protect their vulnerable offspring, while men with bolder personalities would have been more successful in hunting and competing for mates.

It should be noted that there are differences of opinion regarding the 2013 study, and about the views of evolutionary psychologists and their validity – some have argued that social conditioning in early childhood, rather than biological or neurological factors, causes the difference between men and women's brains.

Whatever the cause of the differences, they are still socially predominant and to deny these innate differences is to deny our own individuality as women. And, in turn, the danger is that we forget to be ourselves. We ignore what makes us stand out: so often, women tell me they feel they are encouraged to modify their supposed 'softness' in case it's viewed as weakness and so become brittle, almost rigid. They feel defensive, rather than open. By creating barriers without realising that's what we're doing, we limit our own potential.

It's exhausting having to keep up the charade of a persona that doesn't come close to who you actually are. If you're waking up every morning telling yourself to be tougher than you feel, that can drag you down.

Then there's the absurd double-standards that exist in many workplaces, where women who are confident and self-possessed are dismissed as 'bossy' or 'opinionated' or 'bitchy'. These are value-laden words that carry with them a whole stratum of negative assumptions. Men showing the same behaviour will be lauded for their assertiveness and managerial style. I know very few men who have ever been called 'bossy'.

I believe that your strength comes from inside you – from knowing who you are. It's not an afterthought. True strength doesn't have to be displayed like a peacock fanning its feathers, and it can – and should – be combined with sensitivity. There's a power that comes from authenticity and flexibility: if you embrace yourself, accept all your contradictions, and acknowledge that you can be strong *at the same time* as having softer attributes, you'll probably discover that other people respond better towards you because they can detect you are being more natural and honest. It's not simply a question of putting on pearl earrings; it's about an entire way of being that I call 'tough softness'.

Women should be empowered to embrace their femininity at work: as men and women, we should be able to distinguish between useful emotion, and emotion that doesn't serve us, and sometimes how liberating it is to just let the tears out. Crying is cleansing. I've cried at work before because I've been exhausted or nervous. Occasionally, just after doing a big presentation to a potential client I've been so adrenalised with fear that I've taken myself off to the toilet cubicle to have a weep.

If you do find yourself welling up at your desk, it's probably time to take a proper break and address whatever issue is causing you such emotional distress in a place where you won't have to handle the scrutiny of your colleagues or run the risk of being called 'unprofessional'. It is important to have certain people you can trust – a good friend or a close colleague – with whom you shouldn't be afraid of showing your vulnerability. Sometimes it does all get a bit too much and it's much better to let it out than allow it to fester silently and build up inside you.

I've always told my children that the two most important sounds in a home are laughter and crying because it means you're in tune with your emotions and you're expressing them. You are lifting the lid on the pressure cooker of emotion that can build up and explode in a very destructive manner if always held in.

As women, our emotional intelligence is often instinctive: studies show that female chimps display empathy more often than male, whilst a 2014 study of 8,979 participants in Poland[24] found higher overall scores by females on all facets of emotional intelligence. My eldest daughter, who has special needs and possesses the academic age of six or seven in conventional tests, has always had the most extraordinary emotional intelligence and empathy. She can almost see people's hearts through their eyes. She feels if they are good or bad, if they are telling the truth, if they mean harm. She is not that unusual; I have met many people who register on the special needs spectrum who are like her, who have this different ability.

But we talk ourselves out of empathy because we think we must be technical, tough and dry in our decision-making. To this I say: you must trust your gut first, use your head and heart, and think about doing what is right, not just what is most acceptable or profitable.

These are not sweeping generalisations about gender: both my experience and the data show that men and women

---

24 'TIE: An Ability Test of Emotional Intelligence' – Magdalena Śmieja, Jarosław Orzechowski, Maciej S. Stolarski, *PLOS One*, 2014.

react differently to emotional situations. In my work in the third sector I've often found that when I am talking to a group of male donors together, or individually, they find it very difficult to cope. The raw reality makes them feel so uncomfortable with people's pain, circumstances and vulnerability that they don't want to be there. Some of them have even broken down in tears and asked to leave early.

Women, on the other hand, in general have a bigger capacity or ability to cope with emotion. A 2012 review published in the journal *Neuropsychologia*[25] found that women are better across the board at recognising facial features, and processing others' expressions and emotions. Men were better at recognising anger, aggression and threats. At its best, we women have this emotional intuition that is sensitive but strong.

It took me several years to understand this concept and apply it to my own life. And the person who taught me most about what 'tough softness' meant was not a boss or a colleague. It was my ever so special, special needs daughter, Lucy-Ann.

---

25 'A review on sex differences in processing emotional signals', M.E. Kret, B. De Gelder, *Neuropsychologia*, 2012.

14

A Strong Woman

I've always been a fighter, but having my eldest daughter made me into a lioness.

I was twenty-three when I gave birth to Lucy-Ann. By that stage, I had been married for a year. My husband, Adrian, was ten years older than me. We'd met when I was a seventeen-year-old sixth-form pupil at Moira House School in Eastbourne. It was a very progressive, non-selective school – especially for the '80s – with an unorthodox provenance that instilled in us girls the idea that we could do anything we set our minds to: during games lessons we were allowed to choose cricket or rugby, if we wanted to. I turned out to be pretty good at cricket. This is how we met.

Visually, he was my opposite – he was blond, very English-looking and tall. I was most surprised that we ended up dating, not least because he was much older than me, but despite our superficial differences, we had a lot in common and he became my first real boyfriend. A year later I moved to London to study law.

Adrian also lived in London and worked as head of sales and marketing at a global photographic firm called Konica (in the days before digital cameras). I loved the colour and culture of London. Studying law was fulfilling my childhood dream to follow in my father's footsteps. But by the end of my second year I began to become disillusioned with the possibilities that lay in my future in a profession where my gender and race would close many doors. My lecturers and careers advisers tried to manage my expectations; my father suggested I could finish my degree in a West Indian University then go back to Guyana to work in his chambers. I was torn, confused about my identity and where I belonged.

One evening on my way back home, walking to the Tube in Mile End to Highbury and Islington, where I lived in a house with my eldest brother and five other students, I was brutally attacked.

I managed to crawl into a black cab after the attack, and when the driver saw me he offered to take me to the police station or hospital. I said no – for some reason, which I cannot explain to this day, I just wanted to go home to my bed. I didn't want anyone to see me or know what had happened. I felt dirty, violated and in shock.

The university eventually found out about the attack when I didn't turn up for lectures, and one of the kindly lecturers who felt I was a promising student came to see me at home. It turned out some of the men who had attacked me were also students there. I didn't sit my final law exams and the university presumably didn't want a scandal so they offered to pass me or let me re-sit the following year. But I never returned – not until October 2017, when the same university, totally unaware of my past, awarded me an Honorary Doctorate of Law exactly thirty years to the month of when I would have been receiving my law degree – isn't life stranger than fiction?

Adrian and I decided on a new start, and moved out of London to a small town outside Bristol. Adrian left his job and we set up a business providing photographic services to local estate agents in the property boom of the mid-'80s. When I found out I was pregnant, I didn't see it would change anything much in my ambitions to build a great business. I would just convert part of the office into a nursery. I automatically assumed I'd carry on working, alongside raising my child. I could do anything I wanted to as an entrepreneur, after all! In my naivety, I thought motherhood would fall into place with my career: I was young, capable, full of energy and ideas. I could not have been happier.

I kept working late into the pregnancy. On Thursday, 5th May 1988, I left the office at 10 p.m. Less than an hour after I got home my waters broke, and I started feeling the contractions: the baby was coming three weeks early. I picked up my overnight bag, already packed with the things I'd need, and Adrian and I wanted to drive to Southmead Hospital in Bristol. But when I spoke to my health visitor, she suggested I wait until my labour got more advanced, especially as they were struggling to allocate midwives to mothers. The following day, around noon, we eventually went into Southmead. At first, everything seemed to be progressing as normal.

This was 1988 and the NHS was not in good shape: waiting lists were long, there were staff shortages and a lack of funding. The Conservative government's plans for restructuring had badly affected patient care. When I got onto the ward that afternoon, the contractions were coming every few minutes and making me double over in pain, but I was told there were no midwives available to deliver my baby. Instead, they gave me a drug to slow down the contractions.

I can't remember much of those long, exhausting hours. For much of it, I was in a state somewhere between pain and sluggish incomprehension. I waited. And I waited. And I waited. Finally, on the Saturday morning, they eased the drugs and my labour progressed. I went into the delivery room determined to do it all naturally. But the reality was that after thirty-plus hours I was completely exhausted. At that stage, I needed all the help I could get. They administered an epidural late on in my labour and the needle grazed my spine. At the time, it didn't even register: I was too busy pushing out my baby. Finally, Lucy-Ann was born around 10 p.m. on Saturday night, 7th May. Her name was something I had thought about long and hard. It is a combination of the Latin for 'light' and the original people of Guyana – my birth-land – the Lucayan. I simply rearranged the letters to Lucy-Ann.

I felt a combination of intense happiness and relief. After such a difficult labour I was overjoyed to hold this little bundle in my arms. I got in trouble with the midwife because I refused to put Lucy-Ann in the Perspex cot beside my bed: I just wanted her to lie against my chest, to feel her breaths rising and falling in time with my heartbeat. To smell that smell that only a newborn baby has. I kept looking at this baby, my baby, with surges of pure joy.

I know everyone thinks their babies are beautiful, but Lucy-Ann really was: I was so proud. I couldn't stop staring at her. She had a thicket of dark hair, bright almond eyes and skin the colour of milky coffee. The combination of my Guyanese roots and Adrian's English fairness meant that Lucy-Ann looked almost Hawaiian or Fijian.

The next morning I woke in tremendous pain, unable to move my legs. The agony was so acute I can still feel it now, as I'm describing it some thirty years later. That's when the medical staff realised they'd messed up the epidural. There was a terrible commotion. And yet despite the pain I still existed in a bubble of happiness. I didn't care what happened to me, now that I had this child in my arms. Everything else faded into insignificance.

I wasn't sure if the panic was about me or her. She had developed jaundice overnight and looked an odd colour. Two days later I was discharged to a cute cottage hospital in Chipping Sodbury, then home.

The experience had been traumatic, but when I got home with Lucy-Ann I forgot about it. I had an angel baby. Lucy-Ann hardly ever cried. She was the best baby you could possibly imagine. She would just lie there, content, surrounded by her toys. She slept through the night. During the day, she was so quiet and calm. The other women I knew from my mother-and-baby group struggled to get a night's sleep and were up much of the night trying to settle their babies. I never had problems, and I felt bad when they complained to me about how hard it was because I had nothing to moan about. I thought my life was complete. I thought it was too good to be true. Our innovative photographic laboratory was thriving, I had this beautiful baby and a happy marriage.

This state of blissful ignorance went on for nine months or so. Then I noticed things weren't quite right. When I gave Lucy-Ann toys or books, she didn't respond in the usual way expected of a baby her age. She would either stroke a book or smell it, or appear just to listen to a toy car. The other babies I saw were banging their toys noisily and starting to explore the world around them with boundless curiosity. Their eyes would follow their mothers around the room, and they would become upset if Mum was out of sight. Not my Lucy-Ann. By the time she was one, and the other children were beginning to crawl and walk, Lucy-Ann would just sit there and smile. She made no attempt to move. All the usual milestones passed without my daughter reaching them.

I raised my concerns with the midwife and clinics, but none of the physical examinations showed anything abnormal. So, we carried on. But at eighteen months, the differences between her and the other babies became more alarming. Lucy-Ann didn't want to pull herself up or walk or talk. That's when I started to panic. Again, when I mentioned this to the professionals, they would put me off with a condescending 'all babies are different'.

'You're being paranoid,' they would say. 'It's natural: you're a first-time mum. These things will happen in their own time.' 'Each baby is different: there is nothing physically wrong with her, she'll do it when she's ready.'

By the time Lucy-Ann was two I was beside myself. I knew there was something seriously wrong because she wasn't meeting any of her milestones. I took her to a series of specialists. The specialists presented me with various diagnoses, each of which was deeply shocking. One of them thought she might be suffering from a syndrome called Fragile X, which would mean degeneration and lifelong care. I was terrified my daughter was either going to die or her brain would cease functioning.

But for whatever reason – call it mother's intuition, if you will – that diagnosis didn't sit right with me: I didn't think anything I was being told made sense, so I kept pushing for clarity. I knew the answer had to be out there somewhere. Adrian believed the professionals and thought I was being hysterical. In the end, I went by myself with Lucy-Ann to see a private team of pediatricians and developmental psychologists, who said, 'She has suffered a trauma at birth, which probably means she was starved of oxygen, which resulted in her being brain-damaged. Only time will tell how serious it is.' They suggested that I would find it difficult to cope, being such a young mother with no family around, and should consider putting her in a home or having full-time care.

Adrian didn't know about this private consultation. I remember calmly putting Lucy-Ann back into her buggy, going back to the car park, putting her into her car seat in my old banger of a mini, driving to a park and just sitting on a bench with her in my arms. It was a beautiful spring day, and as she lay there smiling on my lap, I knew. I knew I had to fight for her.

They were so matter-of-fact about me sending her away, almost as if they were discussing a holiday I was going on and would need to send my dog to the kennels; but it was a human *life* they were talking about – my beloved daughter's life.

I've never gotten a satisfactory answer, but it appears that the medicine I'd been given to delay my contractions had resulted in Lucy-Ann being distressed and starved of oxygen during birth. The penny dropped that the hospital had been negligent. I had had a perfect pregnancy and expected a healthy baby, but fate had played a devastating hand for both me and my baby girl. I could have sued, but I knew that I would need all my reserves of energy to look after my daughter. Years later, when Lucy-Ann was more grown-up, I thought again about suing them, but what was the point? To go through a lengthy legal battle would have caused a lot of emotional pain; I could not turn back time, I could not undo her condition. I felt it was far more important to preserve my own sanity, so I could be strong for her. I had to look forwards, not backwards towards blame.

It's not an easy lesson to learn, but since then I've consciously made the choice not to take on battles that will diminish me. Whatever the material gain might be at the end, whatever revenge or satisfaction might be gained, the long-term emotional damage it does to you isn't worth it.

Lucy-Ann's official diagnosis does not fit neatly into any box. She has symptoms of autism, dyslexia and dyspraxia.

I was told she would hardly walk or talk and would need constant, round-the-clock care. When my mother heard what had happened, she suggested sending Lucy-Ann to be cared for in a convent in Guyana. She pleaded with me that I was a young, successful and ambitious woman and she didn't want me to sacrifice my life.

The idea of sending my daughter, my flesh and blood, away because I somehow wouldn't be able to cope hit me like a sucker punch. I couldn't believe what was happening. I cried. I shouted. But quite quickly I realised I had to dry my tears and stand up for her, protect her; I needed to be strong, now more than ever. I was overwhelmed with emotion, but somewhere in the middle of all of it I instinctively knew what I had to do. I had to be the mother my daughter deserved so that she could be the best she could be.

I chose to reject the advice of the medical experts. I said Lucy-Ann would stay with me, the person who loved her most in the entire world, and that I would never even consider the alternative, so they might as well stop suggesting it.

From that moment on, I dedicated my every waking hour to Lucy-Ann. My dedication resulted in me neglecting my husband and the business, which I effectively left for Adrian to run. He had a hard time accepting Lucy-Ann was disabled. He was a proud man and so felt somewhat embarrassed that his daughter wasn't advancing at the same rate as other children. I don't blame him for that. He was older than me, from a very traditional, middle-class English family, and I think he was in a state of denial for a long time. Outwardly she was so beautiful, her behavior flawless – 'too good to be true'. It meant that I had to step up.

*

The first goal was to get Lucy-Ann walking.

Every morning for nearly six months I took her to the local playground, where there was a slide. It had steps up one side, which you had to climb to get to the top. I would place Lucy-Ann at the bottom of the steps and physically move her feet, one by one, onto the rungs. She would then be rewarded for her hard work by going down the slide, which she loved. She often erupted into laughter. Slowly, after a few weeks, she began to learn how to climb by herself.

The second goal was talking – just the odd word would do.

One day I was playing a cassette of nursery rhymes in the car, and I glanced in the rearview mirror and I saw her trying to mouth the words. I began to wonder whether music was the thing she would respond to. On a hunch, I drove to the Early Learning Centre and bought a little drum kit for her and one for me, and a cassette player with a microphone.

I put the drum kits in our garage and I would recite the alphabet, or a word – 'Mama, Dada, water, food' – every time beating out a count on the drum. I would encourage Lucy-Ann to do the same. It was painstaking. There were some days when Lucy-Ann would just look at me, uncomprehending, or she'd scream and shout and put her hands over her ears, and I'd ask myself if I was crazy even to be trying. But somewhere deep down inside I knew this was what we had to do. I kept at it. I kept saying A, B, C. By the time she was four, she could recite some of the alphabet, count to ten and was beginning to learn how to string words together.

Throughout all of this, I was still working. I had turned the office into the nursery / playroom. In the office, I had to be assertive, in control and professional. Along with Adrian, I was responsible for our employees' livelihoods, and that weighed heavily on me. At work, I tried my best to remain calm and composed, and to make sure everything was going as smoothly as it could. At home, I had to be focused entirely on Lucy-Ann. I showered her with love and affection, but I also had to be extremely patient. Sometimes I lost it. I would find a quiet corner of the house and go there to shout or cry into a pillow so that Lucy-Ann wouldn't see how upset I was. I knew I had to be a fighter for her. No matter how many times I placed her foot on a step or recited one, two, three, I could never lose hope. I needed to have enough hope for both of us. There was not much space for me to be 'the good wife'.

These days we all have complex demands on our time, and as women – particularly women with children – these can be competing demands. Sometimes these demands require what seems like a contradictory response: to be commanding at work, yet endlessly loving at home. But I *had* to be both, which meant accepting that these were complementary parts of my identity. I had to be that lioness, caring but sometimes cruel to be kind to her too. I just had to do it. That's also what I mean by 'tough softness'.

We moved back to Eastbourne's Old Town, and when the time came for Lucy-Ann to go to school, the real battle started.

The local authority refused to give her any special assistance at school. Lucy-Ann had worked so hard on her letters and numbers that we had done almost too good a job, and the local authority was reluctant to categorise her as 'special needs', they rejected the idea of a statutory assessment for a statement of her special needs because that would commit them to providing extra care and support until she was eighteen. Obviously they didn't want to spend the money. Instead they tried to fob me off by saying she was just slow. The system was so imperfect back then. I remember, with my legal studies, completely rewriting the application statement form, and eventually I wrote a 'legal' letter to East Sussex Local Authority that I would take them to court unless she was given an assessment.

It was awful. I knew Lucy-Ann wouldn't be able to cope on her own in a mainstream school, so I refused to send her. The beginning of term came and went, and the local authority threatened to take me to court. I saved up to pay for lawyers and was advised that I'd need another specialist diagnosis, as evidence, from someone the local authority would suggest. Increasingly desperate, I used my money to take Lucy-Ann to see doctors across the UK and Europe. Eventually, after a long, hard slog, I found a doctor who compiled a report that would not only back me up but also satisfy what the local authority required to get Lucy-Ann statemented. It took over two years. When Lucy-Ann was seven, she was finally given special assistance and could start school.

But fighting for Lucy-Ann had taken over my life. I had no time to be a wife. Adrian and I had grown apart. My marriage was imploding and later that year it ended in divorce.

I knew I had to pick myself up and start again. So in 1993 Lucy-Ann and I moved to London. I found a tiny one-bedroom flat on Princess May Road in Stoke Newington that I could just about afford. I paid a deposit and a month's rent with the last of my savings. For two years we lived there; Lucy-Ann slept in the bed and I slept on a sofa bed in the small lounge.

I wanted to better myself, as well as give my daughter a secure future. I enrolled at the University of North London to study marketing. I had gone back to doing a bit of modelling, event management and product launch work, and from talking to the marketing team from big brand companies, we both realised I had a natural flair for marketing and communications. One of the directors of BMW UK suggested I enrolled for a degree as well as work part-time in their new commercial fleet division, which they were seeking to expand in the UK.

I got a student loan, but that was not enough to support Lucy-Ann and myself. When I wasn't in lectures, I took every single job I could. Waitressing. Leafleting. Anything I could get my hands on. One of the less pleasant jobs I remember was handing out flyers for a mobile phone shop in Croydon at Christmas time. It was absolutely freezing, and I had to stand there on the street, dressed in a cheerleader outfit, face whipped by the bitterly cold wind, trying to get people to take these leaflets that they didn't want. The other girls dumped the leaflets in bins, but I was determined to do what I was being paid for. It was soul-destroying for me.

In the evenings, I had a job waitressing at my local Pizza Express in London. This too was not a good experience as there was this octopus-armed, lecherous manager whose hands would be all over you if you gave him half a chance. I used to dread going there, but I needed the job so badly I never dared complain. Also, one of the perks of waitressing was that at the end of the evening, you'd get to take leftover pizza and cakes home. I remember taking back carrot cake and a vegetarian pizza, and the following day Lucy-Ann and I stuffed ourselves happily around our tiny kitchen table. I always tried to make sure she ate well, so on the days when I had barely any cash, I would buy the best food I could afford for Lucy-Ann and eat either her leftovers or something out of a tin. I had beans on toast so many times I lost count.

Childcare was another expense. I was lucky in that I could take Lucy-Ann along with me to evening lectures and she would sit quietly at the back, drawing with her crayons while I took notes. I also had a group of girlfriends at university who were lovely and very supportive. We had a study-group at my flat and on certain evenings, when I needed to work or got a last-minute job, one of them would step in and look after my daughter. I couldn't have got through those lonely years without those wonderful young women, willing to help at the drop of a hat.

At home, things were challenging as Lucy-Ann was getting older and more demanding. She was frightened of loud noises or bright lights. When something upset her – a passing police siren, for instance, or a street-lamp turning on, or the neighbours shouting and arguing above our flat – she used to put her arms over her ears and scream. She would run and hide, usually under the little kitchen table, until the fear had passed. I could not cuddle her to make her feel better. When she was like this, she didn't want to be touched or held. Everything became frightening to her because she couldn't understand it – I just had to let it pass on her terms.

One of the effects of her condition was that she found it difficult to entertain herself or just play alone if I was not with her or by her. Her memory was incredibly short-term, so I always had to do things for her. The way she learned how to get dressed was by me putting everything in a certain place, so that she knew where it was. If something wasn't in the right place, Lucy-Ann didn't know how to go about finding it. It meant that last thing at night, no matter how tired I was or how many essays I had to write or textbooks I had to read, I would go around the flat checking that everything was in exactly the right place for the morning: her clothes, her hairbrush, her shoes. That was the only way I knew how to foster her sense of independence. It was important to me that Lucy-Ann felt able to be her own person, whatever her abilities.

There were some very low moments. During the day, I could keep going, keep going, keep going because there was so much I had to do. Attending lectures, waitressing, leafleting, looking after Lucy-Ann, making sure she was all right at school: it was hectic. But at night, after Lucy-Ann had gone to bed, I often stared at the walls of my small rented flat and I felt crushed by having to battle for her on my own. Life seemed to be going on outside for other people, but I was drifting into isolation. I was so scared of what might happen to me and how I would cope in the weeks and months to come. If I couldn't cope, who would look after her – her father, my parents, my siblings? I was not close to them during this time, as their lives were going so well – I didn't want them to feel sorry for me, to have pity on me. I couldn't stand that.

To make the flat look a bit more cheerful and homely, I'd bought a knick-knack from Ikea. It was a green glass object, molded in the shape of a head, and I put it on the top shelf above the TV. One Saturday morning, as I was dusting the shelves, the glass ornament toppled and fell on my head with a thud. I was knocked out cold. I came around hours later, to find Lucy-Ann sitting next to me surrounded by shattered glass.

That's when it hit me.

I often think back to that moment and say to myself, 'My God, if it had been more serious, what would have happened? If I'd died, who would have looked after Lucy-Ann? Who would have found her?' Because the stark truth of it was, while not deliberate, I was not in close contact with my family at this time. My parents were in Guyana, my siblings were at the start of their careers or adult life, and Adrian was not a physical daily presence in our lives.

It was a tricky time.

When I got up from that floor, I looked in the mirror and saw a gash on my forehead. I realised that I had to look after myself better. I needed to be there for my child. I think that carried me through. In many ways my daughter saved me because every time I thought I was too exhausted, or it was all getting too much, she gave me the strength to carry on. I was the only person who would fight for her.

Every day was a battle. To the outside world, I would project a sense of confidence and self-assurance. For Lucy-Ann, I would exercise tough love – to challenge her, to push herself to do better. As soon as she was old enough to understand, I said to her, 'I'm not going to let people feel sorry for you. I want you to be the best that you can be.'

I've always felt that my daughter is not disabled so much as differently abled. The world would be a very boring place if we were all the same. I taught her that she just had to discover what she was good at and concentrate on that.

*

Lucy-Ann turned thirty this year. She has a reading age of six, and she looks a lot younger than she is – probably around sixteen. She can sense when I'm down and will always give me the warmest of smiles and cuddles to make me feel better. She's very black-and-white, which many people find disarming but to me it is ever refreshing in a world where people believe they should say what others perceive as acceptable or will make them more liked. When she sees someone sleeping rough in the streets, she'll immediately want to invite them back to our house to sleep because we have a spare room. To her, it's that simple.

When London hosted the Summer Paralympics in 2012, it was the first time we as a family had seen these terrific athletes compete on prime-time television. My youngest brother and his wife had kindly taken Lucy-Ann on the day the UK won lots of medals. The atmosphere in the stadium was electric and I couldn't wait to ask Lucy-Ann if she had had a great day. When she returned and I said to her how incredible the athletes were, she looked at me and said a single word: 'No.'

I thought that was odd, so I persisted: 'Yes, they are! They're really amazing.'

She replied: 'I don't feel sorry for them. They're not that special because everybody can see their disability. No one can see mine.' Her truth struck me dumb.

I've always impressed on her that she is special, so she is aware of her differences. But it really hit her hard after my two youngest children were born. She went through a tough time then, because she saw them growing and doing things that she couldn't do, and it made her frustrated.

She started to get depressed and angry. One day, to my absolute shock, she asked me, 'Why didn't you just kill me when I was born?'

Can you imagine the pain to hear your own child say this to you? Even now it breaks my heart to think that such a thought ever crossed her mind – her words are still a dagger that strikes my heart.

I love her so deeply that I could never imagine my life without her. With love and understanding, we got through that patch.

When I turned fifty, it really hit me that I had to start the process of allowing her to become more independent. She needs to be able to survive on her own terms, without me, because I'm very unlikely to outlive her. It's not an easy thing to come to terms with because I still worry about her so much, every second of every day.

The fact that Lucy-Ann looks what is deemed 'normal' is a constant challenge. She's slow and takes her time doing things, which means people shout at her in shops, on public transport, even in hospitals. She'll try and use her credit card to pay for something, and she knows now she can tap it and use contactless, but it will take her a while to work it out and there'll be people tut-tutting angrily in the queue behind her, increasingly making some racist comment. In this hyper-connected society, where everything happens at the click of a button, we've forgotten how to be patient, how to think of others. We're too quick to judge. So many people are fighting a private battle we don't know the first thing about.

I've been tremendously lucky to have Lucy-Ann as my daughter. I did not appreciate how prophetic it would be to give her a name that means 'light', what a gift she would be. She has strengthened me in so many ways and honed my ability to fight. To fight against the establishment; against the voices who told me she'd never amount to anything; against all the medical predictions; against my own constant anxieties about what would happen the next day and the day after that. She has always gifted me unconditional love: one of the most powerful forces in our lives.

However difficult things have been, I have refused to allow myself to become bitter, angry or resentful. My first motivation is love and I know I can be both tough *and* empathetic, hard and soft. My experiences have taught me that emotions are not a weakness when they are used as fuel. They have taught me to follow my heart.

Having Lucy-Ann has made me realise I can fight battles without losing myself or my softness. And once you fight one battle like that, it becomes easier to do it again and again. It becomes part of your personality, your thought process, who you are. That's partly why I was able to take on the government over Brexit: I already had inner strength, forged through my years in that one-bedroom flat in Stoke Newington, where I fortified myself on so many days to go out into the world and fight the daily struggle to survive.

When I embarked on my legal challenge over triggering Article 50, Lucy-Ann didn't really understand what was going on. All she knew was that people were getting angry with her mother. She calmly said to me, 'But that happens a lot, Mummy, quite a lot of people don't like you.' It made me laugh.

I wanted to explain it to her in terms she would understand, so I sat her down and said, 'The reason people are cross with me is because I'm doing something they don't like. It makes them think about what they did, but I'm not saying what they did was wrong.'

In her inevitable Lucy-Ann way, she replied, 'Did you do it again, Mummy? Did you tell the truth?'

I thought for a few seconds about how to explain it to her more clearly.

'You know if you go into a shop and you take something off the shelf and you don't pay for it, it's wrong?' I asked.

'Yes,' she said. 'That's called shoplifting.'

'The prime minister, who is our leader, is doing something wrong. She's not taking something off the shelf, but she's trying to do something that is just as bad. She's trying to do something against the law.'

Lucy-Ann didn't even blink.

'Well,' my clever daughter said, 'someone has to tell her she is being bad, and she must stop.'

In that moment, I felt like the strongest woman alive. The proudest of lionesses.

15

Letting Go

Many things I've gone through in life have made me feel guilty and have made me question whether I have done the right thing – not just by Lucy-Ann but all my kids and loved ones. One of the hardest things to do in life is to let go – of guilt, but also anger and regret. Letting go means you must acknowledge that something is over and that you're not going to allow yourself to be defined by it any more. That can be emotional. Even though you know, on a rational level, that the best thing for you is to get out of bad relationships, to protect yourself from toxic friends or to forget past hurts, it's often difficult for your heart to do the same.

It's not just the big things either. It's hard to let go of that dress hanging in the back of your wardrobe, even though you haven't worn it for years, just because it reminds you of a specific occasion or time in your life.

One of the most self-harming things we can do – and I've noticed this particularly in women – is to hold on to negative feelings, on to hurt. It's so damaging to carry a grudge. I always imagine it as having a rat inside you, gnawing away. You can either feed the rat with your own hatred, or you can let it go and be done with it. What I've discovered through the course of my life is that it's much easier to let go and to forgive and to move on because you only have to forgive once. Whereas if you don't forgive, the person you're damaging most is yourself. The rat will still be there, gnawing away from the inside, until you are nothing more than a shell of yourself.

Don't get me wrong, I know that's not an easy thing to do. I learned the lesson of letting go the hard way.

After many years of raising Lucy-Ann on my own, doing everything I could to protect her and to make ends meet, I was tired. I was guilty. I dreamed of giving my precious daughter a loving family. I wanted her to have a consistent father-figure, siblings and a mother who wasn't always worried about where the next £10 would come from.

That's when I met the man who would become my second husband in my final year of studying for my marketing degree. I was asked to help with an event at Legal & General for their top Independent Financial Adviser clients. I jumped at the opportunity, as my final year dissertation was on financial services, and as part of that I really needed some practical experience. Jon was the manager in charge – a charismatic, confident man.

It's hard to explain, looking back through the prism of everything that happened, exactly why I fell for him. But I think it was because he appeared to represent all that I wanted. If I'd had to fill out a form for a dating agency and list all the things I was looking for, Jon ticked every box. He was very close to his family, God-fearing and had three children of his own he absolutely adored. He was Irish, with a twinkly charm. He was kind, supportive, and said and did all the right things in connection to Lucy-Ann. It was the ready-made family I had dreamed of for her.

Jon and I dated for a couple of years while I graduated and started work. Quite quickly, I began to trust him. For the first and last time in a relationship, I was completely honest with my partner, revealing all my weaknesses, all my fears, all the things that terrified me. What I realise now is that, however much you might want to offer up all your darkest secrets to the person you love, it can also give them tremendous power to hurt you.

But back then I was caught up in a heady whirl of romance, and I let my guard down. Jon had a house in Bradford-on-Avon, a lovely Wiltshire town with a community feel, and he started saying that it made sense for me to move there.

'It's a better life for Lucy-Ann,' he said. And I agreed with him. She was having a rough time at school in London – she was bullied for being different and dark-skinned, and even came home with cigarette burns on her arms. It was devastating to be her mother; I felt the need to shelter her even more strongly than before.

I wanted nothing more than to offer Lucy-Ann some sort of long-term security. And here was this man who seemed so kind and trustworthy, so accepting of my daughter for who she was and who said he loved me. I moved to Wiltshire and we got married a year later. Once again I was momentarily happy, but it turned out to be one of the biggest disasters of my life.

*

Things changed when we got married. It seemed to me as if, after two years of courtship, Jon felt he owned me. I'd moved away from my home, my friends and my support network. The very things that he appeared to love me for, he was now determined to undermine and break.

It was small things at first. Emotional abuse often begins like this: it is almost impossible for a victim to be able to point at a specific action and say, 'There. That's when it started. This is what's happening and it's wrong.' I don't think I knew the term even existed. What I knew was I felt like a bad wife:

I was drowning in a world of alcohol, broken confidence, control, confusion.

At first I'd try to confront him, but he'd just laugh off the things he said as 'banter' or say I was being too sensitive. Step by step, without my realising it was happening, I found myself cut off from everybody I loved. I didn't recognise it for what it was. Back then, emotional abuse wasn't talked about. I know that it happened, and I know that I survived it, but in truth I can't explain it. I look back and I don't recognise my own weakness; I still can't recognise that Gina.

From the outside, we had a wonderful life. We lived in a rambling country house, with expensive furniture and a state-of-the-art kitchen. My husband was successful and charming in public. We didn't have to worry about money. I adored his three children – two sons and a daughter – who often came to stay with us. His youngest son was the same age as Lucy-Ann and was just gorgeous.

But scratch the pretty surface and there was an uglier truth nestling beneath.

This is what I remember:

I remember the coldness of the floor.

I remember the hardness of the slate pressing against my side.

I remember the numbness; the absolute incomprehension that this could be happening to me.

This is what I do not remember:

I do not remember the pain.

I shut down. I floated out of myself. It was as if it were happening to someone else entirely. It's a way of coping. You can't process the emotion of a situation like that in the moment: you can't feel, you can only survive.

And for a while it works – even when I woke the next day and my ribs were so bruised that every time I breathed there was a sharp pain in my chest.

Why didn't I leave? Well, I felt guilt and tremendous shame at being a failure as a wife. I didn't want to tell anyone what was going on in case they judged me negatively. Who would believe me?

It wasn't that easy. I had lost who I was. I was losing a grip on myself, on who I thought I was. I compare it to drowning: falling deeper and deeper into the water towards the seabed. I could still see the surface, and the dappled sky beyond it, but I couldn't reach it. Sometimes I felt I couldn't even breathe, as if all the air was being squeezed out of me by an iron fist pushing down on my chest. I kept spiraling downwards.

My confidence dwindled to a point beyond zero. I tried to leave three times; every time I went back because I believed it would be different. He promised it would be different, he promised he would drink less. A pattern of behaviour so many men and women suffering domestic abuse engage in.

Then, one day, it really was rock bottom. Jon and I were having terrible rows once again. I woke up one morning with a terrible gash and pain on my back but couldn't remember what had happened the night before.

I went to Lucy-Ann's room and packed a small case with her clothes. I threw some things into an even smaller bag for me. I wasn't thinking beyond that one present moment of knowing I needed to get us out.

I took Lucy-Ann by the hand and rushed downstairs with the bags. I didn't take a single possession other than the most basic necessities. I stopped for a second and looked around at all the beautiful things which had garnished our supposedly picture-perfect life, and which I had spent hours choosing – the plush sofas, the crystal brandy glasses, the silver-framed photographs, the kitchen with its cold, slate floor – none of it meant anything any more. It was a mirage, a chimera, a hollow shell of something that had never really existed.

We ran outside and threw the bags into the back of my car and drove away from that house without a second glance.

I was lucky because a woman I was friendly with nearby was about to go on a two-week holiday with her family. I called her, she offered me the use of her house while they were away. That's where Lucy-Ann and I stayed. No one knew where we were or what was happening, as I had shared very little with anyone. Sometimes the safest place is right under someone's nose.

After those two weeks were up, I didn't have anywhere to go. I didn't want to go to my family or friends because I thought he'd try and follow me there, and I didn't want anyone to have to lie on my behalf or be involved. It's a fault of mine that I can be very proud. I was too ashamed to ask other people for help. I tried to rent a flat for the two of us, but every time the estate agent wanted my permanent address, my bank account details, where I last lived. I didn't have anything because I had no paperwork. I had no documents. We stayed the odd night in a bed and breakfast. When I ran out of physical cash, Lucy-Ann and I slept in the car, with all our possessions stuffed into a couple of bags in the boot. More than once, we slept in a multi-storey car park. The sounds made Lucy-Ann frightened, so I bought earplugs to help her sleep. They seemed to work a little, but she mainly clung to me, burying her head into me to block out the noise, as well as keep warm.

It was at that point – one of the lowest ebbs of my life – that I thought to myself, 'Gina, you just have to be strong, rebuild your life, for your daughter.' I needed every ounce of my energy to recover from this. And that meant I had to let go of everything and just look ahead.

It was the best decision I could have made.

Women find it so hard to let go. It's partly because we're conditioned to feel guilty about failure, even if that failure is not our fault. And it's also because, in a divorce scenario, we are often encouraged by lawyers and advisers to fight and get as much as possible. But re-living the moments, things and people you're angry about means being constantly riled-up, and that holds you back. The hurt keeps happening; the pain never eases.

Holding on to a grudge is a waste of time, effort and energy. If, like I did, you need to put yourself back together, then you need to refocus all the power you expend on hating someone into more positive efforts. Holding on to feelings of resentment or revenge is like sipping arsenic and expecting the other person to die. If you forgive, forget and forge forwards, you can use your energy to strive, create and rebuild.

I'm not saying it's easy! But those nights sleeping in my little blue car in multi-storey car parks, when I would wake with a stiff neck and a ballooning panic in my chest, forced me to look at my situation honestly. I needed to get on with my life. And I knew I could survive. One thing I've always returned to is that I can work. It doesn't matter what kind of job. I knew that I was strong enough to look after myself and my daughter. That sense of resilience is extremely important. I didn't need anything or anyone. I could walk out of the door and be OK.

In the end, out of desperation, I phoned Lucy-Ann's father Adrian and told him what had happened. I am forever grateful that Adrian listened and immediately offered to help. He said that there was a flat in the same block he lived in for rent in Tooting, South London. He said he would organise everything so that Lucy-Ann and I could live there, and we could split the childcare equally.

I didn't ask Jon for anything. I didn't want his money or his possessions. I just wanted to be free, to become myself once again.

Lucy-Ann and I moved to Tooting. It was a good arrangement: she had a bedroom in my flat and a bedroom in Adrian's, and during the coming weeks and months as I set up my own business, if I had to work late or had dinner with friends or clients, or a networking event, Lucy-Ann could pop upstairs and stay with him. He helped me through. I can't thank him enough for that.

I had not heard from or about Jon for years. Then I read an article in a trade publication in 2010[26] saying that he was to stand for the English Democrats, an anti-immigration political party, at the next general election. The article read:

> [Jon] will stand in the Chippenham constituency of Wiltshire for the party, which proposes that 'no more so-called asylum seekers should be allowed into England' and pledges to withdraw the UK from the 1951 UN Convention on Refugees.
>
> The party also opposes multiculturalism, and pledges to close down all 'politically correct quangos'. 'We want English freedoms and values, not multiculturalism,' it states in an election leaflet. He outlined his support for the English Democrats, which is campaigning for a separate parliament for England. Maguire said: 'They want to say cheerio to the Scots, the Welsh and the Irish – and hooray for that and let England pocket the stupid cash we keep sending across our borders.'

As I read the words, thoughts and memories started tumbling through my mind. This was my former husband. Had I ever really known him?

---

26 http://citywire.co.uk/new-model-adviser/news/jon-maguire-to-stand
   -for-anti-immigration-english-democrats-party/a386621

Slowly, step by step, brick by brick, I rebuilt my life and my shattered sense of self. I think there's a mistaken perception that only a certain type of person suffers from domestic violence: it can only happen to somebody that is weak or from a deprived background who is so financially dependent on their spouse that leaving feels impossible. There's a sense that it doesn't happen to people who've got money, who live in a nice house. There's almost an unwillingness to believe it's true. In the months that followed my divorce, some of my closest confidants would say to me, 'But you were perfectly fine in public'. There is a belief that strong women are never victims. It scares people to know that it can happen.

After many years of burying this period of my life, it was been very upsetting to revisit it, talk to others – friends and family and hear their memories of a woman I do not recognise. What I now realise is that when you feel yourself drowning, you are too emotionally crippled to reach out for help, you feel trapped.

I consider myself a strong woman but this happened to me. And that's what I want anyone reading this book to understand. Because if I can share, then hopefully other women in similarly damaged relationships will be less afraid to speak up.

What I say to these women is: you are not weak, even when you think you are. You are special, you shine and that is what can attract men who feel the need to control or own you. You have more strength than you realise. You can leave, and there is another, better life you can be living. Start by forgiving yourself. Try to let go. Feel no guilt over this. Set yourself free. Focus your energies on making a positive future. It will be a liberation.

It was for me.

16

Is That All You've Got to
Put Me Off?

After my second marriage, it took me a long time to trust a man again.

To be honest, I wasn't even looking. For years, I was focused on providing a stable home life for Lucy-Ann and building up my own marketing consultancy business to secure our financial future. I had a busy work-life and re-kindled several friendships with girlfriends. I had various dates with men but nothing evolved into a serious relationship. I was happy with that. Or at least I thought I was. I didn't plan on meeting anyone.

Then, in October 2002, two of my girlfriends started getting cross with me and complained that I was working too hard and not having enough fun. 'You're always working too hard, being serious or looking after Lucy-Ann. You need to let your hair down for once.'

They persuaded me to go to a Halloween party that was being held at a club they knew, and they even went to the lengths of getting all three of us matching witch outfits. There we were, sitting at the end of the bar in our black outfits with peaked black hats and heavy eye-make-up. Towards the end of the evening, a tray of drinks arrived for us for free. Then a few more arrived. We had no idea where they came from, but presumed they were on the house, so we drank them anyway. It was a good night. I went home, clambered out of my witch's costume and I didn't think anything more of it.

The next morning, my mobile rang. I didn't recognise the number.

'Hello?' I said.

It was a man's voice on the other end of the line and the first thing he asked was, 'How's your head?'

I was baffled and a little taken aback.

'Why do you have my number? Who is this? Who are you? Why are you asking?'

'Oh, I'm the person who bought you and your friends drinks last night,' the man continued. 'My name is Alan Miller.'

There was something about the name that felt familiar, but I didn't know why. I tried to think hard, but I couldn't place it. 'Oh,' I said, worrying whether he was someone important or not. 'How did you get my number?'

'I still had it in my phone from when you did some work for the company I work for,' he said. 'Anyway, I was thinking it would be nice to go for a coffee sometime.'

'Of course, of course,' I replied, distractedly. I didn't want to be rude, but I also wanted to get him off the phone so I could go to work.

We ended the conversation without any concrete plans to meet up. If anything, I thought he was a bit of a weirdo and I didn't want to give him any false encouragement. I dismissed the call.

A couple of days later, I remembered who he was. He was the founding partner of a company called New Star, which was a fast-growing UK asset management company. I had done the launch marketing for Alan's boss, John Duffield.

I felt a twinge of guilt for being so dismissive. After all, this guy had bought us drinks, which I'd never properly thanked him for and called to see how I was! So I called him back and we agreed to go for a coffee a few weeks later. In the meantime, I called Rachel, who was one of the women in the New Star marketing team I had become friends with, to check that Alan wasn't a weirdo or a misogynist – after all, I had not been good at picking men recently. All she said was, 'He's got a heart of gold, he's a good egg.'

When we met, he was self-deprecating, funny, comfortable, clever and I could see and feel the 'heart of gold' Rachel mentioned. It was also clear that Alan was interested in me romantically. But I wasn't interested in a serious relationship. I'd been through a lot. I'd been badly burned by my second husband, who had seemed to offer everything I most wanted. I knew not to trust first impressions, as far as men were concerned.

My guard was up. I said to him, quite clearly, 'Look, I'm not ready for any complicated relationships. I've just found myself again. I'm getting strong. I'm solid where I am now and I don't want or need any more complications in my life.'

We didn't contact each other for a few months. When we met again, he was divorced and we went out to dinner. We talked. We got on, so we decided to meet up again. I started to warm to him, I started to let my guard down. I relaxed a bit in his company. Then, on the third date, I said to him straight away, 'Listen, I have a daughter with special needs. She takes up a lot of my time. If this relationship is going anywhere, you need to be OK with that.'

I had got to a stage in my life where I didn't have any time to waste. I wanted to be direct. I wanted to test this man's mettle before I became any more enmeshed in his life, or he in mine. I knew, by the third date, that I liked him. But I wasn't going to let things develop further unless he signed up for all the baggage I came with.

I put all my cards on the table and told him he wasn't going to get all my attention. I was a committed mother, I was running my own business and I didn't have time for anything that wasn't real, and if he wanted someone fluffy on his arm like so many men in the City appeared to want – that wasn't me. I delivered this long monologue, detailing all the things that were difficult in my life and what a rubbish partner I would be, and at the end of this outburst Alan looked me in the eye and said, 'Is that all you've got to put me off?'

What struck me most about Alan those first few times we met was not his physical looks as much as the sense of quiet self-assurance and humility he exuded. There was nothing threatening about him. He was just comfortable to be around. I didn't feel that he was playing any games. I had learnt to listen to my instincts, to my inner voice, and I instinctively knew I could trust him. I'd never properly felt that before. From the start, Alan made me feel it was OK to be me, cared for and understood.

But I wasn't about to get carried away. I worked in finance and I knew I had to do my due diligence. I was still in contact with a few other women who worked for New Star. I called them up and said, 'Tell me about this Alan Miller. Tell me what he's like.'

Every single one of them replied with a version of the same thing. They all said, 'He's very principled and he's just got a heart of gold.' That was the phrase that came up again and again. Heart of gold.

It was very easy to see that. He was quite black-and-white and uncomplicated about the world, also extremely bright and caring. I was fortunate enough to meet Alan's father shortly before he died, and he was also a wonderful man. I would say the man Alan is has a lot to do with his upbringing – he was raised by loving parents who instilled in him core values and a belief in community; which is often a mark of people from the Jewish faith. In many respects, his parents were like mine. That's what makes us so alike, despite our religious differences.

We fell in love.

Three months into our relationship, I introduced Alan to the other great love of my life, my daughter Lucy-Ann. I was nervous about how they would get on because Lucy-Ann has always been very straightforward and uncompromising. But when she met Alan she instantly bonded with him. I was worried, because even now I wasn't yet entirely sure I wanted a long-term relationship.

But, as time went on, their relationship deepened. Strangers we met used to say to her, 'Oh, you look so like your father,' even though there was no genetic link between them. Clearly, it was just meant to be.

As much as he loved Lucy-Ann, Alan was desperate to have children of his own and I knew it wasn't going to be easy for me. I was over forty and had been told that one of my ovaries had stopped functioning completely, so already my chances were halved. Most of my closest female relatives, including my mother and my aunt, had gone through the menopause in their late thirties. So, as soon as we'd decided that this relationship was worth it, we felt there was no time to lose.

We set about planning for pregnancy with military precision. If you've ever seen the film *Maybe Baby*, starring Hugh Laurie and Joely Richardson as a successful professional couple struggling to conceive, you'll have some idea of what it was like. We both stopped drinking alcohol and started eating more healthily, and I got those ovulation sticks which told me when I was at my most fertile. My bedside drawer was full of all those self-help guides on how to get pregnant, thermometers, vitamin pills . . . Too much.

But weeks went by without success and then the weeks turned into months. We were both feeling exhausted and a bit dispirited by the process. After six months had passed, I thought, 'Enough. I'm sick of having to chart our lives according to when we might or might not be able to have a baby.' It was very stressful having to plan out your life like that, so Alan and I looked at each and said, 'Shall we just ... escape?'

We booked a weekend in Paris. We decided to treat ourselves and to go out and have some fun together and forget all about the rules and regulations. We ate whatever we wanted, we drank all the things we shouldn't have, we laughed, we relaxed. By the end of that weekend, I was pregnant with Luca.

So that's my tip: if you want to get pregnant in your forties, go to Paris for the weekend! Have fun – love and laugh. It helps. I'm joking, of course. But for me there is a nugget of truth within that: I placed far too much pressure on myself, as many women do, to conceive at a certain time in my life, and that stress and tension was never going to help me get pregnant. For me, the most important thing was to relax.

*

In June 2005, Alan and I were married on a beach in Jamaica. By then, I was heavily pregnant and not really supposed to fly, but I'm fairly small, as was my bump, and we knew we'd have five doctors as guests, so we decided to risk it.

The wedding took place at six in the evening, just as the sun was setting. We hadn't told our friends and family what we were doing because we wanted it to be a surprise, so instead of inviting them to a wedding, we told them we were going to have a 'Dressed to Kill'-themed party to celebrate my birthday. Most of the guests turned up in black tie and glittering evening gowns, but one of our friends took the theme literally and came dressed as Dracula, complete with fangs and cape with a bright red interior. It was hilarious – and he certainly stood out in all the wedding photos.

Lucy-Ann wore a floaty yellow dress and was so excited because we asked her to be the ring-bearer. My mother got over her initial fury at not being able to make my wedding cake; my family was all together, singing, dancing. It was a beautiful, happy day.

In the evening, Alan and I danced together as the stars twinkled high in the velvet sky above. As musicians played one of my favourite songs, 'Sway', with the chatter and laughter of our dearest friends and family surrounding us, I could feel the baby kicking in my stomach and I knew the four of us would finally be a family. I remember lying on a deck chair on the beach looking up at the glorious night sky and thinking – happy at last.

Three weeks later, our son Luca was born.

17

Not Playing by the Rules

As you will have gathered by now, I'm a pretty relentless person. I don't sleep much. I'm constantly on the go. Whenever I stop doing one thing, I think of something else that needs my immediate attention. I think a lot of women are like this.

And a lot of the time we're made to feel bad for not following the unspoken rules: we feel pressure to look nice and act kindly, or to exercise every day, putting in strenuous workouts in the gym; we worry that we're not eating regularly or healthily enough, like all the nutritionists tell us we should. There is a whole machinery of social conditioning to make us feel guilty.

I don't believe there is any right or wrong, just a journey of discovering what is right for you. However frantic your life gets, the way you maintain your energy levels is a personal thing. It's important to know what works for you, because who cares what other people think you should be doing? You need to follow your own path.

I tend to eat little and often, and when I know I need it. There are a lot of old wives' tales about how you mustn't eat after a certain point at night and how supper should never be the biggest meal of your day, and I think, 'Where is the medical evidence?' So much of what we should and shouldn't do appears to be designed to make us feel guilty about totally unnecessary things. On the day of the High Court verdict, I got back home at two in the morning, made myself a salad and washed it down with a large glass of white wine. Was I worried about my metabolism? No. I was just hungry and needed to unwind!

I've never really seen the point of following rules that someone else has set. In life, I'm a firm believer in finding what works for you, then sticking to it, no matter what convention dictates or what other people might think.

This attitude was formed quite early on, when I was at boarding school in Eastbourne. I'd been boarding for two years when things started to change back home. When I was nearly thirteen, Forbes Burnham, the dictator of Guyana, imposed currency restrictions: suddenly it was extremely difficult for my parents to send money to the UK to pay the boarding fees and living allowance for me and my fifteen-year-old brother. As a result, they bought a house with the money they did have in the UK. The house was split in two – we lived in the ground-floor flat and the top one was rented to students at the University of Sussex, who had a campus in Eastbourne. The rent from the flat, plus the currency they managed to buy on the black market, just about paid for our day fees and food, but we had to earn our own money for anything else. My parents said it wouldn't last long and told us to be strong and brave – that getting the best education in the world would be worth it.

That is how my brother and I came to be living on our own: we were forced to be adults before our time and began juggling the demands of the situation we found ourselves in. We hid it from our school and the authorities because we knew that if they found out we might be taken into care. It's the kind of thing you can never imagine happening now, but back then the authorities were less questioning.

I was thirteen when I applied for a job as a chambermaid at a local hotel: I had to lie about my age and pretend I was sixteen. I went to charity shops to buy high-heeled shoes and clothes that made me look older than I was. I got the job. Every morning I would wake up at five, get dressed in my charity-shop clothes and then walk down the seafront in the freezing cold morning air so that I would arrive promptly at 6 a.m. When I got to the hotel, I'd be given a list of around ten rooms to turn over by my supervisor. Normally, I would do the rooms that were empty first, to make sure they were ready for guests checking in. These rooms had already been cleaned and all I needed to do was a bit of dusting and make sure there were enough sachets of tea, coffee and biscuits. Then, after the current guests had checked out, I would move on to those rooms. That bit was always harder because people left their hotel rooms in an utter state.

It was hard work and, after being at the hotel for two hours, I would turn up to school at 8.30 a.m. exhausted. I also worked weekends, although my hours were later in the day. I got paid £5 an hour and sometimes got a tip. The more generous guests left a pound or two, but mostly people would leave their small change. I'd collect all the coins and take them home with me and put them in a big jar. When the jar was full, I'd take it to the bank and exchange it for notes.

The thing that has stayed with me most from those days as a hotel chambermaid is my shock at how carelessly people treated a room that was not their own and how little they seemed to care about leaving the rooms in a disgusting mess.

I was young and had never stayed in a hotel before. I thought, when I started working at one, 'This will be a treat because it'll be rich guests and beautiful rooms and they'll behave really well!' The reality was so starkly different; I was appalled. I had naively assumed that well-off people, because of their wealth, would have higher standards than anyone else. In truth, they didn't show better manners or behaviour, and that was quite a leveller for me. It opened my eyes to the fact that money can't instil in you a sense of etiquette or manners

My husband Alan laughs at me, because every time we stay in a hotel I will always tidy up before we leave.

My eldest daughter Lucy-Ann now also has a part-time job in a beautiful hotel. She tops up the food on the self-service breakfast bar, clears the tables and polishes glasses, and then she comes home and has almost exactly the same observations as I used to have: she'll tell me how the rich people are rude to her, how they shout at her for not being quick enough and how they rarely leave any tips. It's funny to see how little has changed, but these are great lessons for her. It will make her appreciate both the value and the limitations of money, just as it did for me.

*

Working in that hotel was how my brother and I earned money to survive. It was difficult, but we had no other choice: we just got on with it. As it turned out, the currency restriction in Guyana went on for longer than anticipated. We didn't think of ourselves as struggling, but lucky. We were privileged to be living in England. When there were so many people in my country with so little, why would I complain? You get on with it and that's what I've always done. My father went from serving petrol at the age of fourteen to being one of the most respected QCs. My mother's father was murdered when she was ten and she had to start helping her mum in their little shop. What did we have to complain about?

I suppose this is when my resilience raised its head. I'm often accused of having no sense of boundaries. Like a child,

I don't tend to hear or understand the word 'No'. I'm more likely to ask, 'Why?'

That mindset and sheer hard work got me through my school years. It also got me through the following decade of raising Lucy-Ann on my own, taking on every part-time job I could and putting myself through university. It was instrumental in enabling me to set up my specialist marketing business for financial services. But it also came into play when my husband Alan and I decided to try to tackle impropriety in UK fund management.

For decades, we had been told that money could only be invested in certain ways – often with high fees and inconsistent returns, and with a plethora of other dubious practices that leave hard-working, prudent people worse off, whilst the industry swells its profit margins. People putting money aside for their pension or their future family security would be hit with enormous operating costs and commissions. The financial services industry was operating like a cartel, facilitating legalised looting whilst successive governments and regulators turned a blind eye.

To put this into context, the average operating margin for a UK drugs company valued at more than £2 billion was recently found to be 23 per cent, as compared to a stonking 45 per cent for a typical UK large fund management company. It is scandalous. For decades, they have been denying savers the basic consumer rights of knowing what they are buying and what they are paying.

Rather than take a strong hand in regulation, the UK regulator has deferred its responsibilities to the industry for years. There were so few checks and balances in place. The result of this dereliction of duty was a complete lack of transparency in fees or holdings, inflated research costs and a high level of risk. It may be connected to the fact that often the senior management of successive financial services regulators would end up in a senior position within one of the same firms they pretended to regulate but with a vastly inflated salary.

There are so many examples of this controversial revolving door, where senior regulators, Treasury staff and financial services companies have too cosy a relationship. I've been calling for a lobbying register so there can be total transparency on who is meeting whom at the Regulator, the FCA, but unsurprisingly I always get some lame answer as to why this can't be done. This old revolving door is still being far too well oiled. They lament that it was best for the industry to regulate itself as much as possible, knowing full well that, like turkeys they were never going to vote for Christmas by telling clients their true fees.

But then, in 2008, the global financial crisis hit. Things had to change.

Alan and I had sold our business interests and decided to take a year out to travel, spend time with Lucy-Ann and our two babies, Luca and Lana (born in 2007), and decide what we wanted to do next. We decided to leave our money with several respected financial institutions so we could relax. Travelling in October that year, somewhat surreally we got the call when we were hiking through the rainforest in Panama with Lucy-Ann and our two young children. It looked like the Royal Bank of Scotland was going to go down over that memorable weekend in October 2008. We dropped everything, flew back to the UK and tried to save as many of our investments as we could. But we soon realised that even we had been sold products that looked low risk that were not. We started getting calls from our friends and family, asking for help. My friend's father was going to lose 85 per cent of everything he had ever saved.

'What do we do?' she asked me, crying over the phone.

We tried to advise her the best we could, but really there was nothing to be done. Even though we were industry professionals, we were shocked at what we found out. It got both of us thinking. Alan was spending time on his hobbies – photography and art – and after so many stressful years in the City he was looking forward to some quality time with our family.

But by December I had started talking to him about whether there could be a different way of doing things, a different sort of investment company, where we could look at every angle afresh – the business model, the investment style, 100 per cent transparency on fees and holdings, and aim for consistent performance based on balancing cost, risk and returns. Not only that but we could use technology as an enabler for efficiency, lower costs and affording clients that 100 per cent transparency.

We could use our combined experience: his as one of a handful of highly respected UK fund managers who had started in the City when 'my word is my bond' and acted with honesty and integrity when they were the values of the day; mine as a business owner who had launched an innovative marketing agency, then consultancy. We could shake up the industry, making it evolve and better fulfil its societal duty of looking after people's money so they wouldn't become a burden on the state or their families. We also had a nagging suspicion that many of the ills that led to the financial crisis would not be eradicated. There would be a lot of lip service and good intentions but culturally little would change. We would put our money where our mouths were, in terms of both investing alongside clients and campaigning for better ethics, more integrity and producing research that would expose what was going on behind the UK investment and pension industry.

Neither of us had been given or inherited our money. We had worked long, stressful hours, but also appreciated how incredibly fortunate we were. I have always felt that with money and success comes responsibility to give back and help the society that affords your success.

I view myself as a responsible capitalist and huge admirer of the great British philanthropists of the past, especially the Victorian ones. I like to tell my children the story of how, in the 1890s, William Hesketh Lever, the founder of Lever Brothers, wrote down his ideas for Sunlight Soap because he didn't want his workers to get diseases. It was, he wrote, 'to make cleanliness commonplace; to lessen work for women; to foster health and contribute to personal attractiveness, that life may be more enjoyable and rewarding for the people who use our products'. This humble bar of soap went on to be a revolutionary product that helped popularise cleanliness and hygiene in Victorian England.

I believe that the rise in populism we are seeing across Western cultures is a reaction to irresponsible people, across all walks of life, who have risen to positions of power or success, and who have been too selfishly and negligently short-termist. Businesses have been too focused on profit, rather than people, planet and profit.

Our money and autonomy meant we could be 100 per cent independent, and once we had come up with our concept for a conscious investment company we applied to the UK financial services regulator to be approved. In February 2009, SCM Private (now SCM Direct) was approved and the first investments made in June 2009. The timing was good, as most world markets bottomed out around March that year.

The investment industry is riddled with opacity, but from day one we decided to publish all our fees and costs in one number – one of only a handful of companies to do so for the next nine years.

I am determined that we will never forget the human face of investment. It is simply not our money. Honouring that responsibility is the only way to stop the rot and endemic self-interest at the core of people's loss of trust in the City.

But trying to do the right thing when all your competitors are not, when there is no level playing field, is basically shooting yourself in the foot. There we were, being fully transparent, but being compared on fees with competitors who were typically only showing half of theirs. That's when we realised we needed a campaign to fight for policy reform and legislative change. Alan would do the research and data work, I would spearhead the fight and be the vocal one. Together we could take on the City and all its vested interests, and win. I never doubted that, because what we were saying and doing was right. The issue was how those vested interests would take it: they would obviously try to discredit us, and our business, say I had just dreamt up the campaign as a marketing ploy, but we were ready for the fight. We were ready for the backlash.

*

In February 2012, we officially launched our 'True and Fair Campaign', calling for an end to rip-offs and dubious practices in the UK investment and pension industry, 100 per cent transparency of fees and holdings, as well as for the introduction of a Code of Ethics. Alan always had more friends than me in the City, and it has been heartbreaking to see how many are no longer there for him since we launched the campaign. Some of his old friends only send an email or text if we've had any negative coverage, or he hasn't done so well on a CNBC interview, or similar.

Emotionally I think I'm tougher than Alan, so the rebuttals and abuse received because of the True and Fair Campaign have never bothered me. In fact, I view them as a sign that we are indeed doing the right thing. As a result of our work and contributions to three EU directives, which will come into force from 2018, over 500 million consumers across Europe will benefit from enhanced consumer protection via MiFID (Markets in Financial Instruments Directive) II, PRIPS (Packaged Retail and Insurance-based Investment Products) and a Shareholder Directive. Now we just need to keep an eye on how the industry, regulators and industry bodies try to water down the rules or bypass them, as I am sure they will make every attempt to do.

Spearheading our campaign hasn't made me the most popular person at parties. Men I'd worked with for years (and it is still, by and large, mostly men) bitched about me behind my back and came up with all sorts of unflattering nicknames for me to discredit my experience and my motives. I was, as you already know, called 'the Black Widow Spider' and 'Director of Lipstick' – and far worse, I'm sure, behind closed doors. But by this stage in my life I was resilient enough not to let it get to me.

My resilience had been built up through the years – from cleaning hotel rooms as a thirteen-year-old chambermaid in charity-shop clothes to running an innovative investment company challenging a powerful City. If you know that what you are doing is for the right reason and principles, it matters less if you succeed or fail. It is about the good fight.

Whenever I have experienced hardship or trauma, or a personal or professional failure, I have set myself an exercise. It is to make a list of all the positives and negatives. I must be as honest with myself as I can be. I revisit the situation and my actions, examine why I ended up in a particular situation or outcome, and then I try to apportion the failure fairly, as well as see what I can learn or do differently next time. Because for me, I know there will inevitably be a next time.

Resilience isn't simply a matter of eating well and getting the supposedly requisite eight hours a night sleep; it's about giving yourself space to sit quietly with your own thoughts and reflect, learn and decide your tactics for next time. It takes real self-honesty to explore and accept your strengths and weaknesses. If you are honest and accept your flaws, then others can't use them as weapons against you. It helps you define your principles and your purpose.

And then you get to a place where it doesn't matter what stories other people tell you about the narrative of your life. It doesn't matter if they don't understand you or they criticise what you're doing. Your reputation matters less than the reality. You will know, in your heart, why you're pursuing your own path. If you passionately believe in what you are doing, negativity fuels your ambition rather than dampens it.

I believe I can make a difference because I believe we can *all* make a difference. It starts with being the author of your own life.

18

Pitching Without PowerPoint

I n 2000, I presented a pitch to a big investment company who wanted to rebrand their image. At the time, I was running an agency specialising in 'below the line' marketing.

There I was, standing at the front of a boardroom filled with their top executives – all men, apart from a marketing assistant (who looked about eighteen). You can imagine the scene: lots of men in grey suits sitting around a table with expectant but slightly irritated looks on their faces, waiting for me to impress them but secretly thinking, 'This isn't going to be good, we'll just humour her'. I could see it on the faces, in their body language, in their man-spreading.

I knew we were the wild-card agency and that there were two other big-name agencies vying for the project. When I stood up and started speaking, one of the executives looked baffled.

'But,' he said, clearly confused, 'where's your presentation?'

The thing was, I had no flashy presentation. What I had was a two-page 'direction of travel' strategic document because I thought their brief was wrong. It almost read as one from an already engaged agency looking to increase their work and hence their fees. The idea that this company should get rid of its iconic brand image did not appear to be grounded in any consumer research but some misguided attempt to flatter and appeal to the new CEO wanting to make a name for himself. I knew this was highly unusual, and I knew the other two agencies would have spent a lot of time and money on their glossy presentations. But, as I explained to this mystified audience, what I wanted to do was remind them of their brand story, their provenance. The reason their sales were falling was not about the brand, but the lack of a strategic advertising and PR campaign.

I told them a story about a basketball. I said that you could design an incredible basketball, using all the best, most advanced materials, and then you could assemble a team of the best basketball players in the world, who would send the ball flying through the hoop with every shot. But if you weren't in a league and you weren't playing in an arena where people could see this extraordinary sporting feat, if you couldn't communicate the benefits, so what? People need to know. You need to keep the ball in play, the team in play. People must want to be fans and support them.

This was a big brand whose tone and communication style had become aloof, arrogant and out of touch. They just assumed everyone knew where they came from and what they stood for.

We won the pitch, not with a lucrative rebranding job but a literature and collaterals update, including better sales literature and product training for financial advisers (IFAs), who were their major distribution channel. I won it without a single PowerPoint slide. It brought home to me, once again, the incredible power of being honest, of telling a story or reminding a company of theirs. Sometimes you win, and sometimes you lose, but you don't have to do the expected and play by the usual rules.

Part of my approach has always been to be a storyteller: to dispense with baffling language or terminology, and get people to buy into a story. Human beings have been communicating for millennia by telling stories – from paintings on the walls of the Lascaux caves to hieroglyphics in ancient Egyptian temples. I grew up in a household which had no television, so I often dreamt up stories to pass the time in an era without the internet, iPads or smartphones. It's something I've taken with me into my adult life, and it's a skill I believe is necessary for communicating in business.

Stories are easier to remember than facts. A few years ago, the behavioural psychologist and Stanford professor Jennifer Aaker conducted an informal experiment[27] where she gave each of her students the opportunity to deliver a one-minute pitch.

Only one in ten students used a story within their pitch, while the others stuck exclusively to facts and figures. Professor Aaker then asked the class to write down everything they remembered about each pitch: 5 per cent of students cited a statistic, but an eye-popping 63 per cent remembered the stories.

'Research shows our brains are not hard-wired to understand logic or retain facts for very long,' Aaker says. 'Our brains are wired to understand and retain stories. A story is a journey that moves the listener, and when the listener goes on that journey they feel different and the result is persuasion and sometimes action.'

A classic story has three key points: the journey, the climax and the denouement. Think of it as a mountain – climbing up one side, reaching the top, then walking back down the other side, knowing that the end is in sight. When you tell a story well, it evokes a neurological response. Paul Zak, a neuro-economist who analyses what guides consumer decisions, has found that our brains produce the stress

---

27 *The Dragonfly Effect: Quick, Effective, and Powerful Ways To Use Social Media to Drive Social Change* – Jennifer Aaker and Andy Smith, 2010.

hormone cortisol during the tense moments in a story[28] (climbing up the mountain). This allows listeners to focus. Then at the climax (the summit) our brains will produce oxytocin, the feel-good chemical that promotes connection and empathy. An uplifting ending (the walk back down) triggers the limbic system, our brain's reward centre, to release dopamine – and that makes us feel more hopeful and optimistic.

Put simply: we are social creatures, and we relate to other people, not to a dry list of facts and statistics. But storytelling isn't just important when it comes to business. It's important as a means of understanding each other. As humans, we often forget to tell the most important story of all – the story of ourselves – even to those we love.

28 'The Neuroscience of Trust' – Paul J. Zak, *Harvard Business Review*, Jan–Feb 2017 issue.

19

Tell Your Story

I talk to my children a lot. I don't mean the odd passing comment when we're in the car and the radio's on in the background, blaring pop songs. I don't mean just telling them what to do or asking them to turn their iPads off or saying it's past their bedtime. I mean real, proper, engaged conversations.

At night, no matter how busy I've been during the day, I try and make time to talk to my children before they go to sleep. I sit at the end of their beds and I check in, ask them to tell me about their day and I let them speak about anything that might be on their minds. It doesn't have to be a long, drawn-out affair – sometimes it's as little as five minutes. But it's important to make this time, because it helps us all make sense of our story as individuals and our story as a family. I don't dictate the questions, but ask how they are feeling rather than what they've done: did anything or anyone make them happy, sad, worried?

Storytelling is so important in all parts of our lives. Parents don't tell their own stories to their children. We want to be perfect mothers and fathers. We want to be the adult, so we don't really let our children into our heads or hearts, or our pasts. Maybe we don't let them understand those parts of us because we're scared of letting them know our true selves – warts, weaknesses and all. But they are the ones who most need to understand the choices we took, the mistakes we made and the experiences that moulded us: because who they are comes from us, the nature and nurturing of ourselves shapes who they will be, how they think, how they form relationships, how they react and how they succeed or fail.

The court case over Article 50 and the subsequent appeal took up a lot of energy. I was working every hour I could just to keep on top of the legal papers – because I was the sole claimant, I felt I had to read everything – and it was exhausting. My children saw a lot less of me during that stressful period, but I still tried my best whenever I could to get home and sit at the end of their beds before they went to sleep. Chatting through the day became as important for me as it was for them.

'Why are you doing it, Mummy?' my son asked me one evening, propped up on his pillow in his pyjamas. When I looked at his expectant face, I felt I had one chance to explain this and to get it right. So I told a story. It was a version of the story I've shared here. I told Luca how my father used to talk to me every evening when he got home from work about the cases he'd taken on that day, about the importance of knowing right from wrong, about helping good people fight the good fight wherever you can, no matter what the personal cost might be.

Then I asked Luca to imagine all the days we're here, living on this earth. We worked it out together: assuming we were going to live to eighty that would mean just over 25,630 days. It's not that many when you think about it: we have less than 26,000 days to make a difference.

'And for me, Luca, I'm so old I have even fewer days left,' I said. 'I have to think: what are we here for? We're here to do something good, and as my old Moira House school motto said "*Nemo a me alienus*" – "Other people matter".'

He nodded. I told him that I wanted to do this for his future, and that of his sisters and his friends. I wanted to make sure the world they would live in would be a kind, caring, fair one. I wanted it to be a world governed by understanding and shared values, not a world driven by division and mistrust. I said I wanted to protect them and the people they were going to become, to make their future as good as it could be in my own small way. That was my battle. That was what I was fighting for.

Luca just smiled and gave me the biggest hug and snuggled down to sleep. I kissed him goodnight, pulled the duvet up to his chin, and turned out the light.

I tell them less serious stories as well, of course. It's not all inquisitions on the Meaning of Life at bedtime! My siblings and I used to tell each other stories all the time. My grandmother, mother and my father were great storytellers too, but they took their material from real life. I grew up listening to the story of their past lives and our shared family history. Even as a child I found it amazing that you could keep history alive in this way. At its simplest and most powerful, storytelling is a means of connecting with another human, a way of bringing people together and binding communities.

Often I'll talk to my children about what I was like at their age. It can make them feel less alone or less weird or less peculiar because they understand that I was once just like them. It helps my children see me as a real person, not just the person telling them it's time to get up and go to school. It can help them understand their own reactions, frustrations and moods.

With Lucy-Ann, I faced a different storytelling challenge. My priority with her was to ensure that the story she was being told about herself was a positive, empowering one. For a long time, it felt as though all the medical specialists were determined to tell me a negative, depressing story about my daughter: that she would never overcome her disabilities and never amount to anything; that she should be institutionalised because I wouldn't be able to cope. I was determined that this version of events would not become Lucy-Ann's own narrative. I told her my own story of who she was and who she could become.

I told her she was special because she was so caring and empathetic and gentle. I told her that these were extremely important qualities and not everyone had them. In fact, many people were so concerned with the superficialities of life – how they look, who likes them, ambition, career, financial success – that they forgot the simple but important things. She was indeed special, and in the most precious ways.

The more I told her this story, the more she believed it about herself, and the more she was able to achieve. She started to feel less different and more like a young woman with gifts to share. She was not disabled. She was differently able.

When Lucy-Ann was five or six, I took her to Guyana, the place where I was born. Her great-grandmother was still alive back then, and she hugged my daughter close to her as soon as she saw her and told her she was 'special'. This was the first time they had ever met, and no one had told my grandmother that Lucy-Ann was born with certain difficulties. She had no idea. She just instinctively seemed to know she was special.

That stuck with me for years. My grandmother was not a conventionally educated woman, she could not read or write well, but she had a wisdom about her.

I am fascinated by old cultures and teachings – Hinduism, Buddhism, the ancient South American tribes – and it turns out that many of these societies valued empathy and emotional intelligence as a strength. They see it as a form of heightened sight. Historically, indigenous women in North and South American societies were the storytellers, tellers of tradition.

African-American women consistently employed oral traditions to relate the pain and degradation of slavery, and to celebrate the subversions, struggles and triumphs of black experience. In African-American or Native American cultures, storytelling is a vital means of shaping identity and community. It's a way of bringing people together. At a time when women appeared to have little power, they held the precious past as part of their duty. They were the ones that passed on memories and truths to the next generation.

Of course, times have changed. But whilst many power structures are still balanced in favour of men, women can still find power through the medium of storytelling. My experience through my campaigning work is that men tend to use words as weapons; they'll deliberately deploy the most complex, technical and supposedly intellectual language to freeze the rest of us out. I do the opposite. I've learnt that I can make things accessible. I translate; I tell a story to engage people emotionally, as well as intellectually. My husband Alan finds it terribly embarrassing when I explain the stock market in terms of a wardrobe of clothes!

*

So often, the business world is dominated by men with loud voices, all talking about how they're the best at what they do. How can we make these sectors more accessible to women and take out the testosterone to create a more responsible, even-tempered culture? How can we add value and improve outcomes for everyone?

One of the ways I try to contribute to a culture change is by running a very flat organisation – flat in the sense that there is minimal hierarchy. My view is that being a good boss means being able to see your employees as whole people: you have to make the effort to find out who they are and what they need. For instance, if someone is having a terrible time at home, or if their child is ill, or if they're suffering from back pain and they're coming into work, then you can't expect them to be functioning at 100 per cent. You have to encourage them to share their lives with you so that you can adapt and be flexible to their needs in order to get the best out of them. You have to care, basically. That's not just touchy-feely claptrap; it's actually something that translates to profitability. Happier staff work harder and are more loyal. They will not leave as soon as the clock strikes five because they're desperate to get out of the office.

We need to reflect the society we live in and offer more access, more equality, more understanding – and I don't mean just for women but all people. I believe it starts with telling your story, because it's your experience and yours alone. That's what makes you unique. No one has lived the life you have lived, so no one has precisely the same insights or learned wisdom. You own your story, so why not use it to inform and enhance your career, your interactions, what you have to offer the world?

Storytelling can be an immensely powerful tool, not just as a means of engaging an audience, but also as a way of changing behaviour. In 2013, researchers from the Penn State College of Medicine started to examine students' attitudes to dementia patients[29], who are perceived as difficult to treat. The researchers found that these students had a markedly more positive attitude towards their patients after

---

29 'TimeSlips: Creativity for People with Dementia' – A. Basting, *Age In Action*, 2013.

they participated in storytelling exercises that made them more sympathetic to the sufferer's condition.

As Harrison Monarth, the *New York Times* bestselling author of *The Confident Speaker*, puts it:

Storytelling may seem like an old-fashioned tool, today – and it is. That's exactly what makes it so powerful. Life happens in the narratives we tell one another. A story can go where quantitative analysis is denied admission: our hearts. Data can persuade people, but it doesn't inspire them to act; to do that, you need to wrap your vision in a story that fires the imagination and stirs the soul.

During my schooldays, I used to have a part-time job at an old people's home in Old Town in Eastbourne. I volunteered to sit and chat with the residents, reading them passages from their favourite books or the newspapers, which meant I was even more aware of the news and what was happening in the world compared to my peers. I would also listen to the stories the residents told about their pasts, their families, their successes and regrets. Many of them had lived through the war and often had lost love ones as a result. I was fascinated by the tales they shared with me and was struck by the sadness that often tinged their voices and eyes when they talked of their families and regrets. One of my real concerns about leaving the EU is that we have forgotten how devastating war is. These are stories that we risk losing at our peril.

That's partly because we're almost at the stage now where there will no longer be a living generation who can tell us first-hand what it was like to experience the First and Second World Wars. Long periods of peace and prosperity create a public complacency, a laziness of thought and deed that makes me think my generation is guilty of dropping the ball and closing our eyes to corruption and excess.

The establishment of the EU is one of the fundamental reasons we have been lucky enough to live through seventy years of peace on our shores. But no institution is perfect, so we need to stay vigilant, refresh and reform, and ensure all stakeholders are being served, not silenced. It also means keeping the stories of our past, those memories, alive.

The EU is just as guilty of not telling its own story to the UK public. This has not been helped by successive UK governments deliberately using the EU as a whipping horse, allowing them to pass the blame of their own domestic policy failings easily on to an entity that does not defend itself as a point of principle. We seem to either forget or not be told the stories of our own history – that Britain underwent economic decline between 1945 and 1973, before it joined the EEC, which was the precursor to the EU.

The Second World War did not cause major damage to Britain's population and industry compared to its European allies. In 1950, our GDP per capita was 28 per cent larger than those of the EU6 – those six nations that would go on to form the EEC (Belgium, France, Italy, Luxembourg, the Netherlands and West Germany). By 1957, when the EEC was created, the GDP lead was 15 per cent. But from this point our economic decline began in earnest. In 1967, Britain's GDP lead was 6 per cent and by 1969, it was minus 2 per cent. The EU6 had overtaken us.

I am obviously not old enough to remember or have experienced the British economy in the '60s and '70s, as I came to the UK in the mid-'70s as a mere girl. What I read and researched is that Britain had appalling industrial relations, short-term management, lack of investment and ageing manufacturing. The NHS was suffering from numerous industrial actions and Britain was being called the 'poor, sick man of Europe'. What I do remember were faeces on the Eastbourne and Brighton beaches because of short sewage pipes, which dumped their contents near beaches and shore. The run-off of manure and agricultural chemicals from farms was also an issue. British bathing water was the second worst in Europe. There were power cuts. Britain was the only country in Western Europe that failed to control pollution from cars, power stations and farming, which tried to undermine European pesticide controls, and evaded nitrate regulations and bathing water directives.

Of course, not all of our economic recovery and growth can be laid at the feet of the EEC. There were other contributing factors, such as the influx of Marshall Aid from America. But the truth is that the EU6 were able to align their national aims and take advantage of free trade, with the result that Britain was able to halt its economic decline before eventually reversing it.

Our membership made us stronger as a country, but it was not a one-way relationship. Britain's membership allowed the EU to flourish and grow too. We sent our top-level civil servants and lawyers and were an integral part of drawing up new directives and making great legislation. Just think of the next chapters in the history of the EU and UK that we could help create if we were members, sitting at the EU table, empowering reform. The EU is not some dark force from a *Star Wars* movie, it is simply an organisational system built to agree how to handle issues that affect all members. Each member state elects MEPs who represent their citizens and will often work diligently on reforms aimed at benefiting them – this process of reform is not some one-off event but a continual process. Of course, perfection can never be achieved, but it can be strived for by making worthwhile reforms over time.

When I tell this story, those with closed minds and hearts say, 'What reform?' – the EU won't listen. Well, here are just a few of the reforms being executed now:

- The removal of administrative obstacles to cross-border trade and strengthening economic development.
- The reform of fisheries policy, with root-and-branch reform of the common fisheries policy, which Greenpeace has hailed as 'the solution to many of the struggles facing local fishermen'.
- Improved transparency and rules governing lobbyists, aimed at making backroom deals in the Commission and Parliament a thing of the past.
- Rewriting of rulebooks about how European laws are made, embedding impact assessments into the legislative process. (Maybe David Davis could learn from this basic principle, as it was he who first claimed that his department had produced fifty-eight of such impact assessments, before – when cross-questioned by fellow MPs – admitting that they never existed.)
- Budgetary reform to refocus expenditure on areas where acting together at a European level rather than a national level will save money, or improve effectiveness.
- The strengthening of environmental protections, forcing large corporations to provide data on their impact on the environment.
- Holding giant global companies to account, such as the EU's record-breaking €2.42 billion (£2.14 billion) fine to Google for abusing its dominance of the search engine market.

We all need to tell our stories – whether it's what we tell our families and friends about where we come from or, on a broader scale, whether it's the EU being able to promote all the good things it has done rather than being diminished by politically motivated negativity.

In both instances, telling your story is about being honest with yourself, coming to terms with your past and being comfortable enough that your history becomes the ultimate protection against the negative opinion of others.

20

Imposter Syndrome

Over the last few years, I've spent quite a lot of time in green rooms. The 'green room' is essentially a holding pen for when you're about to go on television, so-called because, in the theatre where they were originally developed, they were usually painted green.

I don't think I've ever been in a green room that was *green*. Most of them are dingy little areas with unwelcoming sofas, lukewarm tea and stale croissants, nuts and crisps. I've found myself at a place where I'm lucky enough to be asked by television programmes to be a talking head on various issues, from women in business and ethical investment to charities, and latterly, of course, the thorny topic of Brexit.

In the green room, you often meet the other guests who have been booked to opine on varied subjects and I've noticed that there's always a distinct difference between men and women as they wait to go on air. There's a certain type of arrogant man I've become accustomed to. These men will be brimming over with confidence. They'll sit back, spread their legs wide, make sure they dominate any conversations by what they have been doing: the journey in, a sporting anecdote, a name drop of whomever they think will make them seem more connected and important. They're usually accompanied by a couple of cowering, young researchers.

When on air, they are bombastic, avoid a straight answer to most questions, and seldom appear to know many facts and figures.

When they come back into the green room, they'll be happy with their performance. On several occasions they have handed me a signed copy of a book they just happen to have with them. I now have a stack of unread books at home from all these men who think I should read what they've written, whether I'm interested in the subject matter or not.

No woman has ever done this to me. In fact, most women I meet in the green room are of an entirely different ilk. There was one woman I met when we were both waiting to go on a Sunday morning magazine-style talk show. I'd been booked to speak about how social media sites such as Google and Facebook were going to have to take more responsibility for abusive content published on their plat-forms. She was an eminent professor, top of her field, with several publications to her name, and was highly regarded by her peers in academia and beyond.

When I walked in, she was sitting in the corner of the sofa, surrounded by pieces of paper and making frantic notes.

'Hello, I'm Gina,' I said, offering my hand. She shook it distractedly. 'How are you?' I asked.

'Oh,' this woman replied, looking a bit startled. 'I'm just putting my thoughts together and rehearsing what I have to say in my head. Do you mind?'

I realised that she was nervous. *Really* nervous.

I sat down on the sofa opposite and said, 'But you know more than everyone here put together. You could answer this stuff in your sleep. There's going to be – what? – three minutes of chat. Don't worry about it. You'll be perfect. You'll blow them away.'

She looked at me and I could see her entire face start to relax. Her jaw unclenched. She sighed with relief. It was as if what I'd said had punctured a balloon and let all the air out.

'You're right,' she said with a smile. 'Thank you.' And she started packing her notepad away.

Then we both sat back and had a cup of tea together, feeling much more relaxed. The funny thing was that talking this woman out of her nerves had made me forget to feel anxious too, because I do get nervous when I have to go on a TV show or appear at an event or take part in a panel. You'd think it would get easier the more I do it, but I still have a constant level of doubt. Alan will say to me, 'Why are you preparing? You know all of this.' But I will always counter with, 'Do I know enough? Could I have done a bit more? How can I be better?' And then a quieter, but equally insistent, internal voice asks, 'Will I be discovered as a fraud?'

Imposter syndrome – the fear of being found out – is a familiar problem for many of us. No matter how successful we are and no matter what our achievements, we still question ourselves in moments of pressure. We still worry that we're not quite good enough.

I've already written about the abuse I received when I launched my High Court challenge against the government. I've also received hundreds and hundreds of supportive letters from people across the country, of all different ages, from all walks of life. A lot of women tell me I'm their 'hero' or 'an inspiration' and – I'm cringing as I write this – 'a modern-day suffragette'. It makes me feel deeply flattered but also deeply uncomfortable, because I can't relate those phrases to me. I'm just Gina, doing what I've always done.

There are so many brave, extraordinary women and men in the world. A lot of the women – and it is, still, mostly women who write – ask me for advice. They know a bit about my past because of what they've read in the news-papers or seen on television, and I get people telling me about being bullied at work, or having problems with their families, or feeling suicidal and suffering from mental illness. I have received several letters from women in toxic relation-ships wondering whether they're being abused or not. I am incredibly touched to read these letters because they come from a place of genuine trust. I suppose, having put myself out there, I'm seen as a public figure that they can relate to on some level. It's very heartwarming and emotional to know that strangers feel like that about me. But it carries huge responsibility.

I try to answer every single letter or email, and if I can't help them, I try to point them towards someone or some-where they can get help. I don't have a team, so it can be time-consuming and done in the wee hours of the morning, but how can I not respond when people open their hearts to me? I know I'm the woman who found the strength to take a government to court and hold them to account. I know that I withstood an astonishing level of abuse for doing so. Yet, at the same time, when these letters arrive on my desk, I feel unequal to the task. Something inside me keeps asking, 'How did you get here?'

It's like that professor in the TV green room all over again.

My own experiences, and having spoken to many women over many years, show me we are our own worst enemies. We plant the seeds of our own insecurity. We lapse into silence when we should be raising our voices higher. We doubt ourselves to the extent of limiting our power as women. This needs to stop. We need to tackle imposter syndrome, to understand where it comes from so that we can beat it – before it beats us.

*

I know many women will have dealt with the same internal doubt I've just described. Even the most successful among us will have experienced it at some point or other. Facebook's chief operating officer, Sheryl Sandberg, has admitted to suffering from imposter syndrome, saying, 'There are still days when I wake up feeling like a fraud.'

The actress Jodie Foster has confessed she thought someone was going to take away her Oscar because she didn't deserve it, while Emma Watson, Renée Zellweger and many other actresses have all expressed similar sentiments. In 2017, the Foreign Office's first-ever envoy for gender equality, Joanna Roper, said she had a conversation with the American diplomat Madeleine Albright in which they both shared their own experiences of imposter syndrome.

I've been lucky enough to meet several highly successful female musicians and actresses through the course of my work. I tend to meet them in a campaigning capacity, when they want to use their platform to talk about more serious issues. They will, without exception, be nervous and it's always such a surprise to see these women, who are so confident on stage or screen, reduced to a pile of jitters. When I ask them about it, they say that they're comfortable in their art but that this confidence doesn't transfer into other areas. When they're stripped of the performance and have to stand on their own, as themselves, they immediately start to question their right to be there.

I was a great fan of *The X-Files*, so was most interested to read an interview with the actress Gillian Anderson, who has some interesting things to say on this topic. In a 2017 interview with *Harper's Bazaar*, she recalled a particular scene she was required to film as Special Agent Scully in her breakout role for *The X-Files*.

'I was a female FBI agent standing in a roomful of male FBI agents,' said Anderson. 'And I remember hearing my squeaky voice and thinking, "Who do I think I am?"'

Isn't it amazing to think that a woman who embodied one of the toughest, no-nonsense, ball-busting TV heroines of the 1990s was feeling insecure underneath that suited exterior?

In the interview, Anderson concluded that overcoming imposter syndrome was about 'admitting you are where you are. It's not about whether I'm good enough; I'm just sharing my experience. And if another woman is seeing that, that can change how they see themselves and that can be powerful.'

Even the writer Maya Angelou, in whose honour this book is named, once said that every time she wrote a book, 'I think, "Uh-oh, they're going to find [me] out now."' And that's *Maya Angelou*, who published seven autobiographies, three books of essays, several books of life-changing poetry, and who received over fifty honorary degrees through the course of her lifetime. If Maya Angelou feels imposter syndrome, then truly everyone can: we are most definitely not alone.

I do believe it is a particularly female affliction, although I'm aware that certain male friends of mine also experience it, as do the vulnerable. It's something that appears to affect groups of people who are different from the white, male, heterosexual default because we're seen as outliers. We're seen – wrongly – as weak and constantly put down on this basis.

Back in Guyana, there was no TV when I was growing up and my parents were sticklers for us reading 'proper books'. But as a treat we could get one DC or Marvel comic a week. I was fairly obsessed by the strong female hero-ines – Mrs Fantastic, Black Widow, Supergirl, Wonder Woman (the latter was my favourite). Years later, towards the end of 2017, the new *Wonder Woman* movie was coming out and I was as excited as my kids to see it. I was hoping the studios hadn't devalued the character too much. I was not disappointed.

On screen, Wonder Woman was played by the magnificent Gal Gadot – athletic, brave, likeable, strong but sensitive, beautiful inside and out. Then I read an interview Gal gave in the December 2017 issue of *Glamour* magazine as I sat at the hairdressers getting ready for our office Christmas do. She spoke about being crushed by self-doubt and internet trolls. She said, 'Hearing "no" over and over, I was thinking, "What am I good for?" And that's when I got *Wonder Woman*.'

It made me think: never give up, you never know what's just around the corner. Such an almost impossibly perfect woman, with such doubt inside.

In a world defined by centuries of institutionalised sexism, women are more likely to question our place in society and our achievements in that context. A survey conducted in 2017 found that 40 per cent of millennial females (aged between eighteen and thirty-four) felt like imposters, compared with 22 per cent of male respondents[30].

Then there's the added issue of quota systems which, although well-meaning, can lead some women in business to question whether they are there on their own merits or because of enlightened positive discrimination.

A 2013 study commissioned by the shampoo brand Head & Shoulders, and quoted in the *Guardian*[31], found that almost 50 per cent of women surveyed believe they would be further on in their career if they had more self-belief. Ninety-two per cent of the 2,000 British women questioned

---

30 'A third of millennials suffering from "imposter syndrome" in the workplace' – Katie Garret, *Independent*, 18th February 2017, research commissioned by career development agency, Amazing If.

31 'Lack of confidence is holding back women's careers' – Matt Dathan, *Guardian*, 14th August 2013, poll commissioned by Head & Shoulders, conducted by OnePoll.

admitted to having hang-ups, with the most frequent obstacle being anxiety about their appearance. Almost a quarter of women said they'd be at a more senior level in their careers if they were freed of their self-doubt.

In 2011, the UK's Institute of Leadership and Management in the United Kingdom surveyed British managers about how confident they felt in their professional roles[32]. Half the women reported self-doubt about their job performance and careers, compared with fewer than a third of men.

Linda Babcock, an economics professor at Carnegie Mellon University and the author of *Women Don't Ask*[33], has conducted a series of studies involving business-school students and found that men initiate salary negotiations four times as often as their female counterparts. When women do pluck up the courage to negotiate, they ask for 30 per cent less money than men do.

Women in the workplace continue to question whether they are qualified to do a job, even when they are already doing it. We are cursed with a desire for perfection, which often stops us from stepping up and taking risks. We baulk at risking failing our own high standards. Whereas male colleagues are more than willing to take risks: to throw out ideas and see what sticks.

That said, there is much that needs to be done in workplaces to deal with unconscious bias towards women who assert themselves. There are also studies that show that when women do ask for pay rises they are not received as favourably as their male colleagues.[34]

32 'Index of Leadership Trust 2011' – Institute of Leadership and Management and Management Today, 2011.
33 *Women Don't Ask: Negotiation and the Gender Divide* – Linda Babcock and Sara Laschever, 2003.
34 'Do Women Ask?' – Benjamin Artz, Amanda H. Goodall, and Andrew J. Oswald, Warwick Economics Research Papers, 2016.

It's not just women in the workplace either. I've lost count of the number of times I've found myself at a Christmas party or a work do with male colleagues and they'll introduce me to their wives, who are always dressed in beautiful outfits, and they'll talk down to their wife all evening because they think their work is more important. I'll say, 'So, what do you do?' and the man will speak up before his wife and butt in with, 'Oh, she's just at home with the children.' Sometimes the woman herself will talk down her own role, with those endless mitigating qualifiers 'just' or 'only'.

'I'm only a stay-at-home mum,' she'll say apologetically, as if it's something to be ashamed of, as if she's not worthy of anyone else's attention.

'Actually,' I say, 'your role is bringing up strong, young people that are the future and will make society better. Don't say you're "just a mother". You're incredibly valuable and doing one of the most important jobs there is.'

I try to make them feel proud, because they should be proud that they've made that important choice to stay at home. A lot of women waste time mourning the life they thought they would have, instead of seeing all the qualities and gifts in the life they do have. I get cross and upset when people undervalue motherhood. We overlook the fact that, in nature, it's the lioness and not the lion who does all the caring and nurturing and fiercely protects her pride. They're the ones who decide where their den will be, where the cubs will be raised, and they're the ones who make the most important, tough decisions regarding the future and survival of their species. Yet that's been completely misunderstood in our modern human world.

*

Imposter syndrome stems from another womanly trait: our desire to people-please. As a result, many of us become pliant and willing to accommodate others' desires. We end up wanting to be liked and accepted. This can limit us and our professional advancement. The key to tackling this is to develop a workplace persona that is distinct from your private identity, which I've discussed in a previous chapter.

In the office, I have always felt you should be judged on how well you do your job, not on how nice you are. That means not saying yes to unpaid overtime, just because you hope you'll eventually be rewarded. It means not being afraid to ask for a pay rise. It means having the strength to contribute to discussions and put forward your own ideas, even if you're worried that you might come across as bossy or overbearing. Of course, you don't need to be a bitch to get ahead. But being too worried about not being a bitch can end up holding you back.

I always remind myself that who I am at work is my professional persona. Even if I end up being liked less in the office, chances are I will achieve more and be more respected. And if I'm doing what I know is right, then what does it matter if someone else doesn't like me?

How can we solve the problem of imposter syndrome in our own lives, and the lives of our daughters? I believe it starts with young girls. It's important to instil in them a sense of deep-rooted confidence in who they are as people. The challenge is that increasingly we live in a society where superficiality is celebrated. It starts with airbrushed and Photoshopped pictures of supermodels in magazines. It's embedded by the notion that you're judged according to how many Twitter or Instagram followers you have. What a boy says about your figure or face. It's heightened by the lack of good female role models. At times it feels like most girls these days grow up aspiring to be like the Kardashians or a YouTube blogger, many of whose careers have been predicated on their looks or ability to apply make-up.

The media projection of what is valued, what is deemed to be 'female' strength, is viewed through this narrow, surface lens. It's unobtainable for most ordinary young women, who nonetheless start judging themselves against these benchmarks without realising it's a hopeless quest. Striving to be thin, to be beautiful, to have a perfect pout, to flaunt diamonds and sports cars and designer labels . . . none of this is the secret to lasting happiness.

All it does is knock the confidence of those young girls who cannot live up to this supposed 'ideal' (an 'ideal', by the way, which is heavily filtered and manipulated and bears little relation to objective truth). A girl can be quirky and inherently herself at the age of eight or nine, but when she's subjected to an onslaught of media hype about what a woman 'should' look like and aim for, she emerges at the age of nineteen or twenty a completely different person, with much of her individuality quashed in the rush to try and fit in with what society wants. This is often accompanied by a fragility that can lead to bad choices and unfulfilled potentials.

It's for this reason that I'm careful to limit screen-time for my own children. I don't have any women's magazines in the house. It's not that I don't like reading them myself – if we're going on holiday, I'll flick through them on the plane or occasionally there's an article I like in a magazine – but it's the advertising that I think is harmful. I don't want my girls to see images of improbably 'perfect' women selling perfume and for them to think that is something worth aiming for.

When Lucy-Ann was being bullied at school, I remember finding her one evening crying on her bed about not being pretty enough. I sat down beside her, held her hand and brushed her long hair from her face, patting dry her tears as I did so.

'You're gorgeous,' I told her. 'You have inner beauty and that's what being truly beautiful is all about.'

We discussed what it meant to be a beautiful person, rather than simply having an outwardly beautiful shell.

'You're special because of how you care about other people,' I said. 'That's truly beautiful and that will last far longer than any other kind of prettiness or outward beauty.'

She nodded. The next day she went into school feeling much happier. There were no tears that evening. Of course, there are challenges, and she does still get down, so we constantly work on building her confidence, but I think – I hope – my words have stuck with her, in the same way it stuck with me when my parents taught me that it wasn't how I looked that was important; it was who I was and what I did with my life.

*

Overcoming imposter syndrome is also about being able to tune in and listen to your own instinct. It goes back to nature, again: that idea that we were the ones who had to be alert to potential dangers to protect our offspring from predators. In the modern world, it's harder than ever to listen to your internal voice because there's so much competing noise. I've always found it helpful to sit quietly, turn my attention inwards and be quiet. That's often the only way to allow the busy-ness of your own crowded thoughts to calm down and enable your true voice to emerge. It gives you time to assimilate, time to worry, or grieve or regret, or time simply to move on.

Some people like yoga, others prefer meditation – whatever you call it, I have no organised practice time, but I make time for silence. It's a necessary part of my life and there's plenty of scientific research to show that a regular practice of this sort improves well-being and productivity. A 2005 study conducted by the Massachusetts General Hospital in America[35] examined the brain scans of regular meditators and found increased thickness in regions of the cortex associated with higher functions like memory and decision-making.

I try to tune in to my internal voice whenever I can – whether it be at night when I'm struggling to get to sleep or, in the past, when I was on the Tube feeling stressed about being late for a meeting. In my twenties, I loved free-climbing. I discovered the pleasures of climbing up sheer rock-faces, with nothing to rely on other than my own strength and focus, whilst on holiday on the island of Gozo in the Mediterranean. I relished the sense of achievement I got when I reached the top, where there was no noise other than the wind in my ears and the odd squawking of a bird. Climbing also helped me to see how small I was in relation to the world. It gave me perspective.

I've climbed all over the world – from Europe, South Africa, Namibia and Morocco to Snowdonia in Wales and the rock-faces of the English coast. Back in the days when I did it a lot, the technology wasn't very advanced, so all I'd have was a little bag around my waist with sand in it to help my grip and a pair of climbing shoes that were almost like ballet shoes.

When I was living near Eastbourne, I would go to Beachy Head and climb up from the sea-front so that I could sit at the top of the cliff, look out at the waves and just think. My favourite time to be there was first thing in the morning, when there were hardly any other people about. Climbing allowed me just to wander and look at life and watch it. It's an extraordinary thing to do: to watch birds playing off a coast or up on a mountain. It really does take you to a completely different place. You feel connected to the world

---

35 'Meditation experience is associated with increased cortical thickness' – Sara W. Lazar et al, *Neuroreport* November 2005.

around you. You feel your own vulnerability as well as your strength, your self-reliance.

It's for a similar reason that I used to enjoy travelling on public transport: I enjoyed being able to watch mothers of every age, social group and nationality, and to realise that the way they cared for their children or the way they held their hands was essentially the same, to understand that human interactions are fundamentally simple and go beyond superficial division or difference. It's us who've built the walls up to separate ourselves from each other. I miss the freedom to be invisible and watch the world going by. It was just so comforting to know that everyone, deep down, is basically the same.

Without being able to tune into that deeper connection and remind ourselves that we are who we are, away from the media pressure to conform to superficial ideals, we risk losing our power. Our own wants have been crowded out by a media narrative of what it is to be a woman or a man. There are social constructs we're encouraged to follow, comply with and fulfil, without being honest and looking inwardly to who we are, how our uniqueness is strength not weakness. Unless you start by being honest about who you are, I suppose you're always going to feel a bit of a fraud because you're living your life according to someone else's expectations, someone else's values and rules, rather than your own.

But of course, no matter how honest you are with yourself, there will still be moments like that one I experienced in the TV green room with the learned professor. And the only way to deal with these is to step up and claim your power. You can't feel confident all the time, but practise pretending: confidence and courage can become a habit, if practised enough. When you act confidently, you inevitably become more so. Realising that people are fallible, that the women you look up to also struggle, might help.

The columnist Oliver Burkeman cautioned in a 2013 *Guardian* article[36] against 'comparing your insides with other people's outsides'. While we all understand our own internal lack of confidence, we sometimes fail to see beyond the patina of success projected by others. No one is perfect.

Other people's self-doubt might be just as deep-seated as our own.

---

36 'This column will change your life: do you feel a fraud?' – Oliver Burkeman, *Guardian*, 9th November 2013.

21

#MeToo

As I was writing this book, the Harvey Weinstein scandal erupted. More than ninety women came forward to accuse the Hollywood mogul of sexual assault over the past three decades. The circumstances were often the same: Weinstein would allegedly invite young actresses or models into a hotel room or office on the pretext of discussing their career, before placing pressure on them for massages or sex. Often these women would feel beholden to Weinstein and would worry about jeopardising their professional future if they didn't go along with it. For all that Weinstein insists that whatever happened was always consensual, there's no doubt in my mind that he was guilty of a shocking abuse of power.

In the aftermath of those revelations, many women took to Twitter to claim that they too had been the target of unwanted sexual advances from men. The '#MeToo' hashtag prompted millions of people to come forward and reveal instances of harassment from their own past, including many celebrities.

It was an extraordinary tidal wave of female solidarity and, for me, it marked something of a tipping point. I'm of a slightly older generation than the majority (although not all) of Weinstein's accusers, and for years I'd had to put up with differing forms of sexual harassment in the workplace. But, like many women my age, I felt that I should tackle it myself or shrug it off as much as possible. I got on with things. I became tough with a silent motto – show no weakness.

As a woman working in the male-dominated world of finance in the '90s and noughties, I was only too aware of how recently feminist battles had been waged on my behalf. My female colleagues and I were always trying to balance pushing forward in our careers to climb the corporate ladder with the knowledge that if we spoke out about the prevalence of sexist behaviour we'd hinder our own progress. It was a difficult juggling act because sexism was rife and misogynistic culture was normalised under the guise of 'banter'.

When I worked in the City, it was perfectly normal to hear a man boasting about pinching a woman's bottom or commenting on her breasts as she walked past. There would be jokes about the size of a receptionist's cups and if a man liked his coffee black, white or brown (referring to skin colour), or games to see how many times they could get the word 'sausage' into a conversation. It was deemed a 'lark' – a badge of honour even – for these men, with no acknowledgement of how it made the women around them feel. If the women complained, we were told we didn't have a sense of humour, that it was 'just a bit of a laugh'; we'd be called 'frigid' or 'uptight', or they'd whisper under their breath, 'She's not getting enough.' If you spoke out, you were seen as a prude and became the one who didn't fit in, who was in the wrong.

The normalisation of discrimination seeped into cultures in such a way that it became difficult to pinpoint or call it out without a woman sounding churlish. 'Leave, if you don't like it,' was a familiar reaction.

We were encouraged to believe it was simply men being men: it was up to us to impose boundaries on their behaviour, rather than them accepting responsibility for themselves.

If a culture of harassment is normalised, it makes it more difficult to call out. In some areas that culture has been challenged, but in other sectors it still exists, particularly in the worlds of finance, film and politics. Most men in power still come from a relatively small number of the same universities and schools, so that when they enter the workforce there's an old-boys' network already in place. They have each others' backs and they use their power as a means of bullying, belittling and blackmailing women – especially women who haven't come from their 'tribes'. Sex is used as a form of control. For decades, these men would keep silent about each other's indiscretions and give each other tacit permission for their odious behaviours.

A 2017 study by the London School of Economics[37] of 120 years of biographical data in *Who's Who* found that Britain's nine top all-male public schools continue to produce nearly 10 per cent of entrants. This is despite those schools having traditionally educated fewer than 0.15 per cent of pupils aged between thirteen and eighteen, and meant that those boys were ninety-four times more likely than anyone else to reach the highest echelons of Britain's elite. Students from those schools were also twice as likely to go to Oxbridge.

That's a difficult citadel to penetrate if your face doesn't fit – if you're a woman or, like me, a woman of colour. Immediately you are viewed with suspicion, especially if you start to question how things are done or if you stand up for yourself in the face of sexism and discrimination.

---

37 'The Decline and Persistence of the Old Boy: Private Schools and Elite Recruitment 1897 to 2016' – Aaron Reeves and Sam Friedman, *SAGE*, 29th October 2017.

I hope that those brave women who shared their stories about Weinstein and other men will have shifted the public discourse. I hope that our workplaces will react by introducing proper mechanisms whereby you can speak up and be believed rather than dismissed as not having a sense of humour or perspective. I hope that this has, indeed, marked a tipping point. It feels as if the climate is changing, but it's like turning around a tanker – it will take a long time for it to have a trickle-down effect in offices up and down the country for ordinary working women.

There will still be women, in all walks of life, who struggle to call out sexist behaviour. How do we empower ourselves to stand up in the face of this sort of injustice? I think it starts with sharing our own stories so that we all feel less alone. Which is why I wanted to tell you one of mine.

*

When I was in my early thirties I set up a specialist marketing agency for financial services firms. The business had an event management division, which I based on the events I helped BMW organise for their dealership clients. The distribution model for investment products didn't appear very different to me. Intermediaries were the major sale channel and as such this is where more effort and spending were concentrated. I therefore designed an annual event called the Senate Programme.

It was at one of these early conferences I organised that I had one of my most blatant experiences of workplace sexual harassment. The conference was being held at a big five-star hotel in London. As the organiser, I was in contact with key figures from the City.

One of the senior men attending was a tall, striking man. I'd crossed paths with him before and knew him well, but our exchanges had never extended beyond pleasantries.

On the first day of the conference, the agenda finished at around five o'clock. There was then a break of a couple of hours before dinner. During that time, this man – who was very senior in the company he worked for – asked me to meet him upstairs to discuss my agency services.

'Why don't you come to my room, so we can talk about us becoming a client of yours?' he asked.

I thought it was a bit odd, but I was naive and believed people only saw my professionalism. I persuaded myself that I was being foolish and what a boost to our business it would be if they became clients. I knew that business was being conducted in the quiet corners of the hotel event, so maybe this was just normal. I knew he had a suite; after all, my team had meticulously looked after all the VIP attendees, so I imagined that we'd be talking in the lounge area.

Half an hour later, I got the lift to his floor, waited for the doors to open and walked down the heavily carpeted corridor to his door. I knocked. I could hear footsteps shuffling on the other side of the door. Then it was open, and there this man was, standing before me in his dressing-gown. I vividly remember it was a dark red and paisley-patterned, and that it barely covered his knees. It was loosely tied, and any time he moved it gaped open, revealing his chest. It made my stomach turn. It was such a shock to see him standing there, naked underneath his robe, that I stammered out an apology.

'Oh, sorry,' I said, 'but I think I must have the wrong time. I'll come back later.'

He reached out to take my hand, but I stepped back, out of his grip.

'No, no, I was expecting you,' he insisted.

'What do you mean you were expecting me? You're not dressed.'

'No, no,' he said again. 'We can talk, don't worry.'

Instinctively, I knew that if I stepped over that threshold this man would take advantage of me. I felt unsafe and out of control.

'I'm sorry,' I said, although why I thought I needed to apologise is beyond me. 'I'd rather we meet downstairs, I'll see you in the lobby in twenty minutes or so.'

He looked me straight in the eye, unblinking, and said in a low, controlled voice: 'If you don't come in now, you can forget it.'

At that point, I began to feel threatened. I remember thinking, 'What do I do? Is this really happening? Am I reading this situation correctly or am I over-reacting?' It's a difficult thing to process because you simply can't believe someone you respect is acting like that. I was a young woman and this man was at least thirty years my senior and in a position of power.

I left him standing there, robe gaping open, and I turned on my heel and walked as fast as I could back to the lift, half-terrified that he would follow me. My heart was pounding as I walked along the corridor to the lift. I pressed the lift call button, but the lift took far too long to arrive.

He never did make it downstairs for our meeting and I never did get his business. The conference ended without further incident and I went back to my normal working life. A few days later a package arrived addressed to me at my office.

It was a small box, about eight inches tall, and when I unwrapped it I saw that it was a bottle of Poison, a perfume by Christian Dior that was popular at the time. The perfume came with a note. It was from the man in the robe, who had written: 'Sorry for any misunderstanding. The event was a great success.'

I saw it as a cheap attempt to flatter me and get me to shut up. I threw the perfume straight in the bin.

For years after, I heard through the grapevine that he spread negative stories about me, claiming that I was useless, that I wasn't any good at business. He downplayed my abilities for running accounts and gave me various patronising, unflattering nicknames. For a while, he made things difficult for me.

Luckily, his ugly attempt at rumour-mongering had little impact on the long-term success of my business because anyone who had ever worked with me knew of my professionalism and commitment. My reputation ended up speaking for itself.

I saw him over the next few years at various industry events. Like so many men who abuse their power, there was never any retribution for him. I have always wondered how many other women were caught in his web. He was successful and highly regarded in certain circles. But whenever I saw him, I made sure I gave him a long, hard stare so that he knew I remembered. He knew that I could have spoken out and ruined his reputation, and I hoped this would deter him from doing the same thing to other vulnerable young women.

*

Something similar happened a few years after the dressing-gown incident. By this stage, I was becoming more successful, more experienced, more sure of myself. I was at a dinner with Alan and was sitting with an obnoxious fund manager from a big firm. He was a star fund manager, so thought of himself as God's gift because he was so brilliant at what he did. He sat down next to me and, without pause, slid his hand up between my legs. I removed it and said to him, 'If you do that again, I'll tell everyone here what kind of a man you are.' I also pinched the skin on his hands quite hard to reinforce the message.

His response was an interesting one.

'Come on,' he said, 'it's just a joke. I've got a wife and children. If you say anything, you'll ruin their lives.' His wife was sitting almost opposite us at the same table. It was a clever tactic because my immediate instinct was to replace my rage with guilt. I felt bad for his wife and children, so I never did speak out about it. Once again, the onus of blame is placed on the woman – not, as it should be, on the perpetrator.

I found out later that at the same dinner he had told Alan to watch out, I was only interested in him in order to get a British passport, to which Alan told him I had possessed a British passport for many years. This was blatant misogyny and racism.

Sometimes, we are so terrified of speaking up that our silence encourages the aggressors. A few weeks after this fund manager groped me, I was having a get-together with some girlfriends and I mentioned what had happened to a lovely blonde lady from his company's marketing team. She recoiled, looked at me in total disbelief and then said something that has stuck with me ever since: 'No, he can't have done that,' she explained. 'He only likes blondes. He wouldn't go for a woman like you.'

It felt like a slap in the face. Not only was this woman dismissing my experience out of hand, in spite of the fact she knew me well enough to know I wouldn't lie about something so serious, but in doing so she was also expressing racism and jealousy. In a way, it was worse than the attempted groping: this was a woman failing to stand up for a fellow woman. I felt gutted.

What this exchange showed me was that sexism sometimes divides women rather than bringing them together. The perpetrators of sexual assault sometimes use female jealousy to pit us against each other because we're weaker when we're fighting amongst ourselves. That's why the first step in any battle against sexism in the workplace must start with sharing stories, with listening to each other and holding each other up, so that we can make a stand together.

It helps to have a group of girlfriends who might not be involved in your area of work but who can be a sounding board when someone is behaving inappropriately towards you. There was a lot of blatant sexism in my day. It's good that has changed, but it means sexism in the modern world can be insidiously expressed. It's less black and white.

I remember when I went to work on the Tube in London in the early '90s, I used to dread having to stand up in rush-hour because if you were standing in front of a seated man, you were just at the right height for them to 'accidentally' lean over and touch your crotch or your bum. That used to happen a lot – and still does. I told Alan about it recently and he couldn't believe it.

In my day, sexism was often obvious: a boss or client brushing against your breasts, for instance. But these days, with more watchful HR departments, it might be a boss consistently undermining your ability to do your job in all sorts of clever, underhand ways that are difficult to pinpoint. Much progress has been made in the battle for gender equal-ity, but one of the side effects is that there are men who are furious we're now 'on their turf'. It can be tricky to spot immediately, which is why it's helpful to have trusted female confidantes who can give you their own perspective.

The two incidents I've outlined above certainly gave me clearer boundaries. They made me far less likely to tolerate the 'small stuff'. I made a conscious decision to call out sexist language or behaviour wherever I witnessed it and say, 'No, you can't do that or say that. That is not OK.' The more women do this, the more difficult it will become for a man to claim he didn't know where the boundaries of acceptable behaviour lay. That, in turn, will hopefully lead to a culture where the default will be to believe a victim rather than discredit her.

Obviously this is a complex issue, with many shades of nuance. I'd say that women should speak up as soon as they feel uncomfortable, as soon as their instinct – that small, insistent, nagging voice we so often ignore – is telling them something is wrong. But the onus should definitely be on men to behave in an appropriate fashion.

I found that as soon as I'd taken the decision to be very straightforward about calling out sexism it became a vicious circle. I got a reputation for toughness. People called me a bit of a bitch – I'm sure they still do! They thought I was hard as nails. I had to not care about that – and I didn't, not really. I retrenched into my work persona and I only allowed a tight circle of people I loved and trusted to see my home persona. They were the only ones whose opinions mattered to me because they were the only ones whose opinion and love really matters. It meant that at work I couldn't be blackmailed by individuals, threatening to take their big account business elsewhere. Principles before profit always.

Too many of us worry about being liked at work, but that's not why we do what we do. Worrying about what other people think becomes a handicap because what they think might change, or it might be based on incorrect or partial information; and, besides, there are always going to be people who *don't* like you, no matter how hard you try. Attempting to please everyone results in losing yourself.

Understanding that has, I think, helped with the more recent abuse I've faced. I've had to learn to separate the media construct of Gina Miller (which has been drawn up to push a certain political agenda, and is riddled with inaccuracies and often tainted by racism and misogyny) from the real Gina Miller, which is the one my family see when I get home.

RISE

My son, Luca, was watching the news with us when the Weinstein scandal broke. I know there are some parents who don't allow their children to watch the news because they worry it's too much reality, but I think it's important that my kids know what's going on in the world now that they're old enough to have a discussion about it. Otherwise we could end up with a generation of overly fragile children with a lack of resilience, who haven't a clue how hard Mum or Dad work, or what the price of anything is, how tough other people's lives really are: children wrapped up in cotton wool whose fragility can become their focus; who live in a bubble.

When my son started to ask me questions about what Weinstein had allegedly done, I tried to be as frank as I could. I told him it was a form of bullying.

'But why do men do this?' he asked. 'He must have known he was doing something wrong. The addiction nonsense is just rubbish.'

Out of the mouth of babes.

'Because sometimes,' I replied, 'when someone sees weakness in another person they take advantage of them. That's what bullies do. And some men see women as weaker than they are.'

At home, I try to raise my two youngest children without there being any difference between them in terms of gender, whilst also acknowledging their strengths and weaknesses. It's the same way that my parents raised me and my brothers. Luca and Lana know they can do anything they want to do and be anything they want to be, regardless of whether they're a boy or a girl. We bring them up to be caring and understanding, and to see other people as equals, whatever their background. There's no mystery surrounding men and women in our home. There's nothing hidden, or fearful or shameful. There's no secrecy and we talk about everything.

I tell them to challenge what is expected of 'men' and 'women'. The Weinstein revelations were the start of a broader societal reckoning, where women are standing tall and proud, speaking out and sharing their stories.

Conclusion

On the morning of 1st November 2017, I woke up, walked to our kitchen and looked out at the garden beyond. It was a beautiful late autumn day, with clear blue skies and sunshine dappling through the trees. The lawn was scattered, here and there, with russet-gold leaves. The clocks had been turned back and the evenings were drawing in, and it felt as if we would only have a few more of these bright, crisp days before the encroaching wintry drizzle. I reminded myself to make the most of it and took a few deep breaths.

I was nervous for what I knew the day held: nervous, but also excited. Today was going to be the day I received my Honorary Doctorate of Law from the University of East London. When I had studied there, some thirty years before, my life had been very different. Now I was married to a loving, supportive man, I had three children and had built myself a stable financial future. I had a roof over my head. I was lucky enough to be successful in my business, and I do my very best to give back to my community and my country. It felt like quite a journey.

I got ready with care, putting on a simple but smart navy-blue dress and heels, then drove with Alan and Lucy-Ann to the O_2 East London, where the ceremony was being held, and cleared the security arrangements that had been carefully made.

As soon as we walked in, I was awed by the size of the theatre. It was more often used as a concert venue, and there was row upon row of seating, all the way up into the balconies that rose steeply in front of the stage. I hadn't anticipated quite so many people, but I had been asked to make a speech to the new graduates, so I tried to get my thoughts together.

A few weeks before the ceremony, I had been called up by the organiser. She wanted to get a few biographical details from me for the citation and she asked me what I thought my biggest achievement was. I thought for a few seconds. There was a lump in my throat when I answered.

'I think building a career while bringing up Lucy-Ann,' I said. 'I wanted her to see her mother succeeding but also to know that she was loved and that I was there for her, no matter what.'

When the time came for me to receive my doctorate, I felt unexpectedly emotional. I was wearing a university gown in bright red, blue and white with an amusing mushroom-shaped cap on my head. They read the citation with me standing there and as I was listening to the words, all the incredibly flattering things they were saying about my professional, personal and political achievements, tears started flowing from my eyes. I couldn't help it.

Although I'm often tough in the face of adversity, I find it hard to contain my emotions when someone is being nice to me. I've built up an armour against insults and threats, and I find it easier to compose myself when people are being harsh or horrible. I find kindness terribly disarming. I know that sounds odd, but there it is.

The other reason it was particularly emotional was that this was almost exactly thirty years to the day when I should have been receiving my law degree.

As I stood there on the stage, I couldn't help thinking how strange life is. With an abiding love for law and a deep-seated respect for the sophisticated mechanisms of justice, this failed law student had brought the biggest constitutional case for nearly 400 years. This mother fighting for the Mother of all Parliaments. When I came to give my speech, I urged the students in front of me to speak out against dishonesty, injustice and inequality.

'It does not come easy, the society we value – it comes from hard work and it comes from being brave and being courageous,' I said. 'To be silent only adds to the lies. It only adds to the weakness. Do not give in to bullying or belittling or bigotry.

'In the past thirty years I have learned that while we must dare to dream, dare to aim high, we must dare to also face our weakness. True character is not how you face your successes. It is how we face reality, obstacles and failures – that defines who we really are.

'You must find your place in this world. You must find your voice. I chose not to let anyone tell me who I could be or how much I could achieve or where I could speak and what I could say. I encourage you to refuse to let others tell you who you can be.

'And when you do succeed, remember that it comes with responsibility, because other people matter and your caring matters.'

When I sat down, to the sound of applause ringing in my ears, I allowed myself to feel a glimmer of pride at where I was, in that exact moment of time, and where I had come from, all those years before.

*

I wrote this book for many reasons, but one of the prime motivating factors was being able to tell my own story to my children. As I said earlier, it's the story that many of us forget to tell, and yet it's one of the most important. The next generation needs to know who we are and where we come from, so that they can help build a future based on shared values and where they come from too. It is as much their story as it is mine. While sifting through the memories of my past, I've had several conversations with my children about what I'm doing. They are full of questions about it.

One of the most shocking letters I have received over the last year came from a Pakistani woman who has a seven-year-old mixed-race grandson. Her little grandson refuses to go to school because he's being bullied and called racist names. His mother walked in one evening to find him in the bath, trying to scrub off the colour of his skin. He had scrubbed at it so hard he was bleeding. It reminded me of a time, twenty-something years before, when I'd discovered Lucy-Ann doing the same thing. Have we not moved forward in the intervening years? Is this really who we are?

I tell my children to be proud of who they are, to remember that the blood in our veins and the tears from our eyes are the same colour the world over.

In difficult times it is even more important to make our voices heard and to tell our own stories. I am a positive person and have always believed that empathy will triumph over hatred: instead of disappearing into our own silos, let us come together.

I wanted this to be a book about sharing. Remembering that we are the person we are because of the challenges faced, battles fought and won, and the decisions we take. Too many people I've met are walking around in mourning for the life they thought they should have had. True resilience is having the strength to let go of what no longer serves you, whether that be an abusive relationship, a dissatisfying job, a negative view of yourself. Without moving on from bitterness, you run the risk of being defined by it. As I have learned at several points in my own life, anger can eat you up from the inside. Choosing to leave it behind means you can cultivate your own sense of self-worth. Everyone benefits when this happens: you, your family and your friends.

The challenges and difficulties my life has held so far have borne me the most extraordinary gifts and lessons.

I have learnt to speak out, I have learnt to challenge. And while it may seem a contradiction, I have also learnt to be fear*ful*, not fear*less*; but I use that fear to drive me forwards. My fear is coupled with worry about what happens when we see something wrong but fail to speak out.

I wrote this book to share my own past and experiences. I haven't always done the right thing: I have made many mistakes, but they were *my* mistakes.

That's why, despite the bullies and the brickbats, despite the attempts to discredit me and the criticism of my integrity, despite the slurs and the rage directed at me simply for having a voice and daring to use it, I have survived. I will continue to rise.

That's why I know you can do it too. Everyone has strength within them. I am no more special than you.

Please listen to your own voice, be the best you can be and live life with vigour. Claim the place in the world that is rightfully yours. Stand up to the people who seek to drag you down. Speak out where you see injustice. When you are knocked down, dig deep and find the strength to get up again, you are stronger than you might think.

I believe in you. I believe in us.
I believe we all can rise.

Acknowledgements

Where do I begin to thank the amazing people who have helped me put my jumbled life into a semblance of cohesion on the pages of this book? It is said everyone has at least one book inside of them, the art is knowing the sentiments and stories you wish your life to portray.

Without the patient understanding and guidance given to me editorially by Hannah Knowles and Jamie Byng at Canongate I would not have known, as a novice, how to even approach writing this book. It was their encouragement that allowed me to tell my story in a manner that shows you can rise above misery, you can rise above hate and you can find hope. But whatever people may think of the book, without the sheer hard work of the marketing and publicity teams at Canongate, especially Anna Frame and Vicki Watson, it would never have been read. It has been awesome to witness their dedication and professionalism.

But I would never have found Canongate without my agent, Janelle Andrew at PFD. There was an irresistible force that drew us together. Before Nelle I wasn't quite sure what a literary agent did, why would I know? She was the General in the battle to get my book published. She instinctively knew I don't want to emulate or imitate anyone else. I didn't want to be 'told' what sort of book to write, what tone to adopt. It had to be my original voice and my perspective.

Nelle completely understood and identified with my rather unflinching approach. Even when she went off to have her beautiful baby boy, she was on email, on hand and firing from all guns – a virtual powerhouse of organisation and multi-tasking!

When I was confronted with the timelines for the book, my heart sank – it's not as if I don't have a few other demands on my time! Then Nelle had a brainwave and clicked into matchmaking mode. She found the talented and erudite Elizabeth Day, a respected novelist in her own right, to help me write my book. As I've found so many times in my life, the fates were aligned – Nelle didn't know that Elizabeth had interviewed me once before and we had discovered a resonance, and very importantly Elizabeth had time in her diary to accommodate me. Elizabeth, thank you for your calmness, your beauty – inside and out, and for always making me feel special.

In terms of the historic court case that placed me on a platform that increased my voice and ability to help others; I will be eternally grateful to James Libson, Rob Murray, Emily Nicholson, Lisa Tremble, Hayley Giffin and team at Mishcon de Reya for their dedication, professionalism, generosity and kindness. My barrister David Pannick who so eloquently transformed the seemingly dry letters of the law into heartfelt rights. My cornerstones – Jeannie and Sarah, I love you guys!

To my beloved ones – my Alan, Lucy-Ann, Luca and Lana – my life would be incomplete without your love, your hugs, your smiles, your cheekiness and snuggles, and your total support. You are my world.

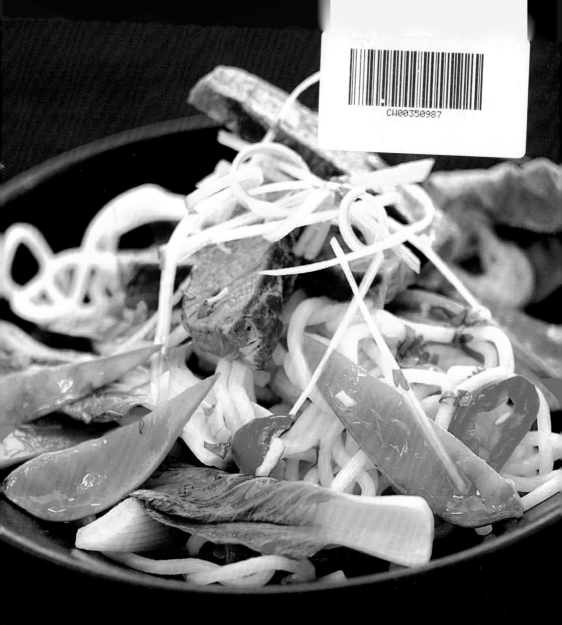

MEALS in moments

Over 60 delicious recipes

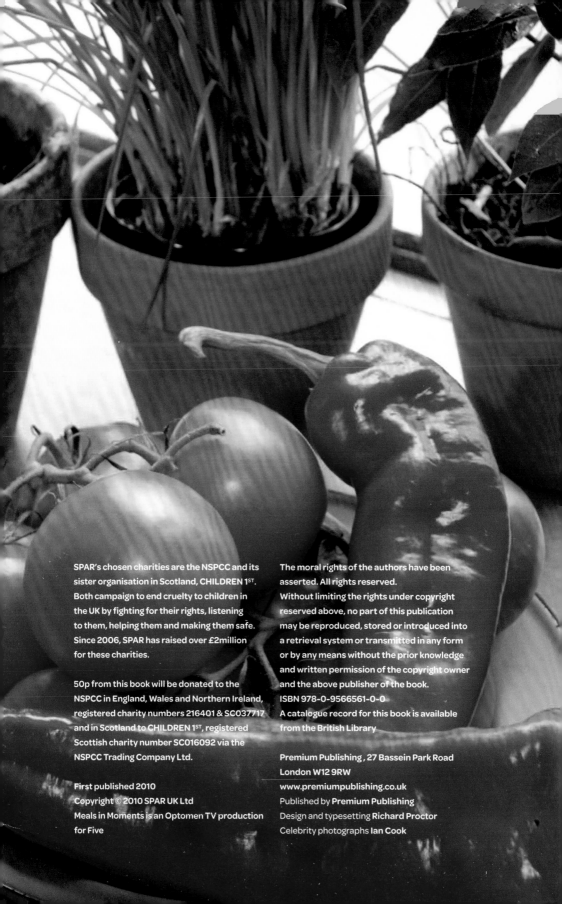

First published 2010
Copyright © 2010 SPAR UK Ltd
Meals in Moments is an Optomen TV production for Five

ISBN 978-0-9566561-0-0
A catalogue record for this book is available from the British Library

Premium Publishing , 27 Bassein Park Road
London W12 9RW
www.premiumpublishing.co.uk
Published by Premium Publishing
Design and typesetting Richard Proctor
Celebrity photographs Ian Cook

Introduction

Looking for something to cook that's quick, easy, delicious and healthy?

SPAR knows that its customers are busy people who don't always have time to prepare elaborate meals. Like the celebrities who have shared their recipes in this book, based on the TV series *Meals In Moments*, you want tasty food you can assemble in minutes from ingredients bought round the corner in your local shop.

If you've never cooked before, don't let that worry you. Many of the stars in the following pages admit to being nervous in the kitchen. Ex-atomic kitten Liz McClarnon used to be terrified of using the oven, and Rowland Rivron burns the chops in his Moroccan Lamb dish. But with chef Simon Rimmer at their side to help them and pass on useful tips, they have produced a set of simple, mouth-watering recipes that will inspire you to start cooking for family and friends.

Most of these dishes are prepared in ten minutes or less, and take under half an hour to finish. There are family favourites like swimmer Sharron Davies's Fish Pie, or EastEnders actress Nina Wadia's Akoori (Parsi Scrambled Eggs). Make it a big occasion with hairdresser Nicky Clarke's Mediterranean Chicken Stew or Hollyoaks star Nick Pickard's Seafood Paella. Or be adventurous with traveller Charley Boorman's exotic Indonesian Fried Rice.

Informal brunch, family supper or a big dinner party: there's a celebrity favourite to suit in these pages. All profits from this book will go to the NSPCC and CHILDREN 1ST, so as well as having fun in the kitchen, you'll be helping children as well.

There's nothing more satisfying than cooking for family and friends, and with a little help from these celebs, anyone can produce perfect *Meals In Moments*!

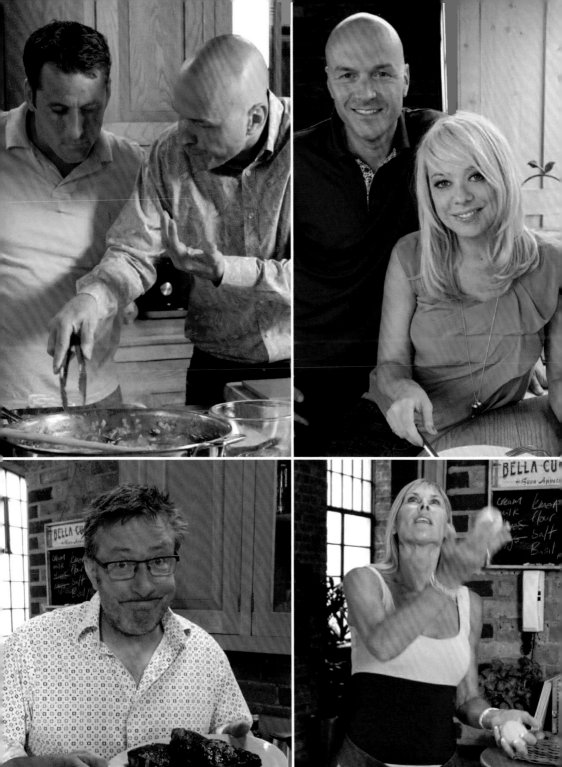

Contents

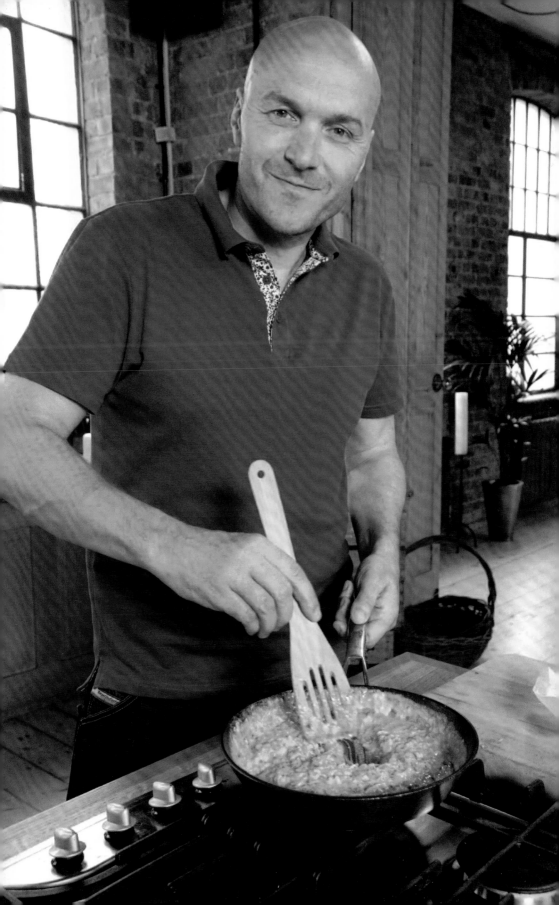

"Welcome to Meals in Moments – the recipe book based on the TV series from SPAR. I've invited well-known faces into my kitchen to cook their favourite recipes and together we will show you how to make fantastic dishes which you can cook in no time at all."

Simon Rimmer

There are two things Meals in Moments chef Simon Rimmer loves in life – cooking, and helping other people to cook. He began his television career with guest appearances, and soon was given his own show. He says: 'Cooking is about exciting people, and that's what makes great TV.'

Although Simon runs two restaurants – Earle in Cheshire and the award-winning Greens in Manchester – when he started in the business in 1990, he had no idea how to cook! He found two cookery books on the shelf, so he thought he could give it a go... and discovered he had a talent for it. Now he hopes that this charity cook book will inspire you to be just as bold in your kitchen, by following in the celebrities' footsteps and trying out some new recipes.

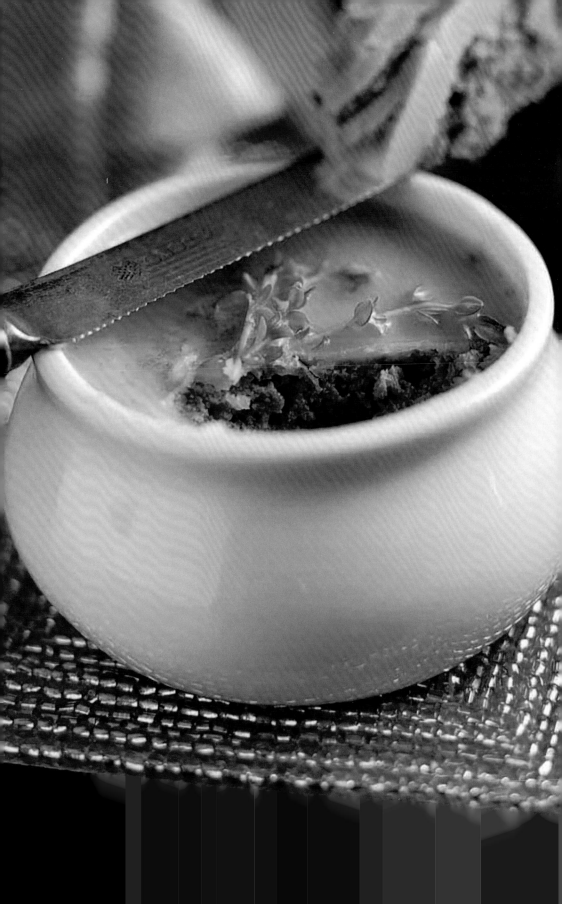

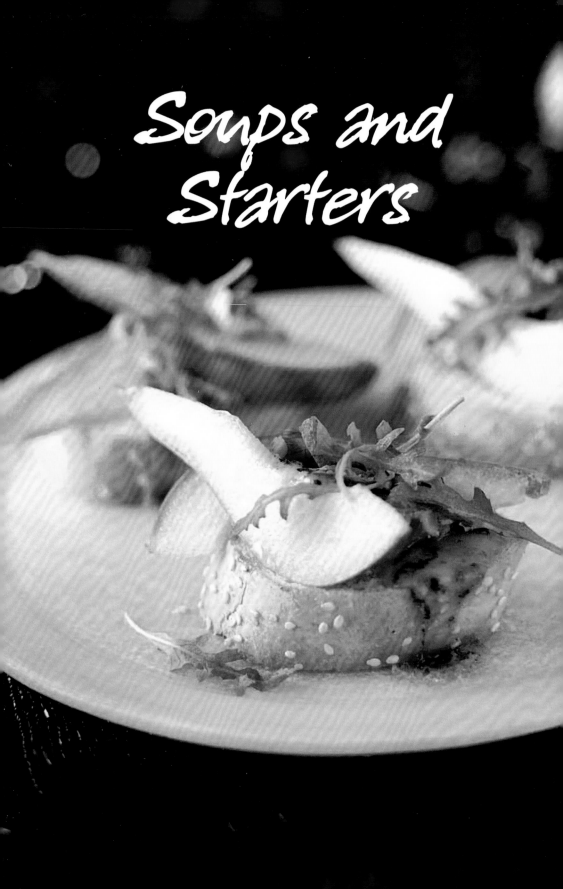

Soups and Starters

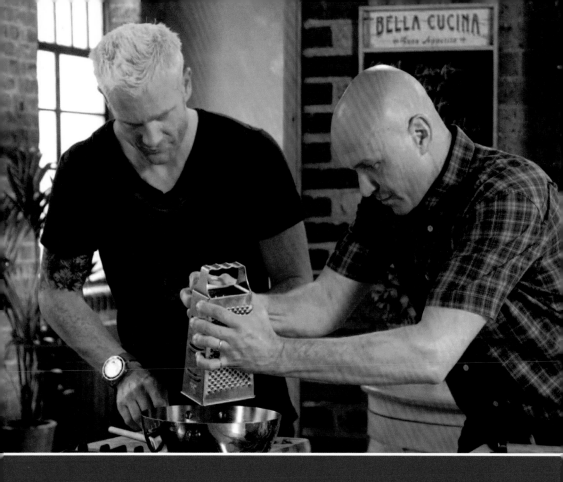

"I love spicy food, especially Asian cuisine such as this recipe – it's a really good cuisine to cook as everything's so quick and easy and it all has bags of flavour."

Iwan Thomas

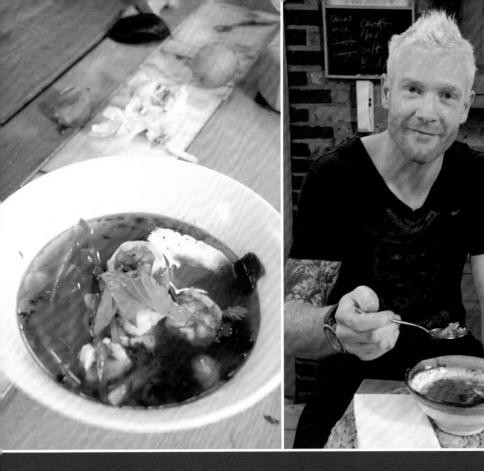

Iwan Thomas doesn't hang about. As one of Britain's finest 400m runners – former European Champion, Commonwealth Champion and current British Record Holder – he likes to do things fast, and that includes food! His guilty secret is that he holds a McDonald's Platinum card, but he's as happy putting together food in his own kitchen, if it doesn't take long. This spicy Asian soup takes only minutes to make using ready-made 'Tom Yum' paste.

Iwan also admits that he'd never taken part in any athletics until he was 16, when he amazed friends by breaking the school record for the long jump first time. Immediately afterwards he had to compete in the 400 metres, and his headmaster told him it was impossible he'd finish, let alone win – but he did, and a couple of years later was running for his country.

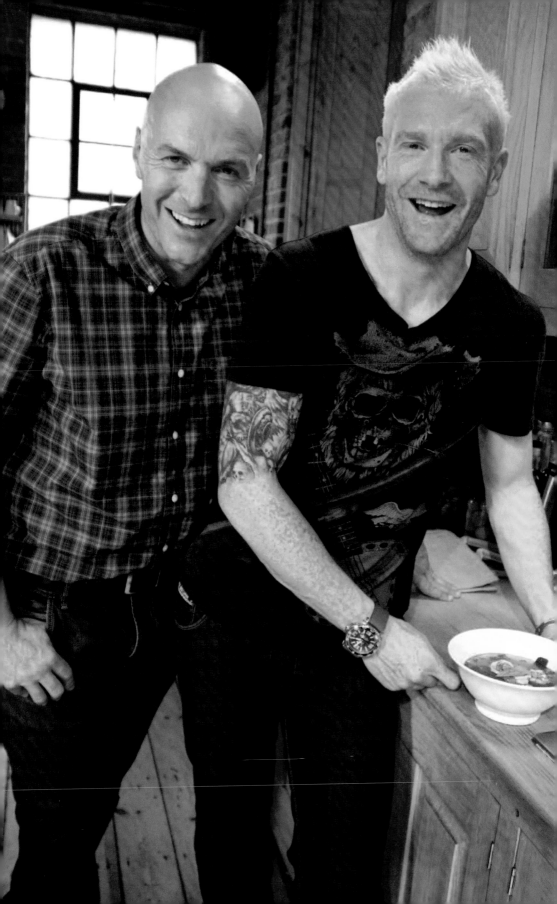

Iwan Thomas – Tom Yum Soup with Chicken and Prawns

Tom yum ready-made pastes are widely available. These are a mixture of herbs and spices (lemongrass, kaffir lime leaf, coriander, garlic, chillies, galangal and shallots are typical) which are crushed and stir-fried in oil before being preserved.

Serves 2
Preparation time 10 minutes
Cooking time 10 minutes

✔ 243 Kcal per serving
✔ Low in fat

1 litre light chicken stock
2 small sticks of lemongrass, outer leaves removed
2 normal shallots, finely diced
1 clove garlic, peeled and finely diced
3 lime leaves, torn in half (optional, you can also buy these dried)
1 long red chilli, sliced into rounds
2.5cm fresh root ginger, peeled and thinly sliced
1 tbsp tom yum paste
2 tbsp fish sauce
A good pinch of palm sugar or light demerara
1 chicken breast, sliced thinly
6 tiger prawns, shelled and deveined
Oil for frying
½ red pepper, sliced into strips
1 small bunch of coriander, stems and leaves chopped
Handful of basil leaves, Thai basil if you can get it but if not normal basil is fine
1 lime, halved

■ Heat a large wok or saucepan and add a dash of oil. Add the shallots, chilli and garlic and fry for a minute then add 1 tablespoon of the spice paste and fry until aromatic. This will take a couple of minutes.
■ Add the stock, lemongrass, ginger and lime leaves if using, bring to the boil and then simmer for 2-3 minutes. Season using the palm sugar and fish sauce – taste and adjust if needed.
■ Add the chicken strips to the broth and simmer for a minute then add the prawns.
■ Finally add the red pepper, pour into serving bowls and garnish with the coriander and basil leaves and finish with a squeeze of lime.

Carrot and Coriander Soup

Making your own soup is a great opportunity to experiment with different combinations of flavours.

Serves 4-6
Preparation time 15 minutes
Cooking time 55 minutes

✔ Suitable for vegetarians
✔ 96 Kcal per serving
✔ Low in fat

125g red lentils
1 bay leaf
300ml water
250g carrots, sliced
150ml fresh orange juice
450ml vegetable stock
2 tbsp fresh coriander, chopped
Salt and freshly ground black pepper

■ Place the lentils in a pan with the bay leaf and the water and boil.
■ Reduce the heat, cover and simmer until the lentils have softened.
■ Place the carrots in a pan and top with the orange juice and stock. Bring to the boil and cook for 15 minutes or until carrots are tender.
■ Drain the lentils and remove the bay leaf.
■ Place the lentils, the carrots and their cooking liquid in a food processor and purée until smooth.
■ Stir in the coriander and season. Reheat and serve with black pepper.

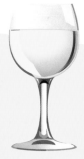

The bold flavours of a southern French Chardonnay with just a hint of apple pie spice from some oak will stand up to the freshness of this dish.

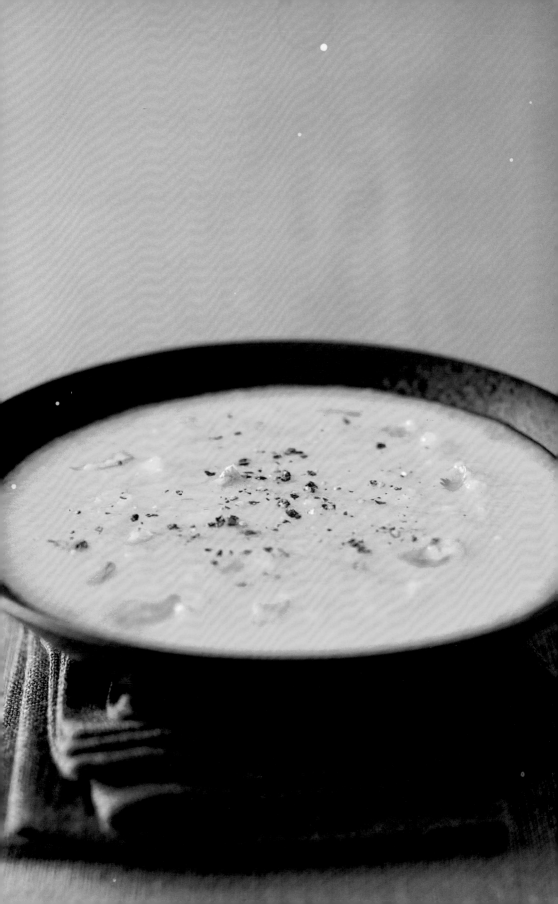

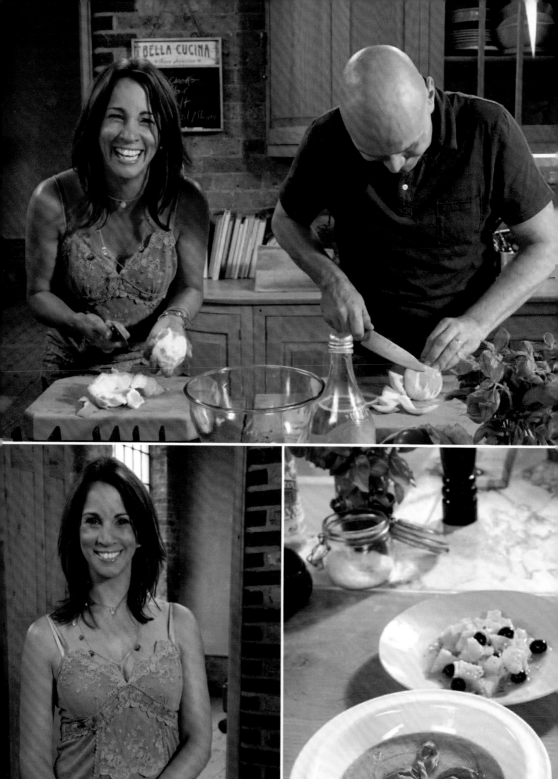
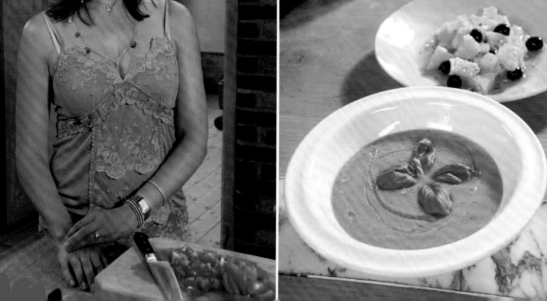

"Once a year I go to Spain with my girlfriends... after a week I said to our lovely chef 'What have we been eating all week?' And he gave me this recipe and I tried it when we got home"

Andrea McLean

One-time GMTV weather girl before becoming host of ITV's Loose Women, Andrea is strong on enthusiasm, but perhaps a little short on kitchen technique – even cutting up the orange for this easy-assembly soup and salad proved problematic! But not to worry, Simon's turned out nice and neat, and really the only skill needed for this dish is simply throwing together the right ingredients.

Born in Scotland, Andrea was raised in Trinidad and Tobago, giving her an unusual mixture of a Scottish/Caribbean accent and a taste for exotic food combinations. And if your orange-slicing isn't perfect either, Andrea says don't worry – like her, you won't have any problems putting the basil on the top, and that's the important bit that finishes the dish to perfection!

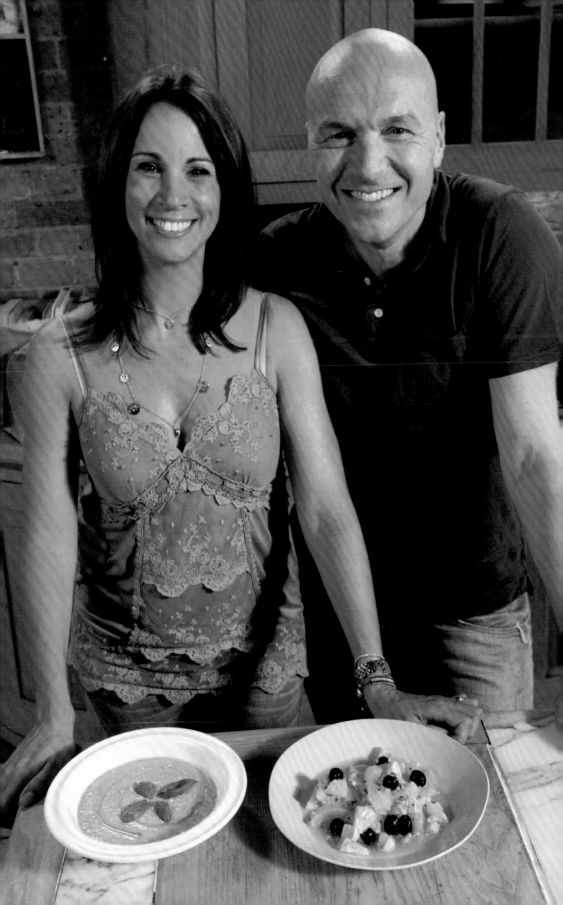

Andrea McLean – Salmorejo (Cold Tomato Soup) with Orange and Olive Salad

This Spanish recipe is perfect for a quick meal because there is no actual cooking involved.

Serves 4
Preparation time 15 minutes

✔ 256 Kcal per serving
✔ Low in fat
✔ Low in salt

For the soup
12 large ripe tomatoes
4 slices of white bread, crust removed
2-3 tbsp of white wine vinegar
Sea salt

Olive oil
Basil
A dash of water if required

For the salad
4 oranges, peeled and segmented
1 red onion
15 black olives
Olive oil
Sea salt and freshly ground black pepper

For the salad
■ Finely dice the red onion and place in a bowl.
■ Segment the oranges over the bowl of diced onion so that all the juices are retained. Add the segments to the bowl along with the olives and a good glug of olive oil. Season with salt and pepper.

For the soup
■ Roughly chop the tomatoes and place in a blender along with the bread and 1 tablespoon of white wine vinegar. Blend well.
■ Taste the soup and season adding salt and pepper and more white wine vinegar if you like. If the soup is too thick add a drop of water. Finally add a handful of basil leaves and a good glug of olive oil.
■ Blend once more and then pour into soup bowls. Garnish with basil leaves and a drizzle of olive oil. Serve with the orange salad.

Spicy Cauliflower Soup

A new idea for an everyday vegetable: transformed into something that everyone should try.

Serves 4
Preparation time 10 minutes
Cooking time 20 minutes

✔ 379 Kcal per serving
✔ Reduced salt

1 cauliflower, cut into florets
2 onions cut into slices
1 tsp cumin seeds
2 tbsp double cream
1 tbsp olive oil
570ml boiling water
Seasoning

■ Place the cauliflower, onion and cumin seeds into a pan along with the water. Season with salt and pepper. Bring to the boil and cook for 10 minutes or until the florets are soft and tender.

■ When cooked, drain, setting aside the cooking water. Reserve a few cauliflower florets also.

■ Pour the remaining mix into a blender along with about two tablespoons of the cooking water. Whizz into a purée adding more cooking water if needed.

■ When ready to serve return to the pan, along with the reserved florets add the double cream and warm. Serve with a drizzle of oil and plenty of black pepper.

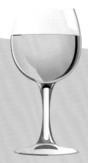

The spiciness of this recipe requires a wine with some structure, and a ripe, strawberry Pinotage rosé from South Africa will do the trick. Vibrant and fresh, with a backbone of summer fruit.

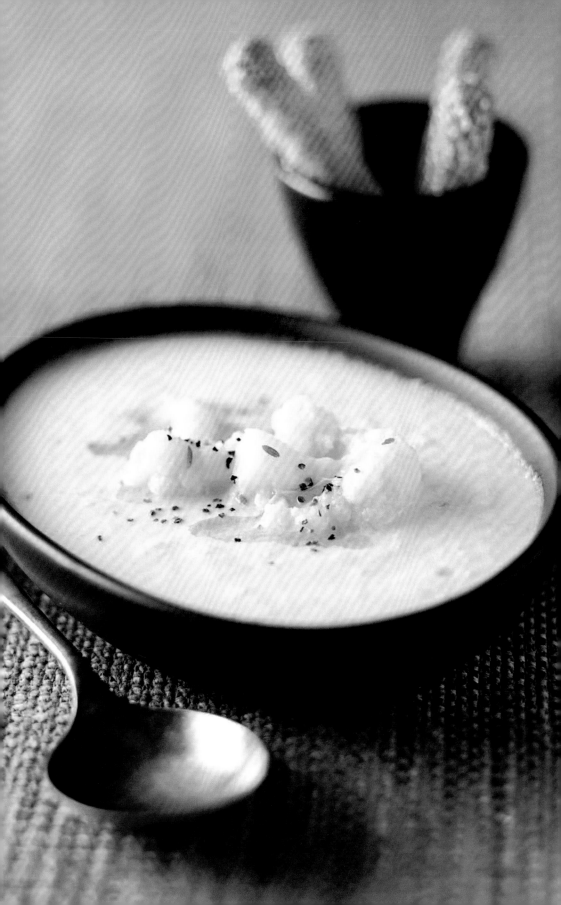

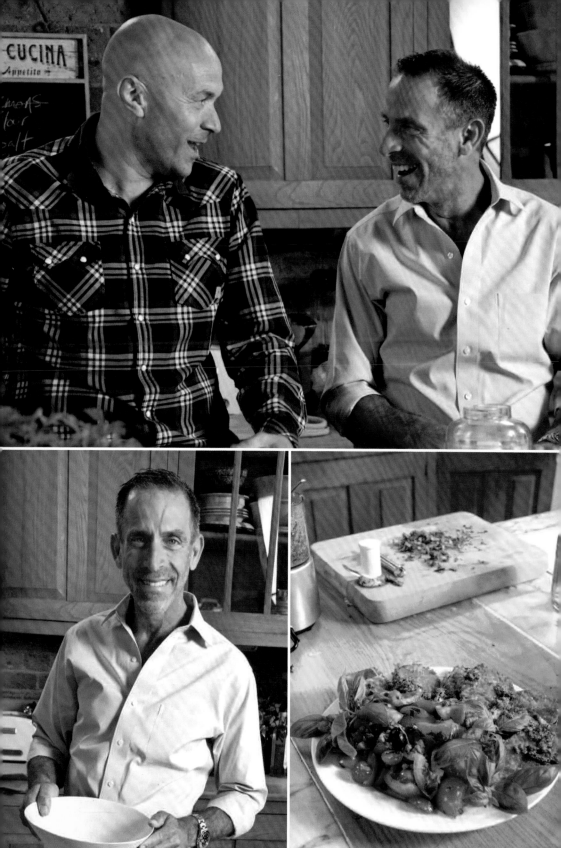

"The heart of our house was the kitchen... it's the love of food and the love of eating. Everything revolves around what we are going to have for dinner."

Ben de Lisi

Top fashion designer Ben de Lisi likes to cook food that looks as good as it tastes – not unusual for a man who dresses the world's most beautiful women and creates elegant, glamorous evening wear and fabulous bridal dresses.

Although people assume lean and long supermodels hardly eat anything, Ben reveals that many have healthy appetites and scoff food backstage at his fashion shows. Not surprising, if it's anything like his favourite dish he cooked for Simon!

Ben loves Southern Italian meals – after a fraught day in the fashion world, they remind him of a less frantic lifestyle in the sun. The best Italian dishes, like this one, are bursting with flavour and freshness, and as Ben points out, amazingly quick and easy.

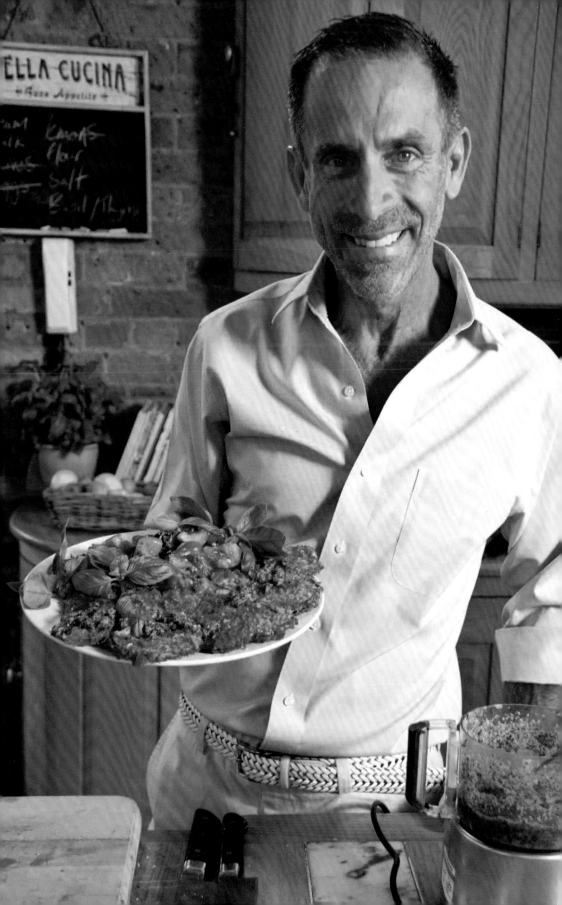

Ben de Lisi – Aubergine Cutlets with Pesto

This recipe came from Ben's Italian grandmother – he loves the simple clean flavours of Italian food. He says this dish is perfect for a quick supper or lunch or even as a sharing plate for weekends with friends.

Serves 4-6
Preparation time 10 minutes
Cooking time 5 minutes

✔ 851 Kcal per serving
✔ Low in salt

For the aubergines
4 medium aubergines, sliced 1cm lengthways
3 eggs, beaten
250g breadcrumbs
A pinch of chilli flakes

50g of grated pecorino cheese
100g plain flour
Salt and freshly ground black pepper
Vegetable oil for frying

For the pesto
1 large bunch of fresh basil
100ml olive oil
The zest of 1 lemon
A handful of pine nuts
2 garlic cloves, peeled
1 bunch of flat leaf parsley

■ Lay the aubergine slices on a plate and sprinkle over a pinch of sea salt – this will draw out the bitter liquid from the aubergines – after about 10 minutes wipe off the excess moisture and salt.
■ Dust each aubergine slice in flour and then set aside.
■ Mix the breadcrumbs, cheese, a pinch of salt, black pepper and the chilli flakes in a shallow bowl or plate.
■ Take the floured aubergine slices and dip in the beaten egg then coat in the bread crumb mixture.
■ Deep fry in batches on a medium temperature until golden, this will take approximately 3 minutes, then leave the slices to rest on some paper towels. Repeat until all the cutlets are fried – if you don't have a deep fryer you can shallow fry in a large pan over a medium heat.
■ For the pesto – Put all the ingredients apart from the oil into a food processor and blitz; while running add the oil until the pesto becomes a drizzling consistency – you will need approx 50 to 100ml of oil.
■ Place the aubergine on a plate and drizzle over the pesto, serve with a tomato salad.

Mozzarella and Parma Parcels

This is delicious served as a tasty light starter or as party finger food.

Serves 4
Preparation time 10 minutes
Cooking time 5 minutes

✔ 191 Kcal per serving
✔ Low in sugar

4 slices Parma ham, halved lengthways
225g mozzarella cheese
Drizzle of olive oil
Caper berries and lemons, for serving

■ Cut the cheese into 8 even-sized pieces then wrap each piece in a half slice of ham. Secure each parcel with a toothpick if needed.
■ Heat the oil in a large frying pan then add the parcels and cook, turning from time to time, until browned on all sides and the cheese starts to melt.
■ Serve immediately topped with a caper berry and a wedge of lemon.

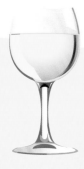

Famous as the wine of Rome, Frascati is a stunning combination of zingy apple and almond flavours. Great with the soft creamy mozzarella and salty parma ham.

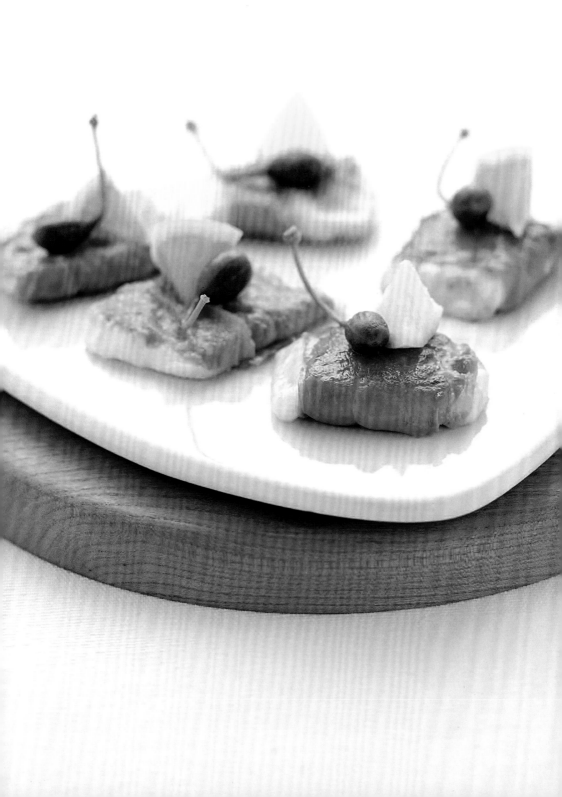

Mini Beef En Croute

Small but satisfying in every way.

Serves 10-12
Preparation time 10 minutes
Cooking time 7 minutes

✔ 204 Kcal per serving
✔ Low in sugar

375g ready-rolled puff pastry
300g beef fillet cut into bite-sized chunks
100g mushroom pate
Handful parsley leaves and redcurrants, to garnish

■ Preheat the oven to 200 °C/400 °F/Gas Mark 6. Unroll the pastry onto a lightly floured chopping board. Cut the pastry into 36 squares. Knock the sides of the pastry with a knife to create an edge.
■ Place the squares onto a baking sheet.
■ Spread each of the pastry squares with the mushroom pate and top with chunks of beef.
■ Cook for 7 minutes. Serve topped with a parsley leaf and a few redcurrants.

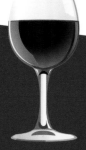

Pick a classic Pinot Noir from Burgundy in France, with lovely raspberry fruit, subtle intensity and ripe redcurrant finish.

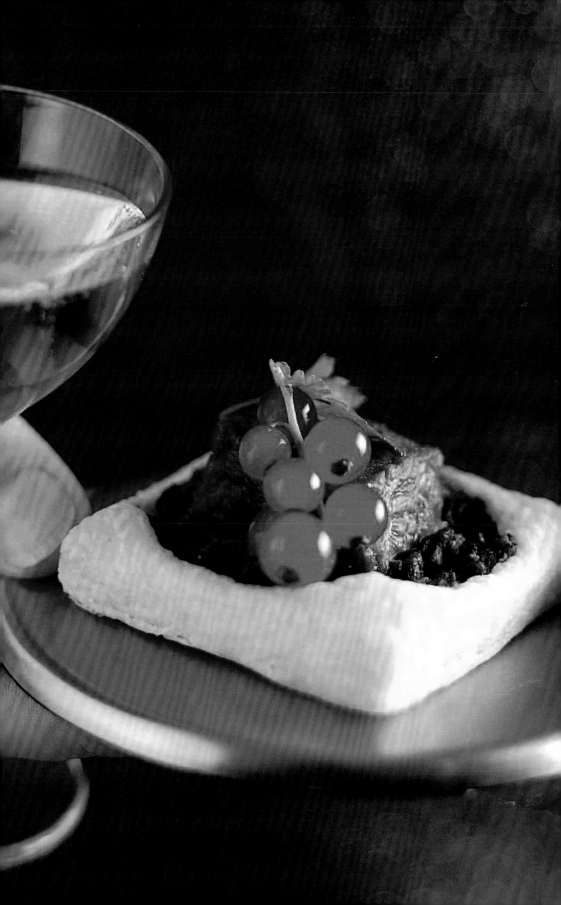

Pear and Stilton Bruschetta

The sweetness of the pear and the strength of ripe Stilton combine beautifully.

Serves 10-12
Preparation time 5 minutes
Cooking time 25 minutes

✔ 244 Kcal per serving

1 French stick, sliced

2 tbsp rocket-flavoured oil
2 small ripe pears, washed
Juice of ½ lemon
200g Blue Stilton
A few additional rocket leaves
for garnish

■ Preheat the oven to 200°C/400°F/Gas Mark 6.
■ Place the bread slices on a baking sheet and drizzle with the oil. Bake for 10 minutes, turning halfway through, until starting to crisp. Leave to cool.
■ Cut the pears into quarters, remove the core. Slice and toss in the lemon juice. Crumble the Stilton.
■ Top each bread slice with 2-3 pear slices and the Stilton. Cook in the oven for a further 12-15 minutes until the Stilton is lightly browned. Cut into quarters, arrange on a serving platter and garnish with the rocket.

See picture on page 9

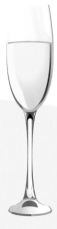

A tricky combination of flavours, best matched by a sparkling wine from Australia. Packed with tropical fruits, and really refreshing.

Chicken Liver Pate

No better way to whet the appetite for a festive feast to come than with a rich pate on crispy toast.

Serves 6
Preparation time 15 minutes
Cooking time 5 minutes

✔ 241 Kcal per serving
✔ Low in sugar

150g butter

225g chicken livers
2 tbsp Cognac
2 tsp mustard powder
Pinch of ground nutmeg
2 cloves garlic, crushed
Seasoning
Sprigs of thyme
Melba toast, to serve

■ Melt 25g butter in a frying pan. Add the chicken livers and cook for five minutes, turning constantly. Remove from the pan and transfer to an electric blender.
■ In the same pan melt 75g butter and add to the blender.
■ Add the Cognac to the pan, just to ensure you collect all the goodness and then pour into the blender with the mustard powder, nutmeg, garlic and seasoning.
■ Blend into a smooth velvety paste and transfer to six small pots. Top with a sprig of thyme. Melt the remaining butter and pour over the pate. Chill until ready to use. Serve with Melba toast.

See picture on page 8

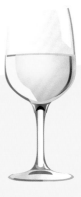

Pair with a bold Chardonnay from somewhere tropical, such as California. Big melon and pineapple flavours, fresh citrus acidity and a touch of vanilla oak.

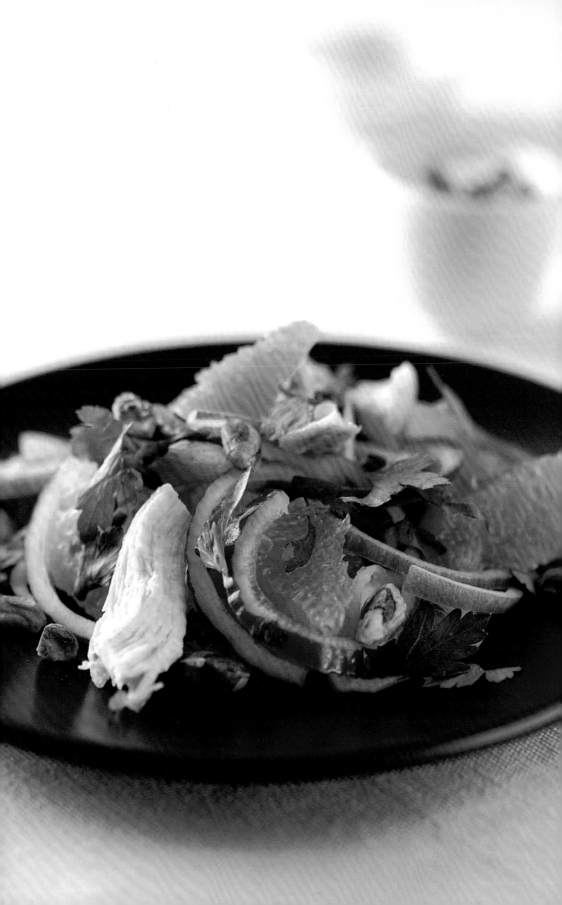

Brunch and Salads

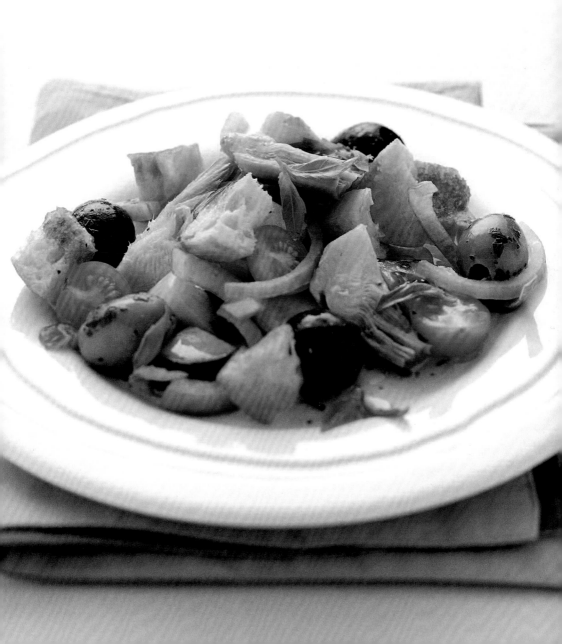

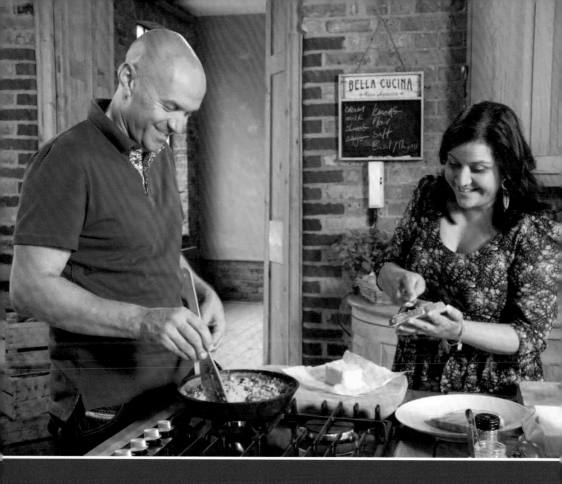

"My Dad used to work for the airlines, and this was a special dish my Mum used to cook for him when he came home. It's real comfort food."

Nina Wadia

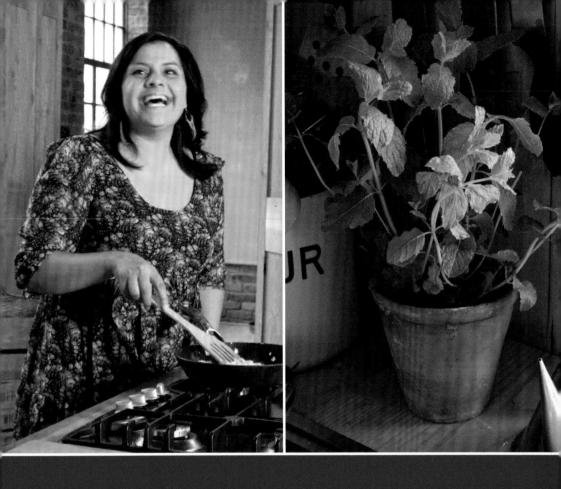

Actress Nina Wadia plays Zainab Masood in EastEnders – a straight-talking business woman who tries to make a living with a catering business. Of course she doesn't really cook the food in the soap because most is brought onto the set ready prepared. But she enjoys cooking at home and chose for Simon a dish that reminds her of the flavours of her birthplace in Mumbai, India, where she grew up in a ground-floor flat that regularly flooded during the monsoon season.

Akoori is a fusion of Indian and British tastes, so it's spicy without being too fierce – unlike some of the dishes Nina's fellow actors have to endure working on EastEnders. She told Simon that she spices up her on-screen husband by sneaking more chilli than reasonable into the meals he has to eat on set!

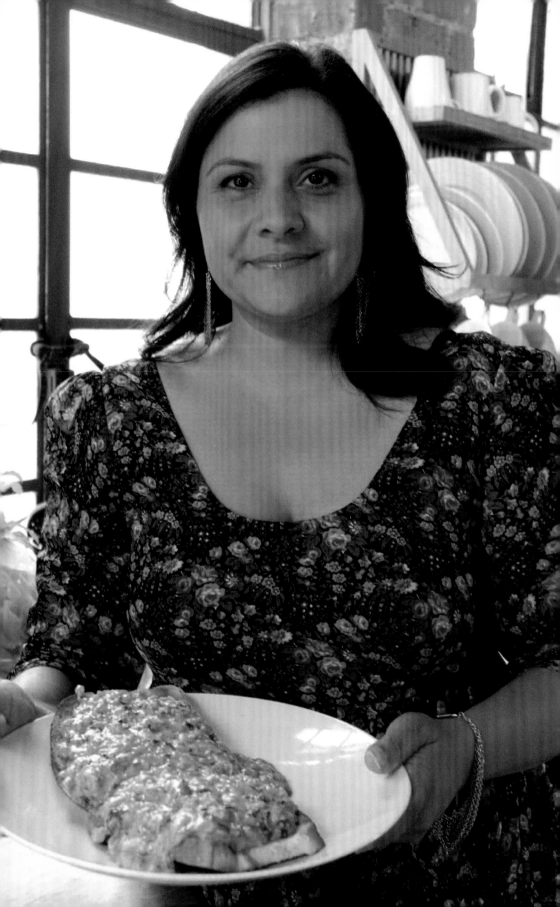

Nina Wadia – Akoori (Parsi Scrambled Eggs)

This recipe was a favourite of my grandfather who used to eat it every day at tea-time.

Serves 4
Preparation time 5 minutes
Cooking time 8 minutes

✔ 205 Kcal per serving

6 large eggs
A small dash of milk
½ tsp cumin seeds
2 tbsp butter

1 small onion, finely chopped
1 fresh chilli (depending on how hot you like) de-seeded and chopped
½ tsp finely grated fresh garlic
A pinch each of chilli powder and turmeric
1 handful of coriander, chopped
1 ripe tomato, diced
Sea salt

■ Heat a frying pan with a little butter, add the onion and fry for a couple of minutes until almost golden brown. Then add the garlic, cumin and chillies.
■ Meanwhile beat the eggs with the milk and a little seasoning.
■ Add the turmeric, chilli powder and tomato to the pan and fry for a further minute or two until the tomato starts to break down. Add in the egg mixture.
■ Turn to a low to medium heat to cook – you want a nice creamy texture so don't stir vigorously. When almost ready add in the coriander leaves and give a stir.
■ Toast some bread, whatever kind you like, and butter generously.
■ Serve the eggs on the buttered toast.

Parma Ham Baskets with Baked Egg

These tasty little dishes are the next best things to a traditional British fry up – but this is a low-fat version you can enjoy guilt-free without worrying about your waistline, and you certainly won't be disappointed!

Serves 6
Preparation time 10 minutes
Cooking time 15 minutes

✔ 208 Kcal per serving
✔ Low in sugar

12 slices Parma ham
6 large free-range eggs
Freshly ground black pepper
A little olive oil

■ Preheat the oven to 200 °C/400 °F/Gas Mark 6.
■ Lightly brush a non-stick 6-hole muffin tray with olive oil. Trim the fat off the Parma ham and use two rashers to line each hole in the muffin tray.
■ Carefully break an egg into each hole.
■ Bake in the oven for 12-15 minutes or until the eggs are just set.
■ Serve hot with a generous sprinkling of black pepper alongside a few roasted tomatoes and griddled ciabatta.

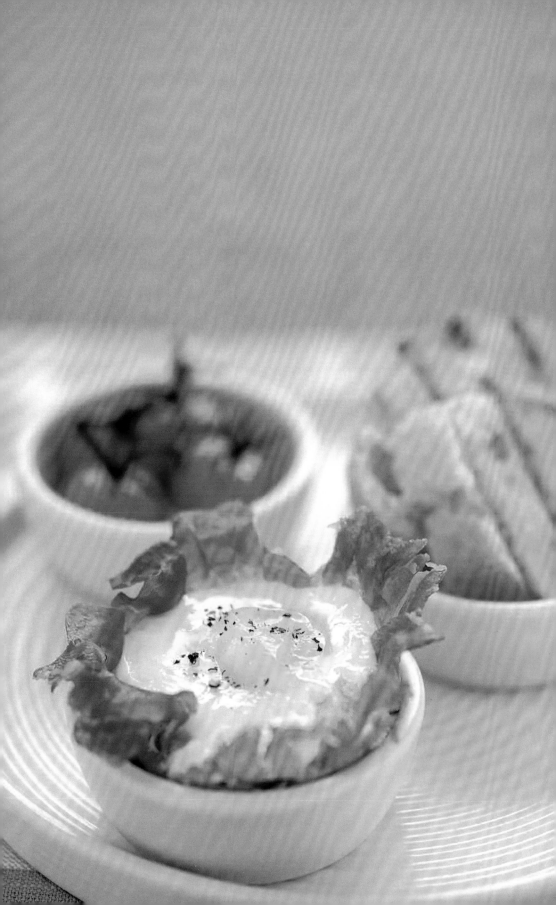

Cranberry and Mixed-Seed Muffins

These wholesome muffins are lovely served warm as part of a family brunch. They're also just as delicious cold, so you can save some to take with you to work the following day as a treat.

Makes 12
Preparation time 10 minutes
Cooking time 15 minutes

✔ 304 Kcal per serving

400g plain flour
100g caster sugar
1 tbsp baking powder
Pinch of salt
284ml carton buttermilk
2 eggs, beaten
85g butter, melted
150g dried cranberries
100g mixed seeds (sunflower, pumpkin, sesame)

■ Preheat the oven to 200 °C/400 °F/Gas Mark 6. Line a 12-hole muffin tray with greaseproof paper or paper cases.
■ Combine the flour, sugar, baking powder and salt in a bowl. In a separate bowl, combine the buttermilk, eggs and butter.
■ Make a well in the centre of the dry ingredients and pour in the buttermilk mixture. Stir until the ingredients are mixed together, do not be tempted to over beat.
■ Fold in the cranberries and most of the seeds. Spoon the mixture into the tins. Sprinkle with the remaining seeds.
■ Bake for 15-18 minutes until risen and pale golden on top.

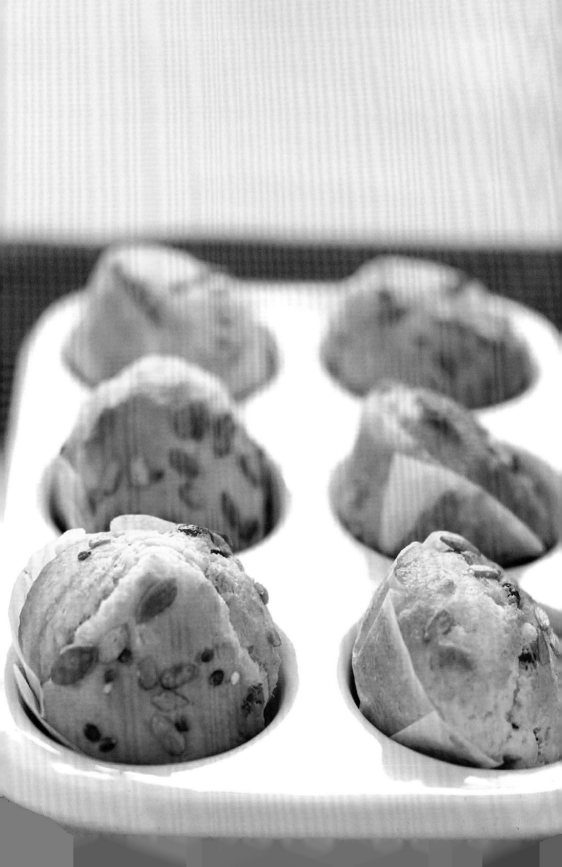

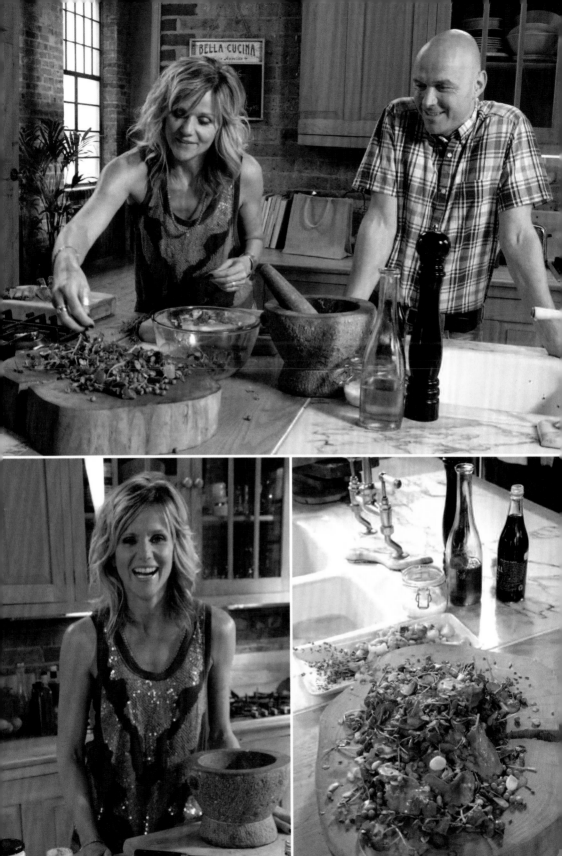

"Dad was a butcher and we were brought up on a cattle farm. So eating meat was a big part of my childhood. "

Linda Barker

Not surprisingly Linda Barker cares passionately about the way food is presented. She began her career as an innovative decorative painter and interior design consultant, and quickly moved into TV where she hosted Changing Rooms and House Invaders. She also has her own successful interiors range.

Her dad was a wholesale butcher, so she loves a good cut of meat. This Italian-style dish is exactly the kind of food she grew up eating and still cooks today, full of flavoursome and healthy vegetables that are the perfect foil for the seared beef. Linda's parents had a vegetable patch in the garden to grow their own peas and beans, but Linda's busy lifestyle doesn't allow time for that, so she pops round to her local SPAR to buy cucumber, avocado, apples, and limes to make juice. She said the SPAR avocados are perfect every day!

Just look at the size of that pestle and mortar – poor old Linda could hardly lift them, and the sound of grinding spices was so noisy that Simon couldn't hear what Linda was trying to tell him. But you'll love the taste of the dressing made in this way.

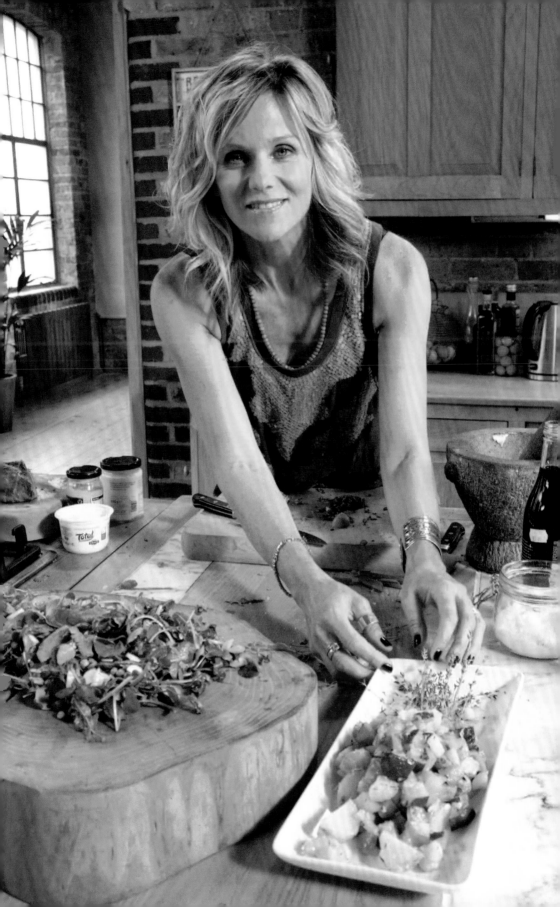

Linda Barker – Seared Beef with Vegetable and Potato Salad

This dish is similar to carpaccio, but with the meat sliced a little more thickly, which makes it more rustic. But if you don't want to use pricey fillet beef for this, you could substitute a cheaper cut such as sirloin. Meaty fish like tuna or salmon also work well, and the dish can be eaten hot or cold.

Serves 4
Preparation time 10 minutes
Cooking time 25 minutes

✔ 458 Kcal per serving
✔ Low in salt

1 x 500g beef fillet
Olive oil
300g sweet potato, peeled and cubed
300g new potatoes, halved if large
a small bunch of thyme

1 tbsp or to taste dijon mustard
2 tbsp mayonnaise
1 bunch chives
A handful of peas – fresh if possible
A handful of pea shoots (optional)
A good handful (1 bag) of rocket
A handful (1 bag) watercress
5 spring onions
A good dash of balsamic vinegar
Sea salt and freshly ground black pepper

■ Divide the new potatoes into two. Bring a pan of boiling water to the boil and boil half the potatoes until tender.

■ Dice the other half of the potatoes and place on a baking tray along with the diced sweet potatoes. Drizzle with olive oil, season with salt and pepper and sprinkle with some fresh thyme. Place in a preheated oven (200 °C) and bake for 20 minutes until golden brown and tender.

■ Boil the peas until tender, drain then run under cold water to refresh.

■ Lightly oil and season the piece of beef then place in a frying pan over a high heat. Let the pan get very hot before searing the beef on all sides until golden brown then set to one side to rest.

■ Make the dressing in a pestle and mortar. Take a clove of garlic and pound into a smooth paste. Add the mustard, balsamic vinegar and 1 tablespoon of mayonnaise and mix well. Finally add enough olive oil until you get a salad dressing consistency. Season with salt and pepper.

■ Thinly slice your rested beef.

■ Scatter the salad leaves on a big platter, sprinkle with a few peas and spring onions then top with the sliced beef and drizzle with dressing.

■ Remove the potatoes from the oven and place in a bowl. Drain the boiled potatoes and mix with the roasted ones along with 1 tablespoon of mayonnaise. Serve alongside the seared beef salad.

Herby Stuffed Tomatoes

If you can, buy vine-ripened tomatoes, they are so much sweeter and juicier.

Serves 4
Preparation time 10 minutes
Cooking time 50 minutes

✔ 379 Kcal per serving
✔ Reduced salt

8 large tomatoes
25g butter
2 tbsp olive oil
1 small onion, very finely chopped

2 cloves garlic, crushed
50g pine kernels
600ml dry white wine
125g Italian risotto rice
2 bay leaves
Sprig of thyme
5 chestnut mushrooms, finely chopped
Handful flat leaf parsley, roughly chopped
Salt and freshly ground black pepper to taste

■ Preheat oven to 200°C/ 400°F/Gas Mark 6.
■ Slice the top from each tomato and reserve. Carefully scoop out the pulp and seeds from the tomatoes and reserve.
■ Heat the butter and oil in a large pan, add the onion and cook for 10 minutes, until softened and beginning to colour.
■ Add the garlic and pine kernels and cook for 2 minutes.
■ Pour 550ml wine into the pan and add the rice.
■ Add the bay leaves and thyme. Bring it to the boil, reduce the heat, cover and simmer for 10 minutes, stirring occasionally.
■ Stir in the mushrooms, parsley, tomato pulp and black pepper, then cook for 5-10 minutes, until the rice is tender and the liquid absorbed.
■ Spoon the rice into the tomatoes, pressing down well. Top with the tomato lid.
■ Place the tomatoes on a double thickness of foil, large enough to hold all of them and to form into a parcel. Spoon the reserved wine over, and fold the foil into a parcel.
■ Place on a baking sheet and bake for 20 minutes or until the tomatoes are softened.
■ Serve with a rocket salad.

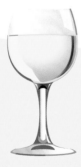

Choose an elegant glass of Italian Pinot Grigio, bursting with floral aromas and citrussy flavours.

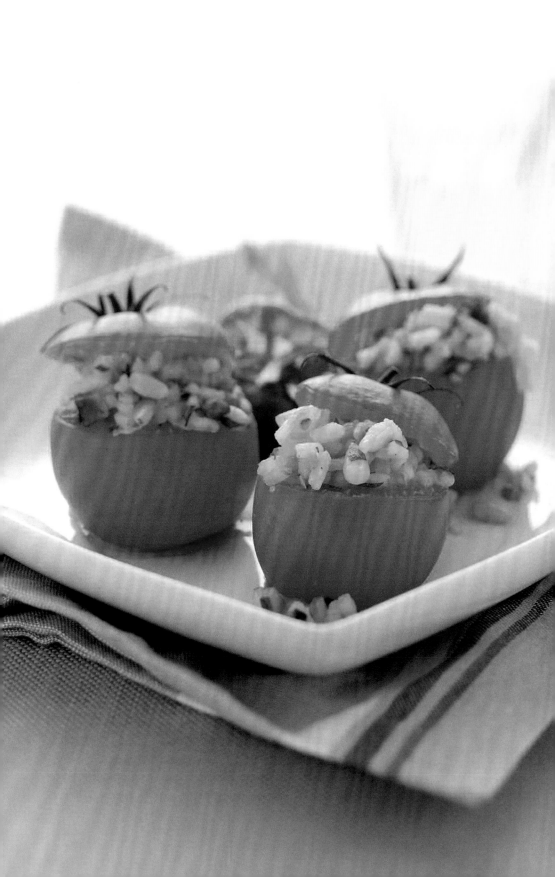

Beef and Thai Noodle Salad

Succulent beef served with vibrant salad, this dish can be served hot or cold, eaten as a main meal or as a packed lunch. You can be as adventurous as you like with additional vegetables such as asparagus.

Serves 4
Preparation time 5 minutes
Cooking time 10 minutes

✔ 334 Kcal per serving
✔ Reduced salt
✔ Low in sugar

4 x 200g fillet beef steak
1 tbsp sunflower oil
2 red chillies, sliced into rings and deseeded
4 spring onions, sliced
100g mange tout, halved
1 pak choi, leaves separated

200g ready-cooked noodles

For the dressing
1 tbsp Thai fish sauce
1 tbsp white wine vinegar
3 tbsp lime juice
1 clove garlic, crushed
1 tbsp caster sugar
2 tbsp sunflower oil
1 tbsp sesame oil
2cm fresh ginger, peeled and cut into strips
1 tbsp coriander, chopped
Spring onion to garnish

■ Make the dressing by mixing the fish sauce, white wine vinegar, lime juice, garlic, caster sugar and oils with the ginger and coriander leaves.
■ Brush the steaks with half the oil. Heat a griddle until smoking and cook the steak for 4-5 minutes each side, until it is well browned on the outside and still slightly rare in the middle. Rest for 5 minutes. When cool enough to handle, slice thinly.
■ Heat the remaining oil in a wok and add the red chilli, spring onion, mange tout, pak choi and the noodles. Stir-fry for 3-4 minutes until just starting to soften.
■ Add the dressing into the noodles and toss until glistening. Serve in 4 separate bowls topped with the thinly sliced beef and some shredded spring onion.

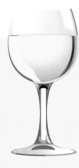

The crisp acidity and tropical fruit flavours of a South African Chenin Blanc work well with the spices in this salad. Enticing citrus blossom and hints of pear fill the mouth.

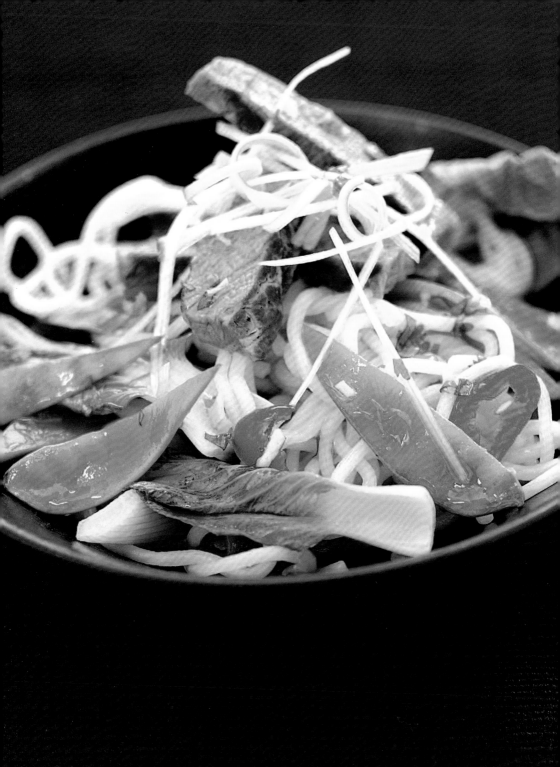

Rustic Italian Salad

This is a very versatile salad and whatever you decide to add – Parma ham and capers make good additions – you should try to keep the look of the dish rustic and chunky.

Serves 4
Preparation time 10 minutes
Cooking time 10 minutes

✔ 193 Kcal per serving
✔ Reduced salt

1 small ciabatta

4 tbsp extra virgin olive oil
2 tbsp balsamic vinegar
6 small vine tomatoes
½ cucumber
1 large red onion, finely sliced
125g artichoke hearts, drained
175g mixed Italian olives
Handful of basil leaves

■ Preheat the oven to 180°C/350 °F/Gas Mark 4.
■ Tear the bread into bite-sized chunks and place in a large bowl.
■ Add 1 tablespoon of the oil. Season and toss to cover the bread in oil.
■ Place the bread over a baking sheet and toast in the oven for 10 minutes until crisp and golden.
■ Pour the remaining olive oil in a small bowl, add the balsamic vinegar and whisk together well. Season to taste.
■ Cut the tomatoes into quarters, peel the cucumber and cut into large slices and quarter. Place in a large bowl and toss with the red onion, artichoke hearts and olives. Add the ciabatta.
■ Add the dressing and toss to combine. Tear the basil into pieces, scatter over the salad and serve.

See picture on page 33

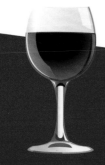

Italian wines match Italian food brilliantly, so find a ruby red Chianti with dark cherry fruit and mouth filling crunchy tannins.

Citrus Chicken and Pistachio Salad

The grapefruit flavours make this dish delightfully refreshing. It's also ideal for a lunch box.

Serves 4
Preparation time 10 minutes
Cooking time 20 minutes

✔ 349 Kcal per serving
✔ Reduced salt

4 chicken breasts, cooked and skin removed

1 pink grapefruit, peeled
1 yellow grapefruit, peeled
50g pistachios, shelled and chopped
½ red onion, finely sliced
2 tbsp virgin olive oil
Sea salt and crushed black pepper
2 tbsp flat-leaf parsley leaves, roughly chopped
2 tbsp mint leaves, roughly chopped

■ Rip the chicken into bite-sized pieces. Segment the grapefruit collecting all the juices.
■ Toss together the pistachios, onion, grapefruit segments and any juices in the olive oil and season well.
■ Add the chicken and herbs, toss and serve.

See picture on page 32

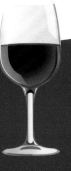

A bold, vanilla and redcurrant Rioja from the north of Spain is the perfect match for the lively citrus notes in the chicken. Red summer berries linger on the palate.

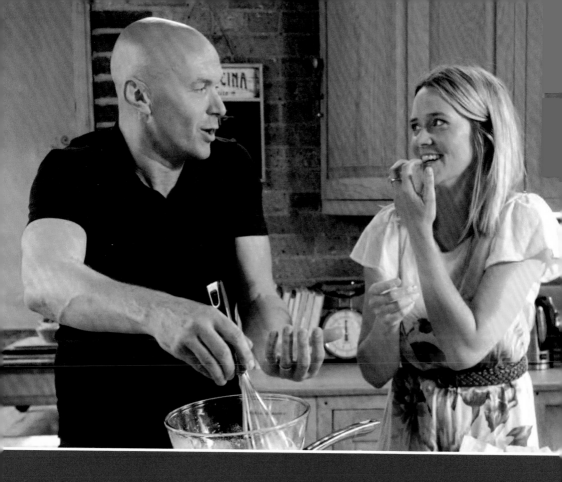

"I used to work in our family hotel and learned this recipe from watching my mother make it for the guests."

Edith Bowman

52

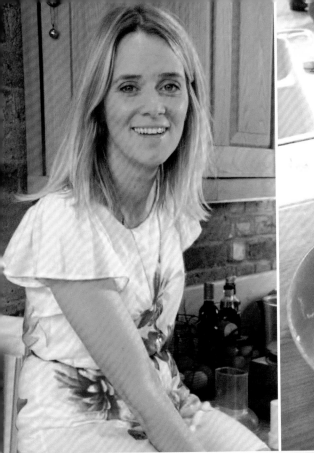
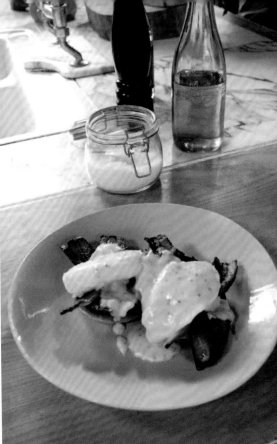

When you work as a DJ for Radio 1, hosting the BBC's television coverage of Glastonbury, Reading and Leeds festivals, there isn't much chance to experiment with elaborate, time-consuming recipes. So when Scots-born Edith Bowman invites a friend to eat, it has to be quick, reliable and simple. Her job makes for late nights, and this dish is a bit like a festival goer's favourite all-day breakfast, only a lot more luxurious than your average greasy spoon offering!

If you feel daunted at the thought of making hollandaise sauce, follow Edith's top tip. Should your sauce look as if it is about to separate, quickly remove it from the heat, dunk the outside of the pan into cold water and whisk very hard. It will usually come round. If it still fails then start again with a clean bowl and fresh egg yolks and add the curdled mixture slowly to the new eggs, beating all the time.

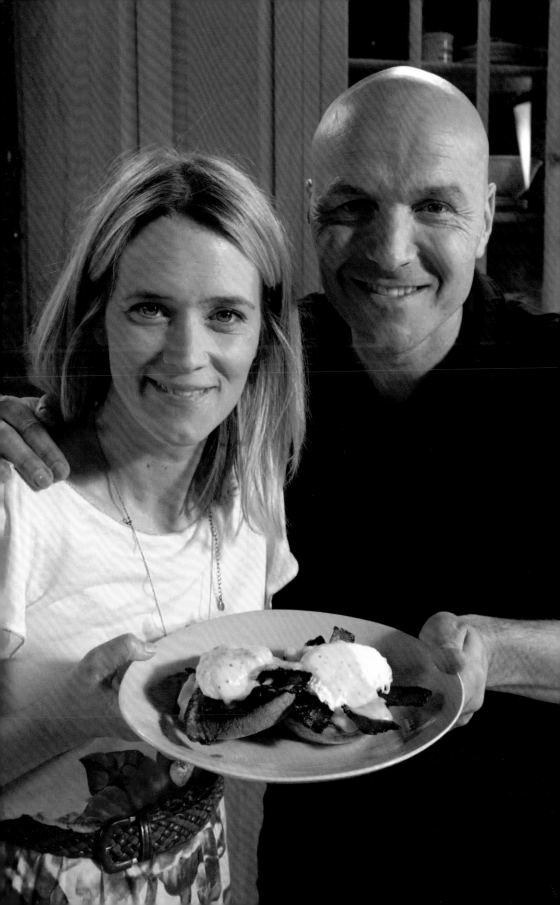

Edith Bowman – Eggs Benedict

There is a knack to making hollandaise sauce, but once you have mastered it you will be making it forever – it's great on this dish but you can also use it as an accompaniment to fish, especially salmon, and if you add some chopped tarragon it becomes béarnaise sauce which is fantastic with steak.

Serves 2
Preparation time 5 minutes
Cooking time 10 minutes

✔ 1264 Kcal per serving

4 free-range eggs for poaching plus 2 yolks for the hollandaise

2 wholemeal muffins
8 slices of maple cured bacon
2½ tsp of white wine vinegar
Approx 1 tsp of Dijon mustard
Approx 1 tsp coarse grain mustard
Approx 150g melted butter
Sea salt and freshly ground black pepper

■ Crack 2 egg yolks into a bowl warmed over a bain marie. Start to whisk then add the melted butter whisking all the time – this will take a few minutes to thicken to a runny mayonnaise consistency and you may not need all the butter. Add 2 teaspoons of white wine vinegar and taste, then half a teaspoon each of mustard and salt and pepper, taste and adjust the quantities to suit then set aside while you make the rest of the dish.
■ Grill the maple cured bacon till it's nice and crisp.
■ Put a pan of water on to boil and when boiling add a good glug of vinegar and salt. With a fork or whisk create a swirl in the pan and add your eggs for poaching.
■ Whilst doing that toast your muffins. By the time the muffins are toasted the eggs should also be ready. Lift them out and put on a kitchen roll to remove any excess water. Split the muffins in half and arrange them on a plate. Put two slices of bacon on each half with an egg on top, then pour over the hollandaise and serve immediately.

Warm Puy Lentil Salad

A light, but filling salad, packed full of delicious Mediterranean earthy flavours. Great on its own or as a side dish.

Serves 4
Preparation time 6 minutes
Cooking time 40 minutes

✔ 323 Kcal per serving
✔ Reduced salt

225g Puy lentils, rinsed
1 small onion, halved

1 celery stick
1 carrot, peeled
2 tbsp balsamic vinegar
5 tbsp olive oil
Salt and freshly ground black pepper
½ red onion, finely sliced
250g baby plum tomatoes, halved
3-4 handfuls wild rocket
2 tbsp freshly cut cress

■ Place the lentils in a pan with the onion, celery and carrot. Cover with cold water and bring to the boil. Simmer gently for 25 minutes. Remove from the heat and stand for 5 minutes.
■ Drain any remaining water and remove the onion, celery and carrot. Place the lentils in a large salad bowl.
■ Whisk together the vinegar and olive oil, season to taste and add most of it to the lentils.
■ Add the red onion and tomatoes and toss gently.
■ Just before serving, add the rocket and cress and serve drizzled with the remaining dressing.

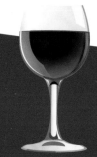

A soft and vibrant red packed full of ripe berry fruit flavours is needed, such as a blackberry and spice Shiraz from South Africa.

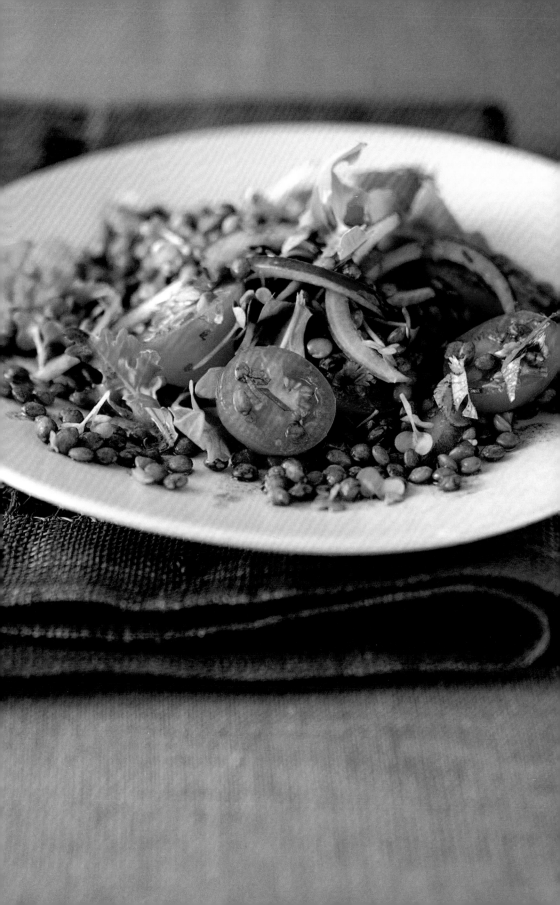

Walnut, Rocket and Clementine Salad

A crunchy salad with some fiery leaves and a Christmas twist of citrus. Perfect.

Serves 6
Preparation time 10 minutes
Cooking time 2 minutes

✔ 263 Kcal per serving
✔ Low in salt

2 tbsp walnut oil
175g walnut halves
3 clementines
85g rocket leaves
85g watercress
3 tbsp balsamic vinegar
Salt and black pepper

■ Heat half the oil in a frying pan; cook the walnuts over a medium heat for 1-2 minutes until lightly toasted. Do not turn your back on these walnuts – if you overcook them they will taste bitter and also will burn very easily.
■ Peel the clementines, removing all the pith, and slice. Collect all the juice and place in a little bowl.
■ Place the watercress, rocket and clementine slices into a bowl with the warmed walnuts; toss together, cover dish until required.
■ Whisk the remaining oil with the reserved juice and balsamic vinegar. Season and drizzle and toss over the salad just before serving.

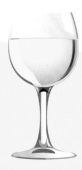

The citrus fruit in this salad calls for a zingy Sauvignon Blanc from Chile. Grassy and herbal, very intense and wonderfully refreshing.

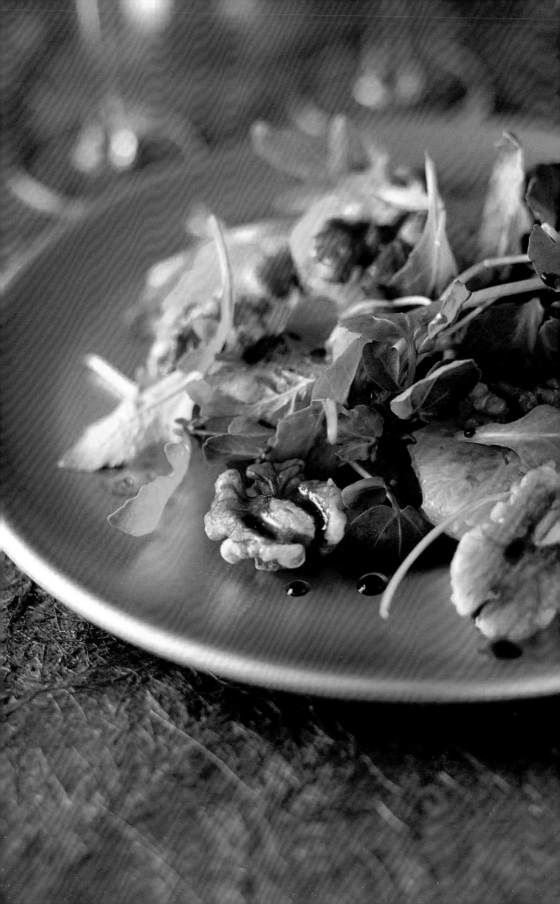

Red Pepper Houmous with Crudités

Houmous is simple, delicious, cheap and healthy. Adding chopped up red peppers gives it extra sweetness and crunch. Serve with griddled pitta or a selection of vegetable crudités.

Serves 4
Preparation time 12 minutes
Cooking time 15 minutes

✔ 158 Kcal per serving
✔ Low in fat

2 red peppers, halved and deseeded

2 garlic cloves, crushed
1 x 400g can chick peas, drained
Juice of 1 lime
125ml very low-fat or fat-free fromage frais
1 tbsp fresh coriander, chopped
Sea salt
Black pepper

- Preheat the grill to a high heat. Place the red peppers under the grill and cook until the skins are blistered and beginning to char.
- Remove from the grill and place the peppers in a polythene bag until cooled. When cool enough to handle, peel off the skins and roughly chop the flesh.
- Place the red peppers in a food processor with the garlic, chick peas and lime juice. Whiz into a slightly rough mix. Stir in the fromage frais and coriander until well blended and season to taste with a little salt and fresh black pepper.

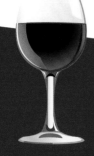

Juicy red fruits and lively acidity combine in the young red wines from Valencia in Spain, perfect with the roasted peppers in this dish.

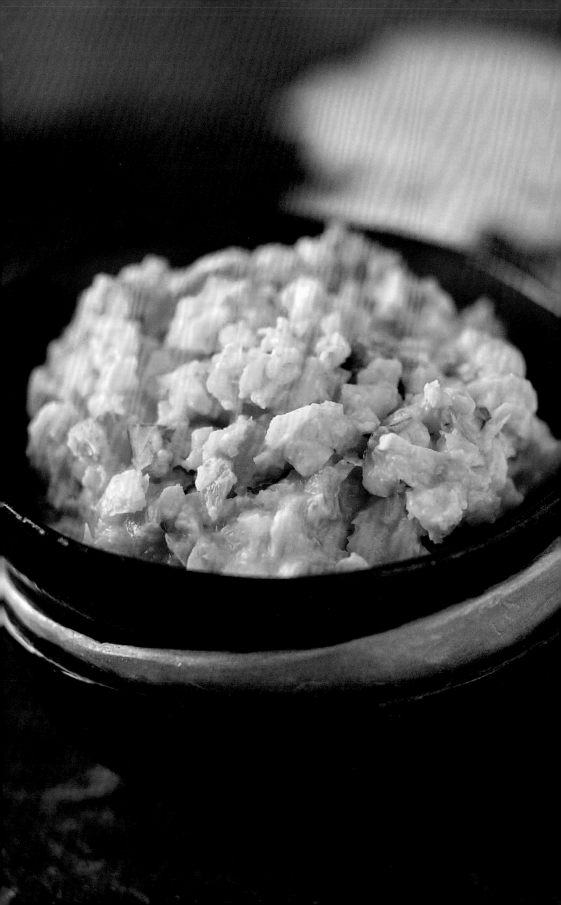

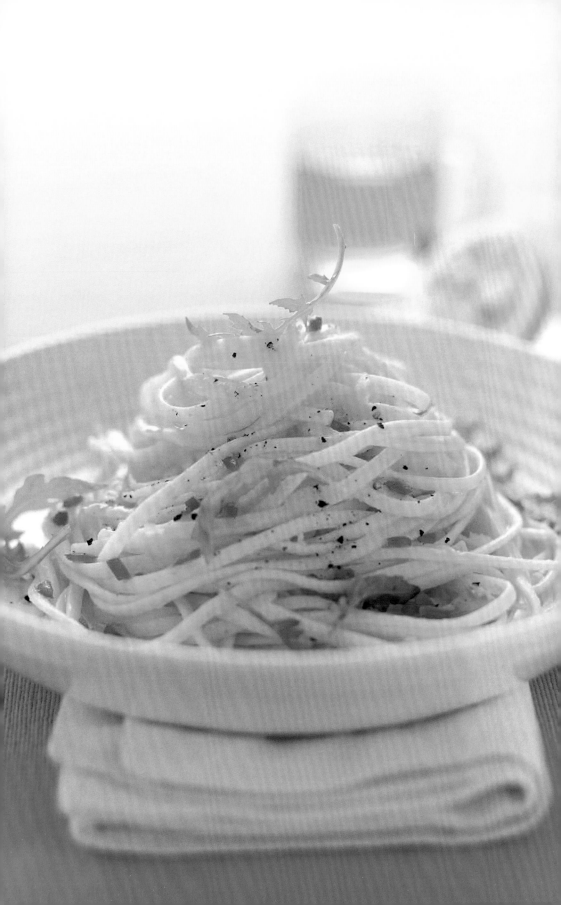

Pasta and rice

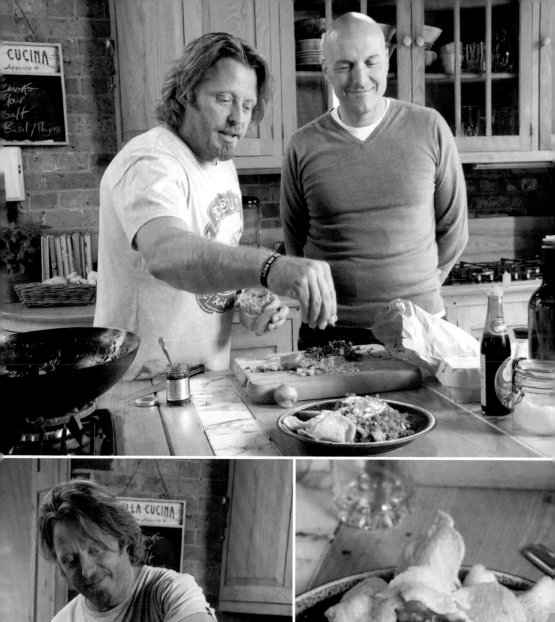

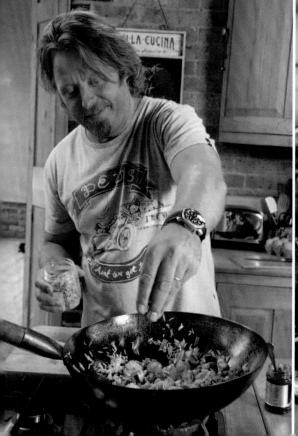

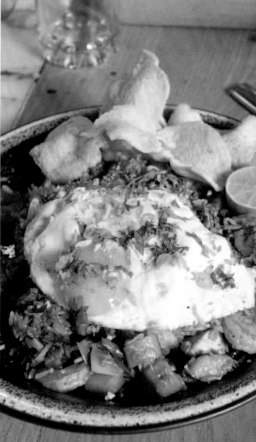

"In this recipe you can use any leftover meat or vegetables depending on what you have in your fridge. If you don't have Indonesian soy sauce, Chinese works just as well. I especially like adding the fried egg on top of the rice."

Charley Boorman

Travel writer, actor and adventurer, Charley walked into Simon's kitchen with his crash helmet still on, and admitted that he doesn't do much cooking. Best known for his motorcycle trips around the world, from London to New York via Europe and Asia with Ewan McGregor, and more recently from Sydney, Australia up the coast to New South Wales where he was joined by an enormous cavalcade of other motorbikes, Charley likes to keep meals quick and simple. That's not surprising when 1,500 other bikers might drop by for supper.

What Charley loves about this dish is that it's a real traveller's supper, adaptable to local ingredients and leftovers. He can keep the key ingredients in his bike panniers, and then just add hot water to bring the rice to the boil. If that's too complicated (and sometimes on his travels it's even too difficult to get water boiling), Charley will use ready-cooked rice. A good tip for anyone who wants a meal in a moment, topped with a fried egg!

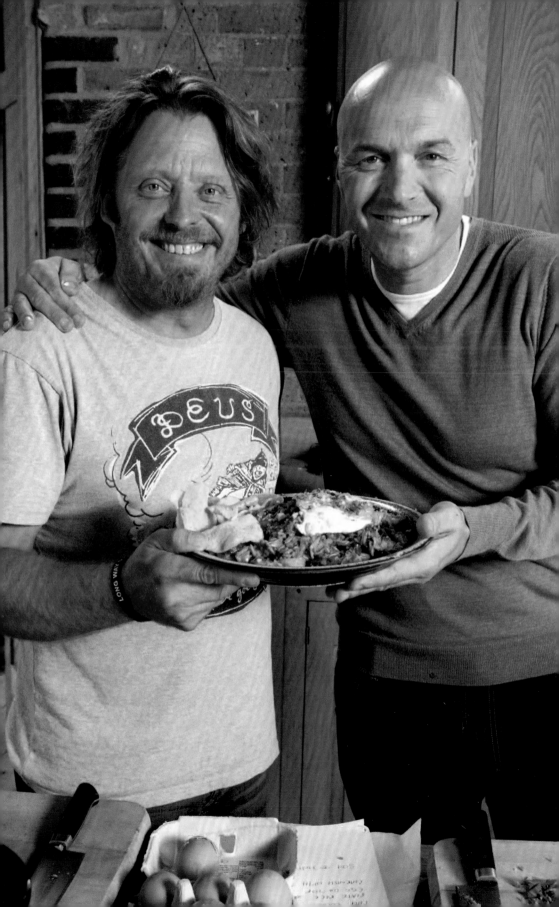

Charley Boorman – Indonesian Style Fried Rice (Nasi Goreng)

Charley learned this dish on his travels and it became one of his favourites. It's quick, adaptable and delicious – if you don't want to make a spice paste, a few spoons of curry paste work just as well.

Serves 4
Preparation time 10 minutes
Cooking time 10 minutes

✔ 486 Kcal per serving
✔ Low in sugar

2 tbsp vegetable oil
2 skinless chicken breasts, sliced into strips
2 tbsp medium hot curry paste
300g cooked rice

200g prawns, shelled and deveined
4 spring onions, sliced
½ cucumber, peeled and diced
A handful of fresh coriander, roughly chopped
4 eggs
75g peanuts, chopped
Lime wedges to serve
A handful of crispy shallots
Soy sauce
Kecap manis (a thick sweet Indonesian soy sauce), to serve (optional)

■ Heat the oil in a wok until almost smoking, add the chicken and fry for a few minutes until cooked through, then add the curry paste and stir well. Add the prawns and spring onions and fry for another minute.
■ Add the cooked rice and stir until it's all incorporated – you can add a few tablespoons of water at this point if it becomes a little dry and starts to stick.
■ Meanwhile prepare the cucumber, coriander, peanuts and lime wedges and fry the 4 eggs.
■ Sprinkle a handful of the crispy shallots into the rice along with a dash of soy and kecap manis if you are using and stir. When everything is heated through you are ready to serve.
■ Divide the nasi goreng between 4 bowls, top with the egg, shallots, cucumber , a lime wedge and peanuts.

Hot Three Tomato Pasta Frills

Tangy tomatoey sweetness and fiery chilli give this Italian-inspired dish an interesting kick.

Serves 4
Preparation time 4 minutes
Cooking time 12 minutes

✓ 320 Kcal per serving
✓ Reduced salt

2 tbsp olive oil
1 clove garlic, finely chopped

1 red chilli pepper, deseeded and finely chopped
1 sprig fresh thyme
450g tomatoes, skinned and quartered
50g sun-blushed tomatoes, drained
250g pasta
350g cherry tomatoes
Black pepper

■ Preheat the oven to 220˚C/425˚F/Gas Mark 7. Heat half the olive oil in a pan and gently cook the garlic and chilli for 2-3 minutes until soft, but not coloured.
■ Add the thyme and skinned tomatoes to the pan. Heat gently and simmer uncovered, for about 10 minutes until the tomatoes are reduced to a fairly thick sauce. Stir in the sun-blushed tomatoes. Meanwhile, cook the pasta according to pack instructions.
■ Put the cherry tomatoes in a roasting tin and drizzle with the remaining olive oil.
■ Shake the pan so the tomatoes are evenly covered. Roast the tomatoes in the oven for 6-7 minutes or until they start to split.
■ Drain the pasta and stir in the tomato sauce. Divide between four plates then gently fold in the roasted tomatoes. Serve immediately.

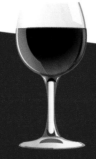

Tomatoes call for wines with structure, so try a Valpolicella from the north of Italy, with waves of cherry and eucalyptus flavours rounded off with a hint of nutmeg.

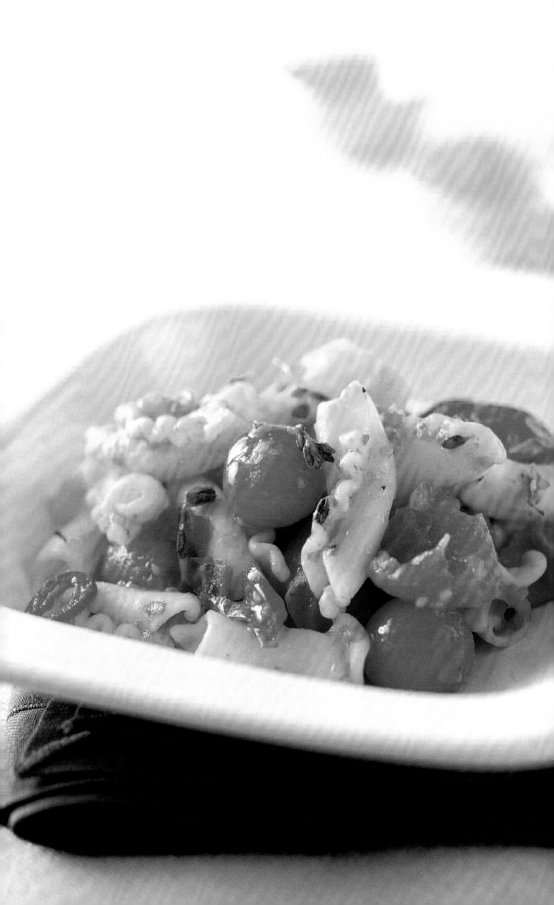

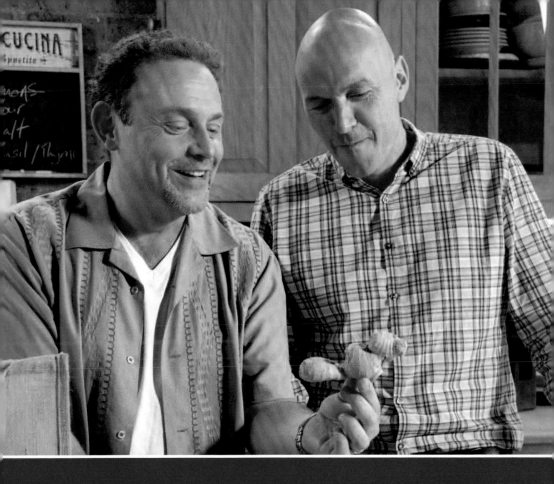

"When I was 21, my Mum and Dad said 'What do you want to eat?' and I said 'Thai'. My Dad said 'Have you had it before?' and I said 'No... but I'm going to!' And now Thai is my favourite food!"

John Thomson

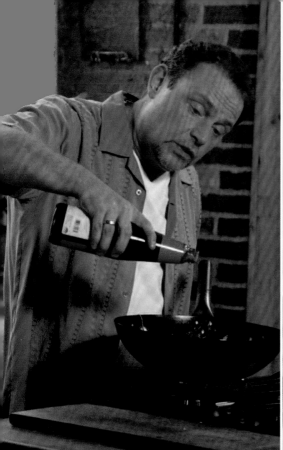
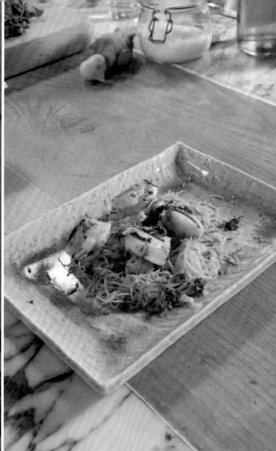

Comedian John Thomson has always loved to cook, and usually finds something to laugh at in the kitchen – just look at the shape of this piece of ginger... what does it remind you of?

Probably best remembered for his portrayal of Pete Gifford in Cold Feet, for which he was nominated Best Actor at the Comedy Awards, John has enjoyed twenty years of success in film, theatre and radio. He's pretty successful in the kitchen too, and is a big fan of all-in-one dishes. This dish is his wife's absolute favourite, and one he created himself – he says the scallops are the star so all the other flavours should complement them.

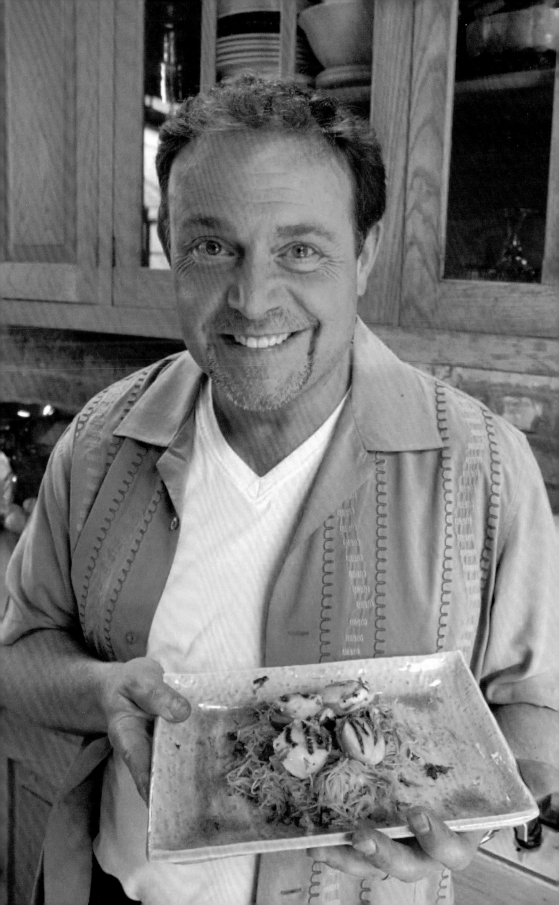

John Thomson – Seared Scallops with Ginger and Spring Onion Vermicelli Noodles

The secret of this dish is the oyster sauce, which brings all the other flavours together. John uses fresh vermicelli rice noodles, though he says that dried are fine if that's what you have in your cupboard.

Serves 2
Preparation time 5 minutes
Cooking time 6 minutes

✔ 405 Kcal per serving
✔ Low in fat

8 scallops, removed from shell and cleaned
6 tiger prawns, shelled, deveined and diced
Groundnut oil for frying

300g cooked rice vermicelli noodles
6 spring onions
1 thumb size piece of fresh ginger, peeled and finely diced
1 clove of garlic, peeled and finely diced
1 red chilli, diced
2 tbsp dark oyster sauce
A small bunch of coriander, finely chopped
Sea salt and freshly ground black pepper

■ Heat a griddle and a wok over high heat, pour a little oil in the wok and then add the ginger, garlic and chillies and cook for a minute.
■ Add the spring onions and prawns and stir well then add the noodles, tossing all the time, finally add the oyster sauce and toss again until all coated well.
■ Put the scallops in a bowl and coat with oil – place on the hot griddle and cook for a minute each side – no longer.
■ Serve the scallops on top of the noodles, garnish with the coriander and season if required.

Sweet Jewelled Rice

A semi-sweet salad with a Moroccan twist. Serve on its own or as a fragrant accompaniment to a spicy lamb dish.

Serves 6
Preparation time 8 minutes
Cooking time 28 minutes

✔ 499 Kcal per serving
✔ Reduced salt

500g brown rice
Seeds of 1 pomegranate

50g dried cherries
50g dried cranberries
50g dried apricots
50g sultanas
4 tbsp orange juice
2 tbsp rose water
2 tbsp fresh mint, chopped
100g flaked almonds nuts, chopped

■ Combine the orange juice and rose water. Add the cherries, cranberries, apricots and sultanas and mix together well.
■ Bring a large pan of water to the boil. Stir in the rice. Return to the boil and stir well, cover and lower the heat to a fast simmer. Cook for 25 minutes. Drain well and leave to cool.
■ Add the dried fruit, the pomegranate and all of the liquid to the rice, and mix thoroughly. Just before serving, add the mint and almonds, then toss and serve.

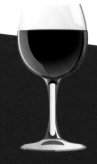

A chunky red from Italy, such as a Montepulciano d'Abruzzo, with lively redcurrant fruit and a firm backbone is a great combination with the sweetness in this recipe.

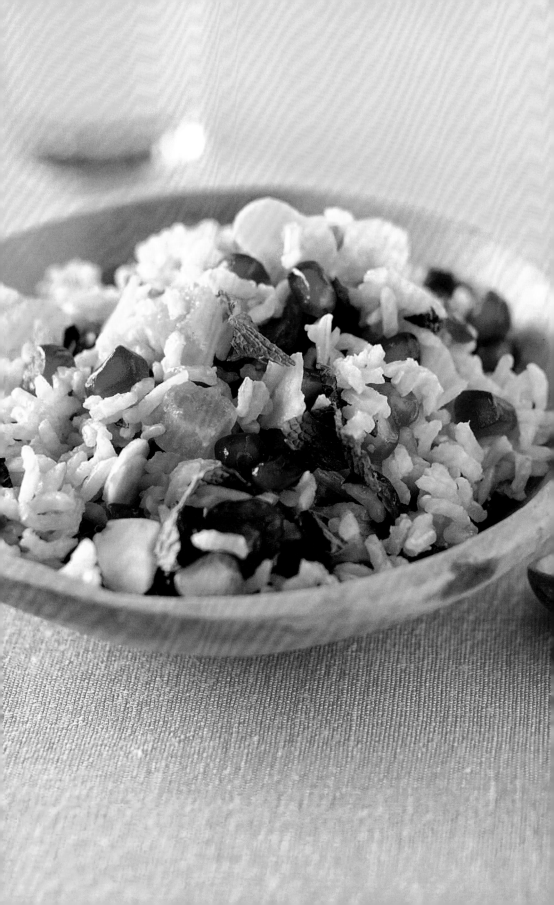

Large Pasta Shells with Walnut Pesto

Many stores sell these over-sized pasta shapes. But if you can't find them, you can use any regular pasta.

Serves 4
Preparation time 10 minutes
Cooking time 15 minutes

✔ 278 Kcal per serving
✔ Reduced salt
✔ Low in sugar

1 large bunch parsley
Handful of thyme sprigs
Handful of mint leaves
1 clove garlic, diced
2 lemons, zest finely grated
50g walnut halves
6 tbsp walnut oil
Salt and freshly ground black pepper
20 large pasta shells

■ Strip the parsley leaves from their stems and place in a food processor.
■ Add the thyme and mint leaves. Whizz until finely chopped, then add the garlic, lemon zest and walnuts and process in quick bursts until they are roughly chopped.
■ Continue to process and add the oil a tablespoon at a time until you get a thick paste consistency. This paste can be kept in the fridge for a few days.
■ Bring a large pan of water to a rolling boil.
■ Add the pasta shells and cook as per pack instructions. Drain, reserving some of the cooking liquor. Return to the pan and add the walnut pesto and toss. Serve immediately.

See picture on page 63

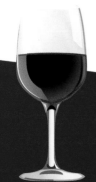

Ideal with a chunky southern Italian red such as a Nero d'Avola from Sicily. Packed with sunshine ripened dark plummy fruit.

Rocket and Chilli Linguine

This is a delicate pasta dish, ideal if you are not a fan of heavier cream sauces.

Serves 2
Preparation time 4 minutes
Cooking time 13 minutes

✔ 309 Kcal per serving
✔ Reduced salt
✔ Low in sugar

175g linguine
1 tbsp olive oil
1 red chilli, deseeded and sliced
2 garlic cloves, crushed
Finely grated zest and juice of 1 lemon
1 small packet wild rocket leaves, roughly chopped
Handful of basil leaves
Salt and black pepper

■ Bring a large pan of salted water to a rolling boil and add the linguine. Boil for about 10 minutes (check the pack for exact time) or until the pasta is just tender but still retains some 'bite' (al dente). Drain well.
■ Heat the oil in a large pan and add the chilli, garlic and lemon zest.
■ Cook for 1 minute without colouring the garlic. Add the lemon juice, rocket and basil.
■ Toss lightly for 1-2 minutes to heat through and allow the leaves to wilt.
■ Stir in the drained pasta and season to taste. Serve immediately on its own or with grilled fish.

See picture on page 62

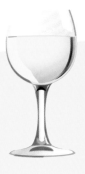

Go for a classic white burgundy from the Chardonnay grape. Elegance and subtle apple flavours with a firm backbone are ideal with the pepperiness of the rocket.

Risotto Bianco

This is the classic risotto and its simplicity is still hard to beat.

Serves 4
Preparation time 6 minutes
Cooking time 28 minutes

✔ 447 Kcal per serving
✔ Low in sugar

25g butter
1 tbsp olive oil
1 onion, finely chopped
325g risotto rice
150ml dry white wine
900ml hot stock
Salt and coarse ground black pepper
25g Parmesan cheese, shaved

■ Heat the butter and oil in a wide shallow saucepan. Cook the onion for about 5 minutes, until it is soft and golden. Add the rice and stir over the heat for a further 2-3 minutes.

■ Pour in the wine and cook over a high heat, stirring, until it has been absorbed.

■ Keep the stock hot. Add one-third of the hot stock. Cook until the stock has been absorbed, stirring constantly.

■ Add another one-third of the stock and cook until the stock has been absorbed, stirring constantly.

■ Add the last one-third of the stock and continue to cook until the stock has been absorbed, stirring constantly. This will take about 20 minutes and the risotto should be quite wet and creamy.

■ Taste and season with salt and pepper. Serve topped with a sprinkling of Parmesan cheese.

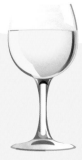

Use a good quality white to make this dish, and to drink with it. Try a crisp, aromatic white from the north of Italy, such as Pinot Grigio from the Veneto region. Floral and citrussy.

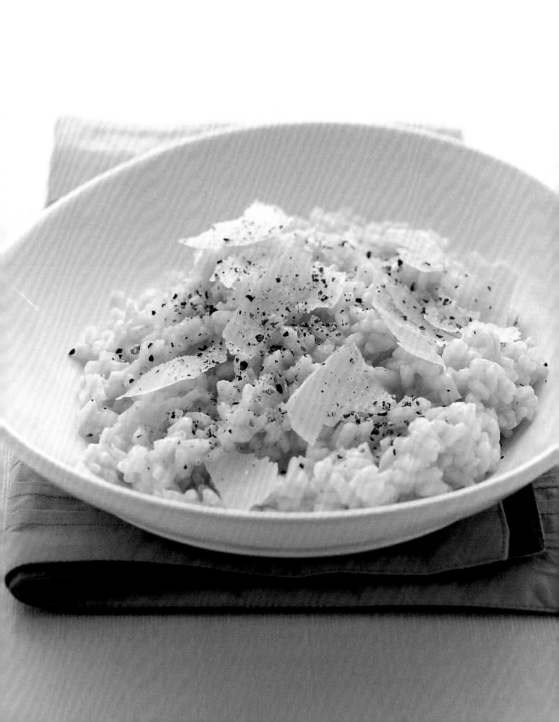

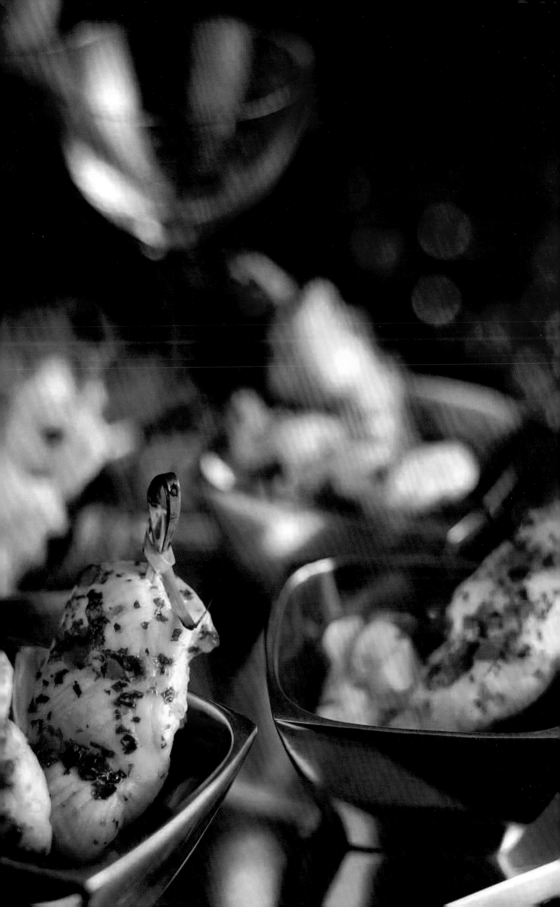

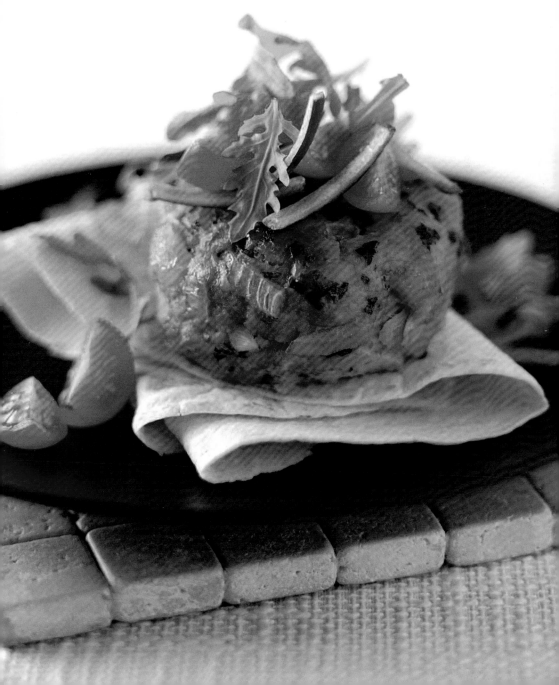

Main
courses

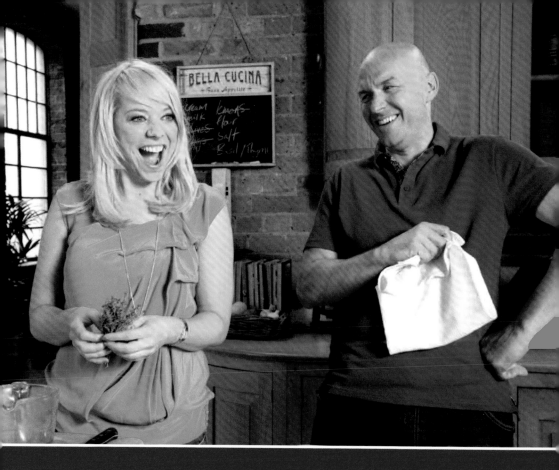

"I absolutely love red meat.
This is a more simple version of
my usual Beef Wellington, so you
can easily cook it at home."

Liz McClarnon

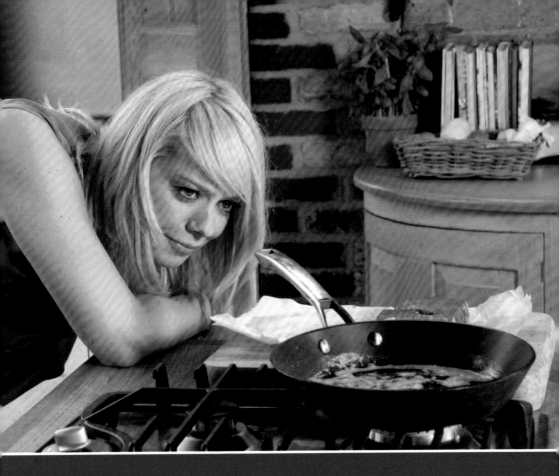

Liz, best known for being part of girl-band Atomic Kitten, has travelled the globe on sell-out tours, eating in the world's finest exotic restaurants, but when the chips are down, her vote is for classic English food like Beef Wellington. She used to be a nervous cook, and confessed to Simon that until she won Masterchef she was absolutely terrified of using the oven. That cheeky grin of hers reveals that this is rather a naughty dish – Liz used to have a high cholesterol level and had to get her mum to hypnotise her to stop eating crisps, but by being strong-willed about high-fat nibbles she can indulge herself now and again in her favourite meals.

This is a celebration dish rather than for everyday, but we all deserve a treat, and it's just the kind of dinner to cook for an intimate night in. With a rich velvety red wine to go with it, your dinner guest will be purring!

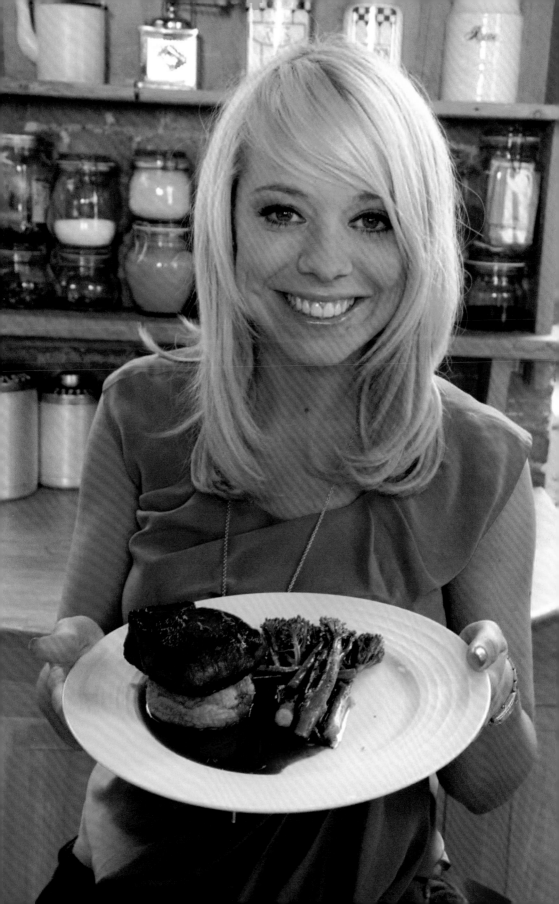

Liz McClarnon – Simple Beef Wellington

Because it's far less involved than a classic Beef Wellington, you can fool your dinner guest into thinking you have been slaving away in the kitchen for hours.

Serves 2
Preparation time 10 minutes
Cooking time 15 minutes

✔ 485 Kcal per serving

2-3 tbsp olive oil
2 cloves garlic finely chopped
1 shallot finely chopped

1 tbsp fresh parsley chopped
125ml port
1 beef stock cube
150g puff pastry sheets (pre-rolled)
125g button mushrooms finely sliced
2 x 175g medallions of beef fillet
Few sprigs thyme and rosemary
Freshly ground salt and pepper
A dash of truffle oil (optional)

■ Preheat the oven to 200°C/400°F/Gas Mark 6.
■ Heat 1 tablespoon of olive oil in a small pan on a medium heat, add the garlic and shallot then cook for 1-2 minutes until soft and golden. Add half of the parsley and port and boil until the liquid has reduced by half (this will look a little syrupy).
■ Use a saucer to cut out two circles of pastry and lay on a non-stick tray. Bake in the oven for 12 minutes.
■ Dissolve the stock cube in ½ pint of boiling water and add to the pan with the remaining port. Gently leave to simmer whilst preparing the rest of the dish.
■ Heat the butter in a small frying pan until just melted, add the mushrooms, season with salt and pepper. Then cook gently until slightly soft in texture. Once cooked add a drizzle of truffle or other flavoured oil and keep warm.
■ Place the remaining oil in a heavy ovenproof frying pan or skillet, heat until it's just about to smoke. Next, add the beef, allowing it to sear for 1-2 minutes. Season with salt and pepper, then turn the fillet over using a pair of tongs. Sear again for 1-2 minutes and season. Add the thyme and rosemary and place in the preheated oven for 6 minutes. Remove from the oven and allow to rest for 5-10 minutes in a warm place.
■ To serve – Place the cooked pastry circles on two warm plates. Poke a hole in the centre and fill the pastry with the warm mushroom mixture. Place the steak on the pastry and pour over the sauce. Serve with seasonal vegetables.

Lamb and Mint Koftas

Make large koftas and serve them as a main course, or smaller ones to enjoy as part of a mezze.

Serves 4
Preparation time 38 minutes
Cooking time 15 minutes

✔ 256 Kcal per serving
✔ Reduced salt
✔ Low in sugar

500g very lean minced
British lamb
1 small onion, finely chopped
2 cloves of garlic, finely chopped
1 tsp ground coriander
3 tbsp fresh mint, finely chopped
Salt and freshly ground black pepper
12 wooden skewers soaked in water

■ Place the lamb in a bowl and mix with the onion, garlic, coriander, mint and seasoning until well combined.
■ Divide the mixture into 12 portions and shape them around the wooden skewers forming a sausage shape. If time allows leave to rest in the fridge for 30 minutes.
■ Preheat the grill.
■ Place the koftas onto the grill rack over the grill pan. Cook for 15 minutes, turning regularly until thoroughly cooked, the juices run clear and there is no pink meat.
■ Serve with tzatziki and pitta bread.

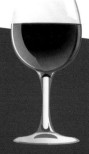

Matching wines with mint can be difficult, but a vibrant, blackberry packed Shiraz Cabernet from Australia should do the trick, with a hint of eucalyptus and menthol.

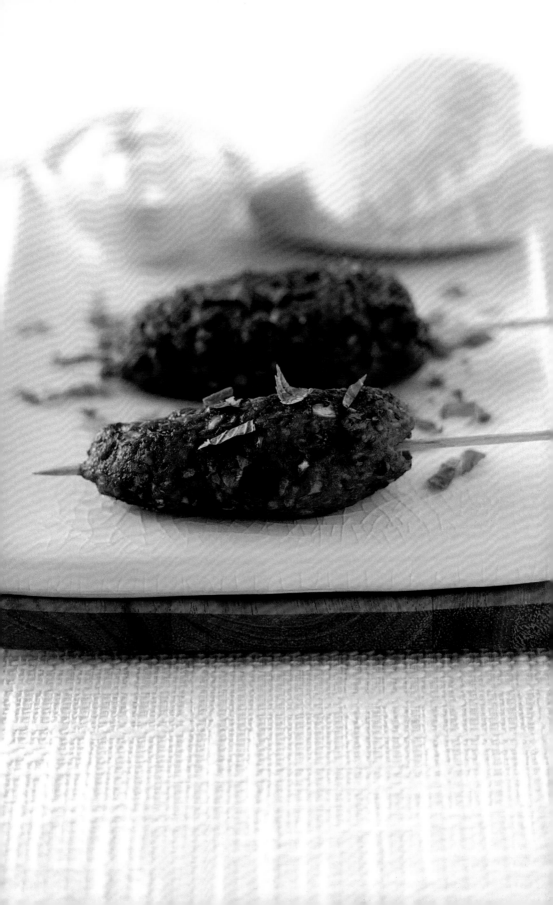

Creamy Squash Curry

Simple yet somehow decadent, with a richness beyond its ingredients.

Serves 4
Preparation time 8 minutes
Cooking time 16 minutes

✔ 180 Kcal per serving

2 tbsp sesame oil
3 tbsp curry paste
250ml low-fat coconut milk

400g spaghetti or butternut squash, peeled and diced
3 courgettes, sliced
150g whole unsalted cashews
400g baby spinach
Juice of 2 limes
Pinch of salt
A handful coriander, chopped

■ Heat the sesame oil in a large pan. Add the curry paste and cook until it starts to caramelise. Stir in the coconut milk and simmer for 1 minute.
■ Add the squash, courgettes and cashews and simmer for 15 minutes. Stir in the spinach, lime juice and salt. Cook for a minute.
■ Serve sprinkled with coriander alongside poppadoms.

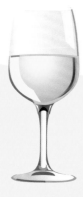

Mild and creamy curries work really well with aromatic white wines with structure – try a Viognier from Australia or the south of France. Rich yet fresh enough to balance the coconut milk.

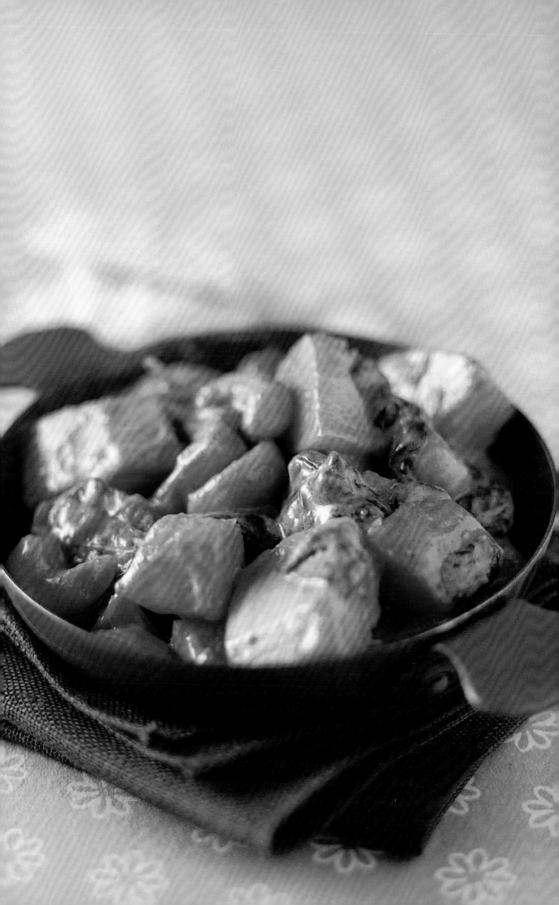

Cajun Pork with Pineapple Salsa

This spicy rub works with steak or salmon. If you like your food hot, don't hold back – go for the extra chillies!

Serves 4
Preparation time 35 minutes
Cooking time 6 minutes

✔ 289 Kcal per serving

4 British pork chops, trimmed
1 tsp sweet paprika
1 tsp crushed chillies
3 cloves garlic, crushed

½ tsp sea salt
1 romano (or an ordinary red) pepper, deseeded and finely diced
½ medium pineapple, peeled, cored and finely diced
¼ cucumber, finely diced
2 tbsp fresh coriander, finely chopped
2 tsp extra virgin olive oil
Rice to serve

■ Trim any excess fat from the pork. Mix together the paprika, chilli, garlic and salt and rub it all over the pork. Leave to stand for 30 minutes.
■ Mix together the pepper, pineapple, cucumber and coriander. Add the olive oil and leave the flavours to infuse.
■ Heat a griddle pan until smoking and cook the pork for 5-6 minutes each side or until thoroughly cooked.
■ Serve the pork with the salsa on a bed of rice.

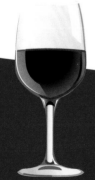

The strong spice of this dish requires a bold red, such as a Cabernet Sauvignon from Coonawarra in Australia. Rich, ripe blackcurrant fruit and black pepper combine in the intensity and layers of flavours.

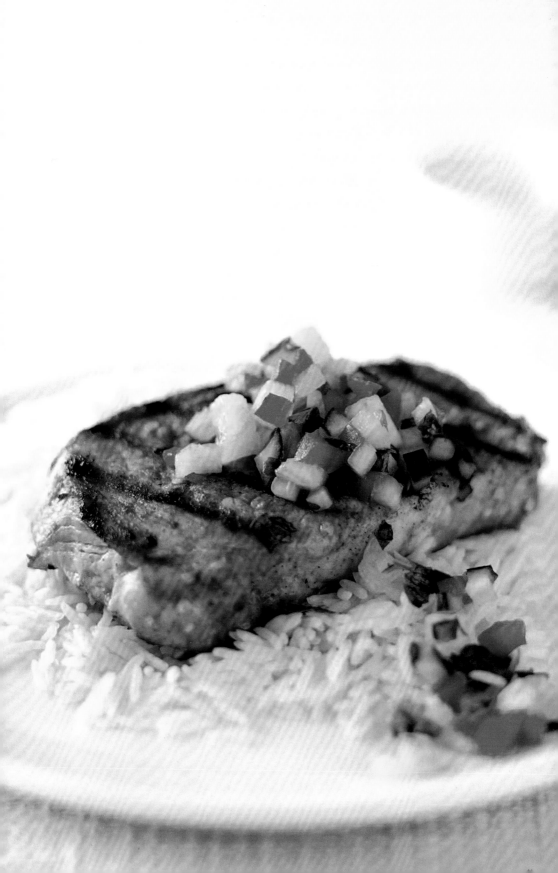

Stuffing Kebabs

A twist on the most important of all the turkey's trimmings.

Serves 6
Preparation time 15 minutes
Cooking time 30 minutes

✔ 616 Kcal per serving

1 tbsp oil
1 small onion
450g (1lb) pork sausage meat
125g dried apricots, roughly chopped
1 medium egg, beaten

50g shelled pistachios, chopped roughly
1 tsp dried thyme
1 tsp ground cinnamon
½ tsp ground nutmeg
¼ tsp ground cloves
1 small onion, chopped
12 rashers streaky bacon
12 chipolata sausages
Orange zest and thyme to garnish

■ Preheat the oven to 200 °C/400 °F/Gas Mark 6.
■ Cook the onion in 25g butter until softened. Set aside to cool.
■ Mix the remaining ingredients together with the onions.
■ Roll into walnut-sized balls and chill. Cut off the bacon rind and stretch each slice, using the back of a knife, before cutting it in half. Roll up half the bacon and wrap the remaining bacon round some of the chipolatas.
■ Place the bacon, stuffing balls and chipolatas onto a small skewer. Bake in the oven for 30 minutes or until cooked. Serve sprinkled with orange zest and thyme.

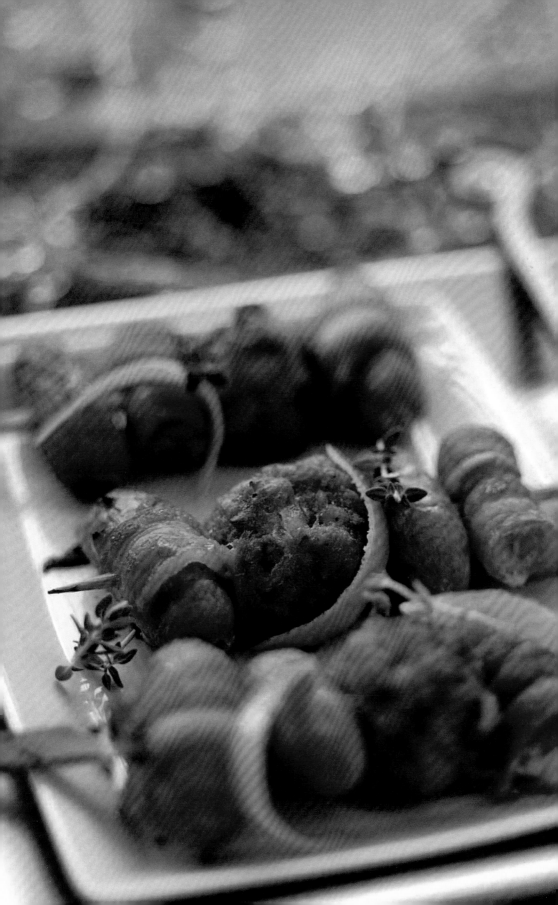

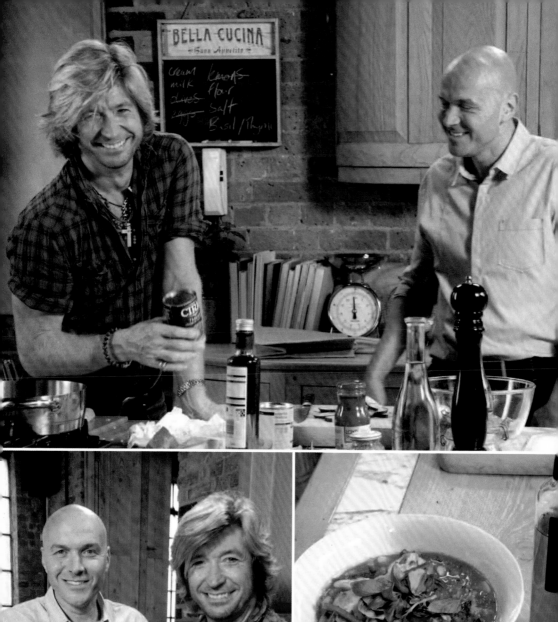

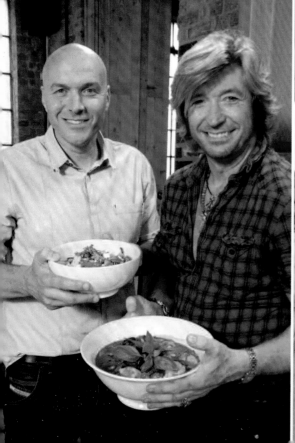

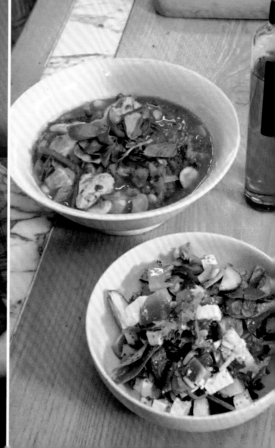

"Giving a dinner party, I always try to do the least amount of work. I tend to do things that I can put into a big pot and maybe even cook the day before."

Nicky Clarke

As personal stylist to movie stars, pop icons and princesses, Nicky Clarke is one of Britain's most famous and trusted hairdressers. He won't reveal his clients' secrets, but he's happy to share his favourite dish for entertaining friends. The trick, he says, is to make it in advance and reheat it on the day, so you can spend as much time as possible with your guests – they've come to see you as well as admire your culinary skills! So don't be shy about accepting a helping hand by using a bought sauce – Nicky certainly isn't averse to making life easier in the kitchen, as there are some amazing quality ready-made sauces on the shelves these days.

Here's a useful tip – cooking in a hot kitchen can make your hair go flat. Luckily a fan was at hand in Simon's kichen to cool them both down and to blow back Nicky's hair into a soft windswept style!

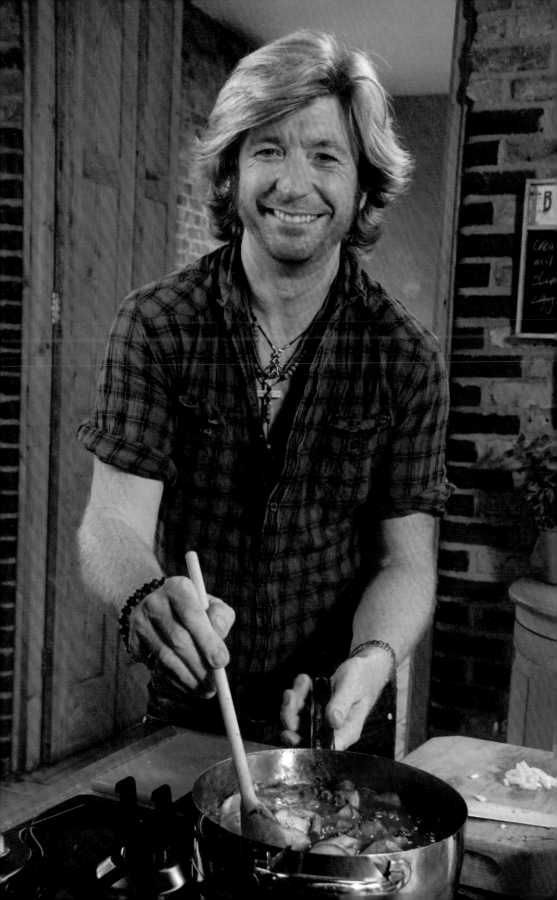

Nicky Clarke – Mediterranean Chicken Stew

Nicky's ideal is to make up a big main dish and serve it so everyone can help themselves. That gives him time to make an effort with the presentation and surroundings, which are equally important to him.

Serves 4
Preparation time 10 minutes
Cooking time 25 minutes

✔ 559 Kcal per serving
✔ Low in sugar

4 chicken breasts
1 clove garlic, peeled and finely chopped
1 onion, sliced
Oil for frying
A selection of herbs (thyme, bay, rosemary, oregano)

1 tin chopped tomatoes
1 jar of ready-made tomato sauce
1 tin of butterbeans, rinsed and drained
200g selection of garden vegetables
Greek olive oil
1 bag of mixed salad leaves
¼ cucumber
1 green pepper
A handful of pinenuts
100g feta cheese
A dash of white wine vinegar
Sea salt and freshly ground black pepper

■ Heat a wide-bottomed pan with a little oil and gently fry the garlic and onion for a few minutes. Slice the chicken breasts into two or three so they remain in large pieces and add to the pan, fry for a few minutes sealing all over.

■ Add whatever of the herbs you have to hand to the pan and fry for another minute.

■ Add the tomatoes and jar of tomato sauce and stir well, cover and cook for 10-15 minutes while you prepare the rest of the dish. Towards the end of cooking add the butterbeans and any garden veg you might like to use, cook for another few minutes until all the veg are cooked through.

■ For the salad, toast the pinenuts, and slice up the cucumber and peppers.

■ Toss with the leaves and crumble in the feta cheese and dress with a simple vinaigrette.

■ Serve the stew in a bowl alongside the salad.

Lamb Cutlets with Apricot and Aubergine Relish

Succulent lamb and juicy apricots complement each other nicely. For extra tang, add a chopped apple to the relish.

Serves 4
Preparation time 10 minutes
Cooking time 15 minutes

✔ 301 Kcal per serving
✔ Reduced salt

8 lamb chops, fat removed
Salt and freshly ground black pepper

1 tbsp olive oil
1 small red onion, chopped
1 aubergine, chopped
55g dried no-soak apricots, chopped
100ml white wine
Splash of white wine vinegar
1 tbsp mustard

■ Preheat the grill to a moderate heat. Cook the lamb chops for 5-6 minutes on each side. Season with salt and freshly ground pepper. Remove from the pan and keep warm.

■ Meanwhile, heat the olive oil in a heavy-based saucepan. Add the red onion and aubergine, and cook gently for 3-5 minutes, taking care not to let them colour.

■ Add the dried apricots, 100ml white wine and the white wine vinegar. Simmer gently until the wine has reduced.

■ Mix in the mustard and season with salt and freshly ground pepper. Place two chops on each plate and serve with the aubergine and apricot relish.

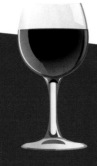

With spice from the Syrah grape, and deep dark fruit flavours of brambles from the Grenache, a classic Côtes du Rhône from the south of France is ideal with lamb.

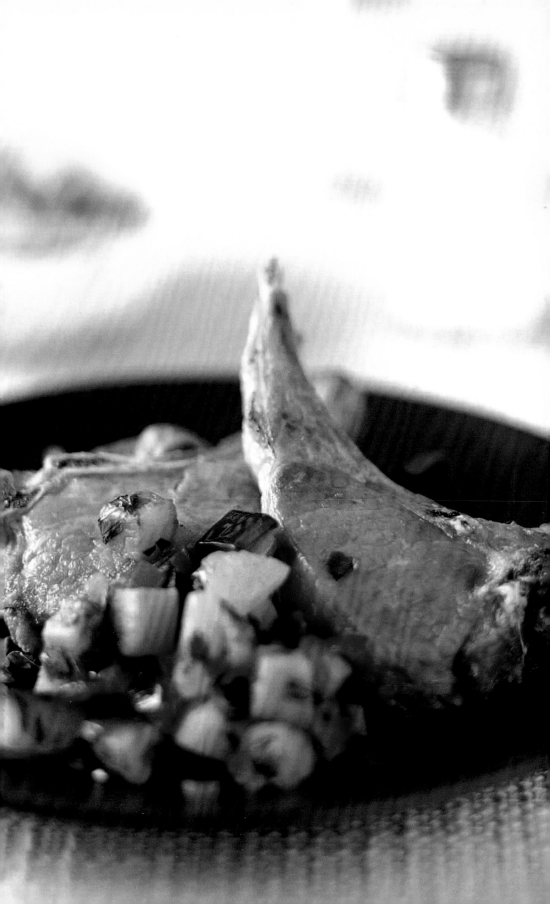

Mediterranean Roast Chicken

This all-in-one dish makes the most of all of the combined flavours and cuts down on washing-up!

Serves 4-6
Preparation time 10 minutes
Cooking time 40 minutes

✔ 335 Kcal per serving
✔ Low in sugar
✔ Reduced salt

1 medium whole British quality chicken
2 tbsp olive oil

Grated zest of 1 lemon
Sea salt and freshly ground black pepper
1 red pepper, deseeded and quartered
1 green pepper, deseeded and quartered
4 courgettes, cut into large chunks
4 tomatoes, halved lengthways
3 garlic cloves, halved
Fresh thyme, to garnish

- Preheat the oven to 190°C/375°F/Gas Mark 5.
- Place the chicken in a roasting pan and brush with a tablespoon of olive oil. Sprinkle over the lemon zest and season with the salt and pepper.
- Arrange the peppers, courgettes, and garlic around the edge. Drizzle the remaining oil over the vegetables and season well.
- Roast for 20 minutes per 500g, plus an extra 20 minutes. Serve the chicken surrounded with all the vegetables and garnished with thyme.

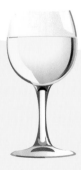

The flavours of the Mediterranean are perfectly matched by an aromatic white from southern Italy, such as a Grillo Chardonnay from Sicily. Brilliant with the herby flavours.

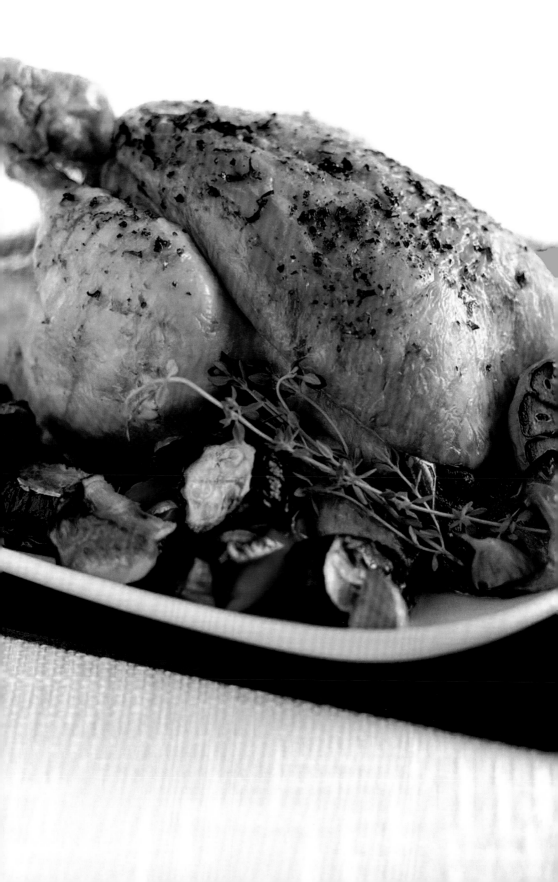

Turkey Satay Kebabs

Turkey can be bland on its own, but you can transform it into a wonderfully fragrant dish with some Thai flavours.

Serves 4 (makes 8)
Preparation time 30 minutes
Cooking time 15 minutes

✔ 376 Kcal per serving
✔ Reduced salt

500g pack turkey breast steaks, cubed

1 large mango, peeled and cut into chunks
1 red pepper, deseeded and cut into large bite-size chunks
2 tbsp organic crunchy peanut butter
100ml coconut cream
2 tsp red Thai curry paste
1 tbsp fish sauce
1 tsp soft brown sugar

■ Soak 8 wooden skewers in water for 30 minutes.
■ Thread the wooden skewers alternately with the turkey cubes, mango pieces and red pepper, then place a single layer in a shallow roasting tin.
■ To make the sauce, place all the remaining ingredients in a saucepan and heat gently, stirring to form a smooth sauce. Brush the sauce over the kebabs.
■ Preheat the grill.
■ Grill the kebabs for 10 minutes, turning often until golden brown and beginning to char at the edges. Check the turkey is cooked through.
■ Serve with a crisp green salad.

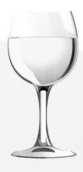

A crisp, grassy and asaparagus flavoured Sauvignon Blanc from New Zealand will be fresh and zingy in the mouth, and stand up to the strong flavours of the satay.

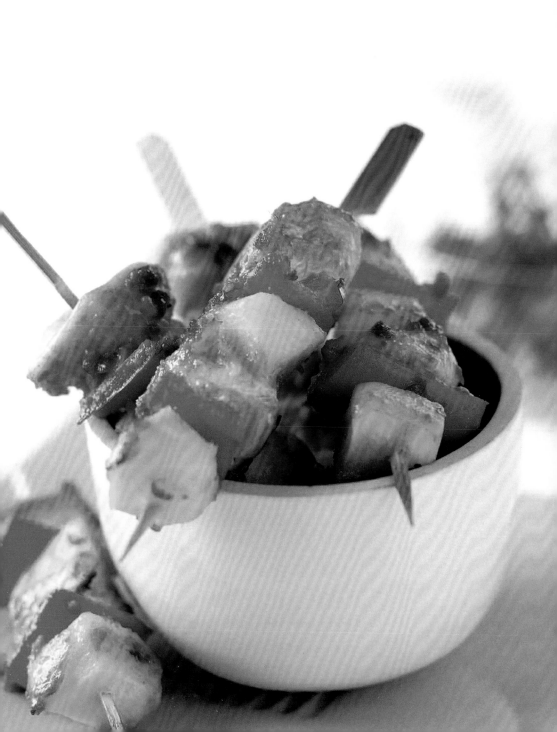

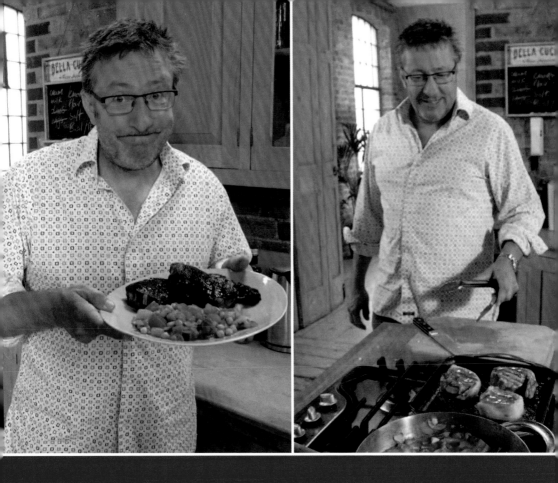

"I got the maple syrup idea when I visited Morocco where they combine meat and sweetness. Ever since then, I've liked it."

Rowland Rivron

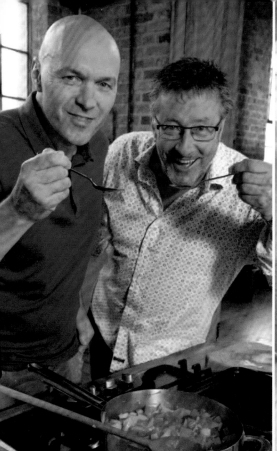
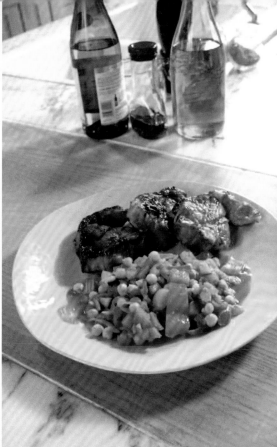

Oops! Why is it that with some people, you just know things are bound to go wrong? Writer, presenter, comedy actor and musician Rowland has built a whole career making us laugh at his mishaps, so it was no surprise that under pressure in the kitchen, he managed to set the grill temperature just slightly too high and burnt the outside of the maple-glazed lamb. But Simon was there to save the day with a less, er, crispy version!

Rowland's tasted delicious, though, and the burnt bits added that 'je ne sais quoi' – but his wife wouldn't have approved – she's a chef.

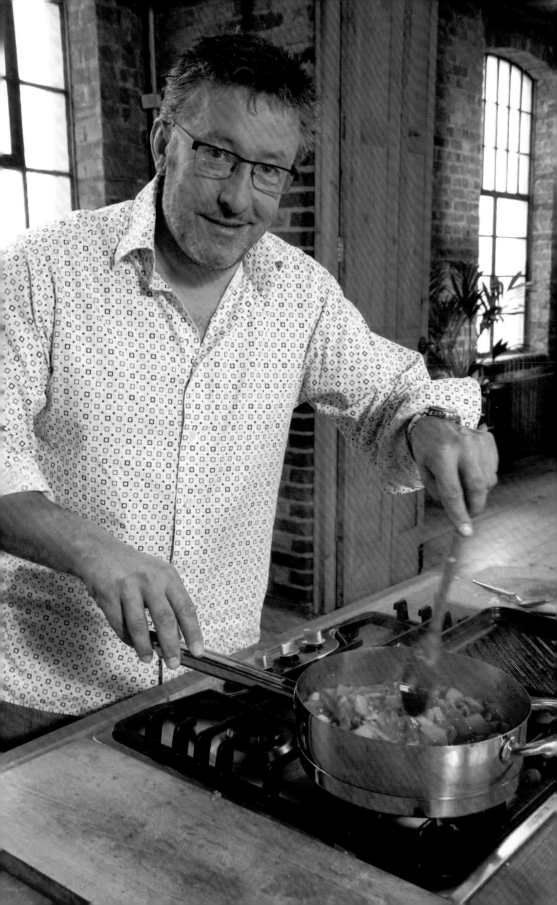

Rowland Rivron – Moroccan Lamb with Chickpea and Vegetable Stew

Rowland devised this recipe after a visit to Morocco where he thought the food was disappointing, so he did a bit of research and this is what he came up with.

Serves 4
Preparation time 10 minutes
Cooking time 25 minutes

✔ 1215 Kcal per serving
✔ Low in salt

Lamb chops, 3 per person
1 jar of maple syrup
Olive oil for frying
1 white onion, sliced
3 sticks of celery, diced
3 cloves garlic, finely diced

2 small red chillies, diced
250g baby tomatoes
1 courgette, diced
½ each red, yellow and green pepper
A good dash of white wine
300ml stock
A squeeze of tomato puree
1 tin chickpeas
A pinch each of ground cumin, coriander and paprika
1 pinch of saffron
Sea salt and freshly ground black pepper

■ Cover the lamb chops with the maple syrup, oil and a little seasoning and set aside.
■ Heat a wide base pan and fry the onion for a good 10 minutes – then add the garlic and spices, the chilli and the other vegetables, fry for a few minutes more then add the wine, tomatoes and tomato puree – leave this to simmer for 10 more minutes.
■ Meanwhile heat a frying pan till medium hot, add the lamb chops and cook turning frequently for 6-10 minutes depending on how well done you like them – be careful not to let them burn as the maple syrup colours quickly – simply reduce the heat if this happens.
■ Finally add the chickpeas to the stew and stir.
■ Serve with the lamb chops.

Chicken Saltimbocca

This dish is usually made with veal, but chicken or even turkey work equally well.

Serves 2
Preparation time 6 minutes
Cooking time 8 minutes

✔ 199 Kcal per serving
✔ Low in sugar

2 chicken skinless breasts
2 slices Parma ham
2 large sage leaves
2 slices lemon
Flour for dusting
2 tsp olive oil
Juice of ½ lemon
Salt and freshly ground black pepper

■ Put each chicken breast between 2 sheets of greaseproof paper and beat with a rolling pin until it is about 5mm thick.
■ Place a slice of Parma ham on each breast, top with a sage leaf and finally, a slice of lemon.
■ Secure with a cocktail stick and dust very lightly with flour on both sides.
■ Heat the olive oil in a large non-stick frying pan, and add the chicken.
■ Cook for 2-3 minutes on each side, until it is cooked and slightly golden brown.
■ Serve the chicken drizzled with a little lemon juice.

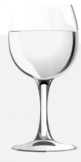

Wonderful mediterranean flavours call for a soft, aromatic white wine such as a Pinot Grigio from Italy. Fresh and enticing, with citrussy flavours to balance the parma ham and sage.

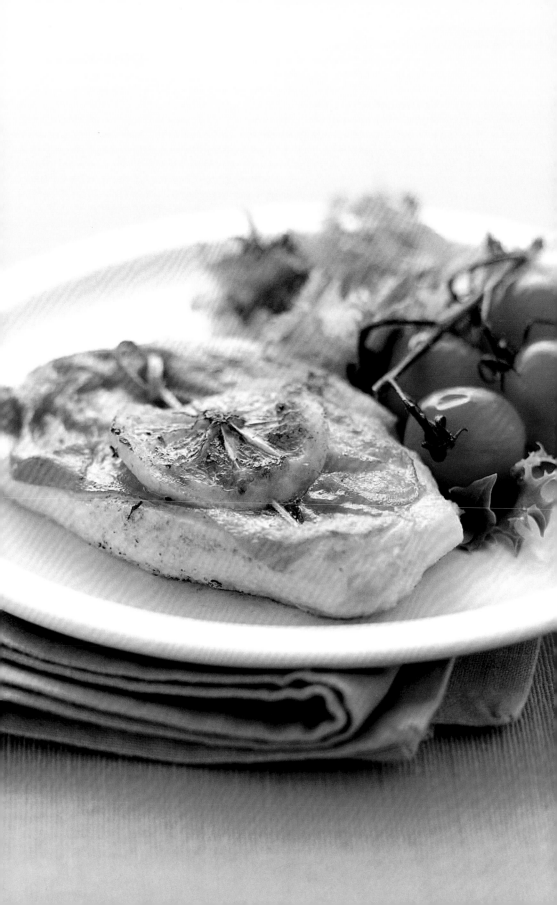

Fruity Turkey Burgers

These low-fat, fruity burgers are a dinner-time treat and will be an instant hit with the kids.

Serves 4
Preparation time 30 minutes
Cooking time 8 minutes

✔ 164 Kcal per serving
✔ Low in fat
✔ Reduced salt
✔ Low in sugar

125g ready-to-eat apricots, finely chopped
Grated zest and juice of ½ an orange
2.5cm piece fresh root ginger, peeled and grated
500g turkey breast mince
1 small red onion, finely chopped
15g fresh coriander, chopped
2 tsp oil, for brushing

■ Place the apricots in a small bowl and add the orange zest, orange juice and ginger. Stir, then leave to stand for 5 minutes.
■ In a large bowl, mix together the turkey mince, onion and coriander, then stir in the apricot mixture. Season, and mix well until all the ingredients are thoroughly combined. Divide the mixture into 4, and with wet hands, shape into burgers. If time allows chill for 20 minutes.
■ Preheat the grill.
■ Brush the burgers with the oil and cook for 6-8 minutes on each side until thoroughly cooked.
■ Serve with flour tortillas and a simple salad.

See picture on page 81

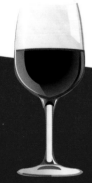

Try with a delightfully yummy Merlot from Chile, packed with flavours of plums and blackberries, easy and approachable.

Chicken Skewers with Dip

Perfect finger food, with the citrus zest of a snappy marinade.

Serves 10-12
Preparation time 5 minutes
Cooking time 25 minutes

✔ 149 Kcal per serving
✔ Low in salt
✔ Low in fat

6 chicken breasts, skinned and cut lengthways into four strips

For the marinade
50g coriander, chopped
3 limes, juice and zest grated
Dash of soy sauce

1 tsp grated ginger
1 tbsp honey
½ red chilli, de-seeded and finely chopped
Dash of vegetable oil

For the dip
150ml fromage frais
1 tbsp grated ginger
1 mango, finely chopped
1 handful coriander, chopped
Dash of sweet chilli sauce
1 lime, juice only
2 limes, zest only

■ Soak skewers in water for 6 hours if you are using bamboo.
■ Mix all the marinade ingredients together and marinate the pieces of chicken in the mix. Thread the chicken onto 24 short skewers. Cook under a preheated grill for 7-10 minutes turning frequently for even cooking.
■ To make the dip, mix all the ingredients together stirring the juices in lightly.

See picture on page 80

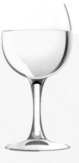

A big aromatic wine is needed to balance the spices in the dip, so try a Viognier from the south of France. Filled with peach and apricot flavours, yet crisp and clean.

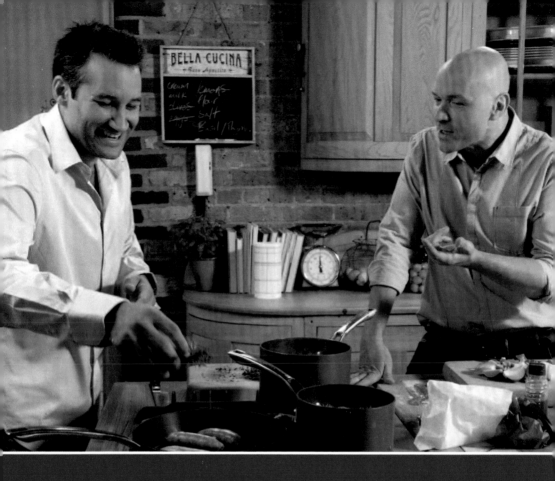

"My Nan got me into the whole Bubble and Squeak thing and ever since... I've loved it!"

Dane Bowers

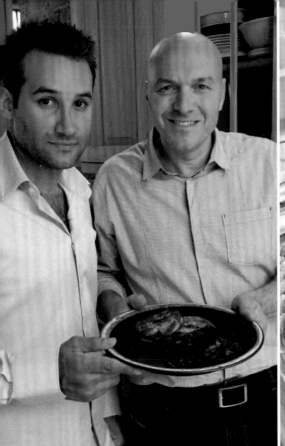
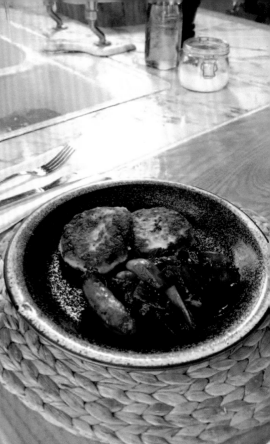

Celebrity DJ and former boy-band singer with Another Level, Dane Bowers has notched-up platinum-selling albums and singles. He went on to a solo music career which included the smash-hit duet 'Out Of Your Mind' with Victoria Beckham, which Dane also wrote, demonstrating his talents as a songwriter.

Now it's his turn to prove his talents in the kitchen. Dane had a somewhat chequered career at school, and while cooking with Simon he told the story of how he was expelled for taking his headmaster's car and driving it onto the school cricket pitch... why? Well, he was trying to impress a girl! Perhaps it would be safer and easier to impress with his cooking – this is a foolproof recipe that will have girlfriends, boyfriends, visiting aunties or kids clamouring for more.

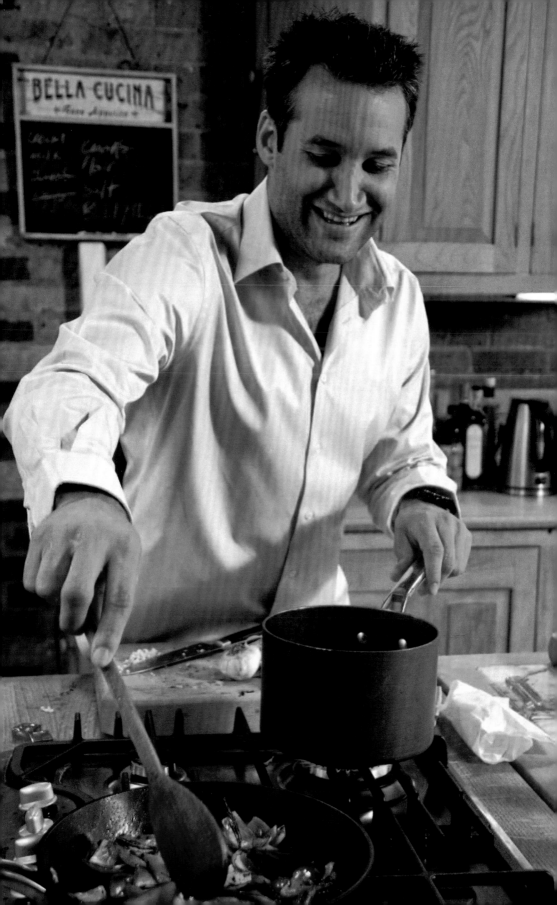

Dane Bowers – Bubble and Squeak Cakes with Sausages and Onion Gravy

Bubble and Squeak is a traditional British dish, which consists of potatoes and some type of green vegetable. With added sausages you can create a champion meal.

Serves 4
Preparation time 10 minutes
Cooking time 25 minutes

✔ 472 Kcal per serving

1kg floury potatoes
½ Savoy cabbage, shredded
1 clove garlic, crushed and finely chopped
A knob of butter
Oil for frying
8 sausages
A drizzle of runny honey
2 red onions
A sprig of thyme
A good slug red wine
250ml beef stock
Sea salt and freshly ground black pepper

■ Peel and boil the potatoes until just soft, drain well, roughly mash.
■ Place the sausages in a frying pan along with a little oil, fry over a medium heat for few minutes, slice the onions into wedges and add to the pan with a sprig of thyme – cooking together for a further 5-10 minutes until the sausages are golden.
■ When the sausages are cooked, remove from the pan and place on an oven tray – drizzle with a little honey and cook for a further 15 minutes in a medium oven.
■ Continue to fry the onions for 10 minutes until they are caramelized then deglaze with a little red wine and then reduce till almost disappeared, add the beef stock and simmer for a couple of minutes until starting to thicken. You can use a knob of butter or a little cornflour to thicken further if needed.
■ Cook the cabbage in boiling water for 3 minutes or until just tender. Drain thoroughly. Place the cabbage with the mashed potato in a large bowl, mix together and season well then shape into patties (alternatively you can use a chef ring) Fry in a little oil or butter for 4-5 minutes either side until golden brown and crisp.
■ Serve the sausages with the bubble and squeak cakes and pour over the onion gravy.

Normandy Chicken

A real belly-full of well-being, with rich flavours and a dash of je ne sais quoi.

Serves 4
Preparation time 6 minutes
Cooking time 28 minutes

✔ 372 Kcal per serving
✔ Reduced salt

4 chicken breasts

Salt and black pepper
Knob of butter
2 tbsp olive oil
2 pears, quartered, cored and sliced thickly
150g chestnut mushrooms, halved
90ml calvados or brandy
5 tbsp crème fraîche

■ Season the chicken with the salt and pepper. Heat the butter and half the oil in a large frying pan. Add the chicken and cook for about 10 minutes over a high heat until browned all over and partly cooked.
■ Remove and put to one side on the plate.
■ Heat the remaining oil, add the pears and cook for 1-2 minutes until browned. Remove and add to the plate with the chicken.
■ Add the mushrooms to the pan and cook over medium heat for about 4 minutes, stirring well, until lightly browned and slightly softened. Return the chicken and pears to the pan.
■ Pour in the calvados or brandy, ignite using a long match. When the flames have gone, add the crème fraîche, and stir until smooth and bubbling. Cook for a further 10-12 minutes until the chicken is cooked. Serve with vegetable of your choice.

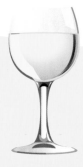

The creamy sauce and fresh apples marry well with a soft Chilean Chardonnay, full of melon and pear flavours, with a tropical twist.

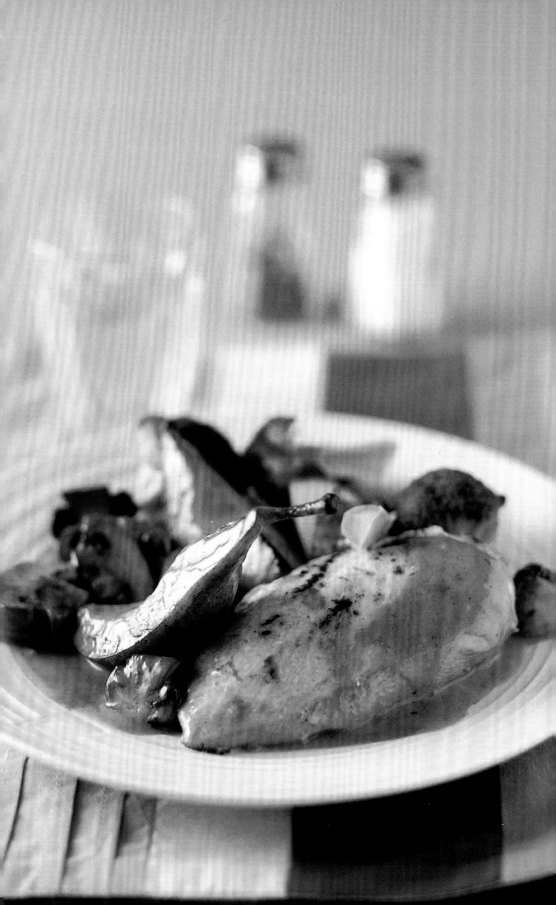

Creamy Turkey and Chickpea Stir fry

Turkey is surprisingly inexpensive and a low-fat meat, so good for the pocket and the waistline.

Serves 4
Preparation time 8 minutes
Cooking time 10 minutes

✔ 460 Kcal per serving
✔ Low in salt
✔ Low in fat

1 tbsp olive oil
285g turkey strips

6 spring onions, sliced
1 clove garlic, crushed
150g can chickpeas, drained
1 x 400g can chopped tomatoes
150g pot natural Greek yogurt
1 tbsp freshly chopped thyme, chives
or parsley
Salt and freshly ground black pepper
150g spinach leaves

■ Heat the oil in a large frying pan or wok. Add the turkey and stir-fry for 2-3 minutes.
■ Add the spring onions and garlic and cook for a further 1-2 minutes stirring frequently.
■ Stir in the chickpeas, tomatoes, yogurt, most of the herbs, and season. Add the spinach and cook for a further 3-4 minutes until thickened and smooth.
■ Serve immediately garnished with the remaining chopped herbs.

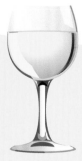

A crisp, dry, mouthwatering Sauvignon Blanc from Chile will balance the cream in this dish. Zingy and fresh, with a touch of herbs.

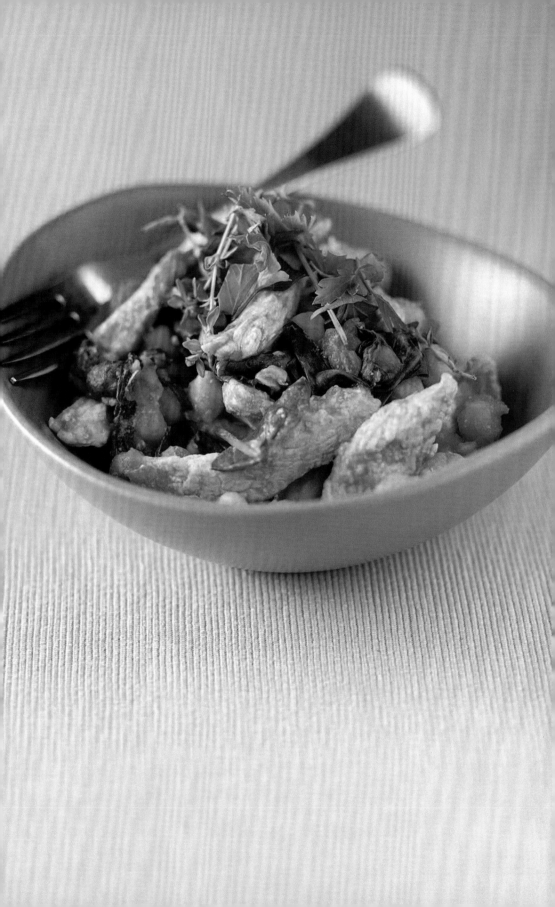

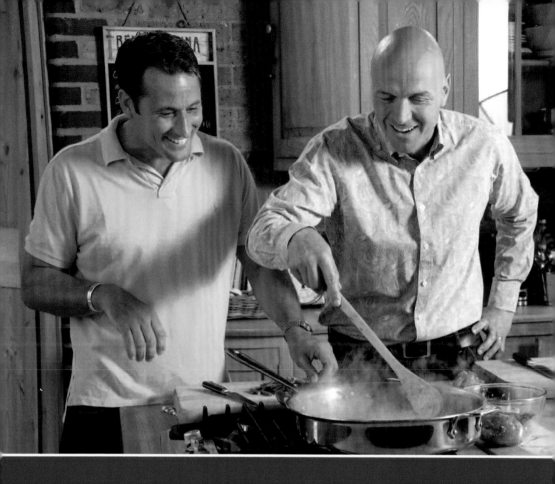

"I run the Hollyoaks football team, and when the lads come round after a match it's either curries or this paella."

Nick Pickard

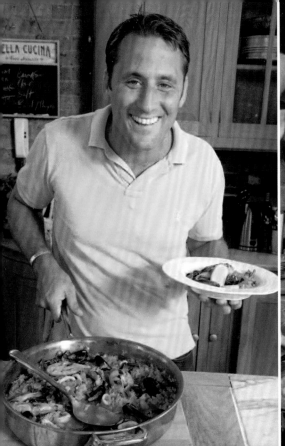
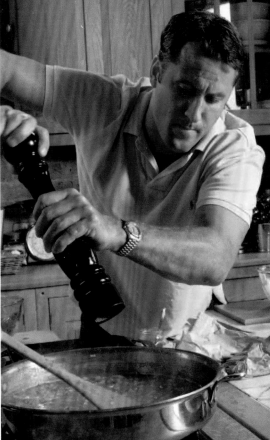

Best known for his role as Tony Hutchinson in Hollyoaks, Nick Pickard is the show's longest standing cast member. His half-brother in the soap, Dominic Reilly, is played by his brother in real life, John Pickard.

Nick knows his food, and he and Simon found plenty to chew over regarding the ups and downs of creating delicious meals in moments. For this recipe he used fresh fish, but agrees that it's just as good with frozen seafood out of the freezer cabinet in your local shop.

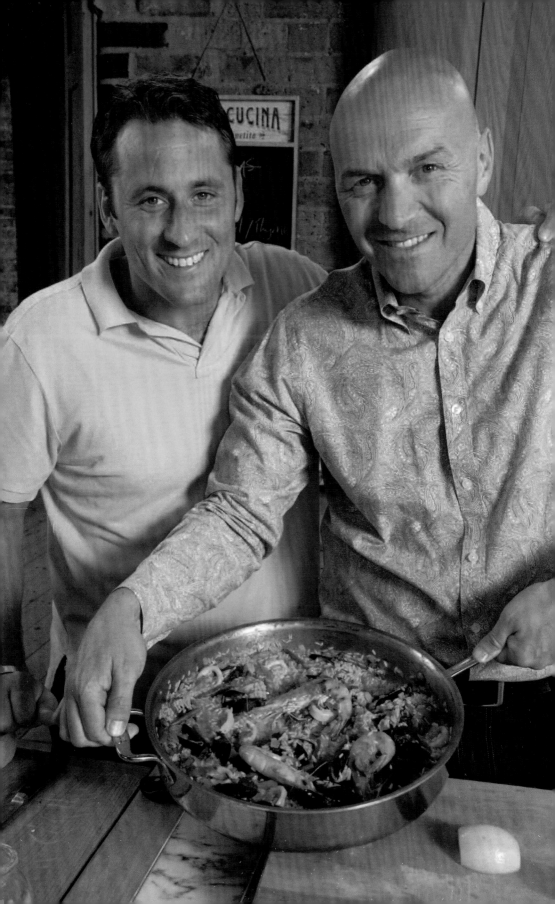

Nick Pickard – Seafood Paella

This is a great meal for a group of hungry guys. You might find they drop round more often when they know you are a great cook.

Serves 4
Preparation time 5 minutes
Cooking time 20 minutes

✔ 714 Kcal per serving
✔ Low in salt
✔ Low in fat

2 tbsp sunflower oil
1 large onion, finely chopped
1 red pepper, de-seeded and sliced
2 garlic cloves, finely chopped
400g can of chopped tomatoes

A good pinch of turmeric
500ml long grain rice
2 pints of veg stock
300g squid, cleaned and cut into rings
500g mussels in their shells
12 raw tiger prawns
200g green beans, halved
Sea salt and freshly ground black pepper
2 lemons, 1 cut into wedges, the other juiced
Bunch of flat leaf parsley, chopped

■ Heat the oil in a large-bottomed pan over a medium heat, add the onions and pepper and fry for a minute or so until starting to soften. Add the garlic, tomatoes and turmeric and cook for another minute or so until it's heated through.

■ Tip the rice into the pan and stir to coat in the juices, continue to stir for another minute until well incorporated then pour in the hot stock. Simmer uncovered for 8 minutes. Add the mussels and green beans and cook for another 3-4 minutes or until the rice is cooked and the mussels are open – if it starts to look dry add a little water.

■ Meanwhile heat a frying pan or griddle until really hot. Toss the prawns and squid in a little oil and seasoning, place on the griddle and cook for a few minutes until done – the prawns will take a little longer than the squid.

■ Slice the squid into rings then add to the rice along with a good squeeze of lemon juice and the chopped parsley, season to taste and. Add the prawns and the lemon wedges and serve.

Caribbean Chicken Curry with Rice and Beans

The classic taste of sunshine when all about is cold, damp and dark. A real lift.

Serves 4
Preparation time 5 minutes
Cooking time 18 minutes

✔ 659 Kcal per serving
✔ Reduced salt
✔ Low in fat

½ tsp salt
½ tsp turmeric
½ tsp ground cumin
2 tsp mild chilli powder
1 tsp crushed dried chillies
50ml water
4 chicken breasts, skinned and cubed
2 tbsp oil

1 small onion, peeled and finely chopped
4 cm piece root ginger, finely sliced
4 garlic cloves, crushed
2 red peppers, sliced
1 small pineapple, peeled and cubed
1 large mango, peeled and cut into chunks
200ml coconut milk
Juice of 1 lime
Handful of coriander, chopped

For the rice and beans
350g long grain rice
130g can kidney beans, drained and rinsed
100ml coconut milk

■ Place the salt, turmeric, cumin, chilli powder and crumbled chillies in a small bowl, and add the water. Mix to a paste.
■ Heat the oil in a large frying pan. Stir in the ginger, garlic and red peppers, and stir-fry for 5 minutes – until the peppers have softened and just begun to colour. Add the mango and pineapple, and cook for a further minute.
■ Spoon in the spice mix and continue frying for a minute.
■ Add the chicken and pour in the coconut milk and bring to the boil. Reduce the heat and simmer for 5 minutes until the chicken is cooked through.
■ While the curry is cooking, prepare the rice and beans. Cook the rice as per pack instructions. And 5 minutes before end of cooking, add the coconut milk and beans.
■ Drain and pile the rice onto plates. Serve topped with chicken curry.

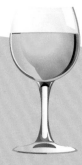

Try a delicious dry rosé from the south of France, full of summer fruit notes.

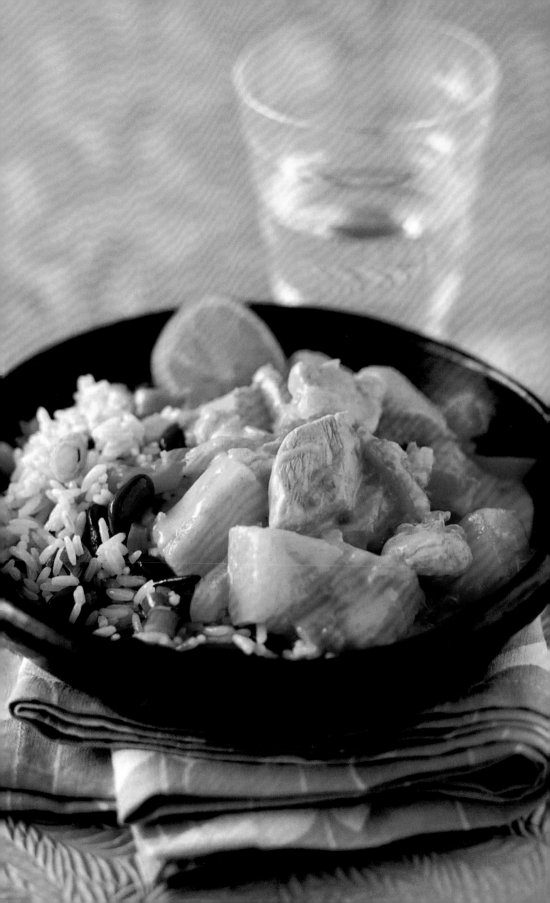

Orange Chicken with Herby Rice

Tickle the tastebuds with some zest, some garden herbs and a twist of imagination.

Serves 4
Preparation time 5 minutes
Cooking time 30 minutes

✔ 439 Kcal per serving
✔ Low in fat

4 tbsp plain flour
Salt and black pepper
2 tbsp sunflower oil
250g chicken breast fillets, cut into chunks

1 large carrot, peeled and sliced
1 large onion, peeled and chopped
2 sprigs thyme
300ml chicken stock
Zest and juice of 2 oranges, zest of 1
150ml white wine
200g white rice
2 tbsp mint
1 tbsp parsley

■ Season the flour and place 3 tablespoons in a large plastic bag. Add the chicken and shake until covered with the flour.
■ Heat half the oil in a large pan. Add the chicken and cook for about 4-5 minutes. Remove the chicken.
■ Add the remaining oil to the pan, along with the carrot and onion. Cook for 5 minutes.
■ Return the chicken to the pan with the rest of the flour, and the thyme.
■ Stir well and add the stock, orange zest, juice and wine.
■ Cook for 15 minutes. Cook the rice according to the pack instructions. Drain and stir in the parsley and mint. Serve alongside the orange chicken.

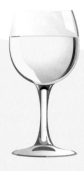

Explore the wines of the Loire in France to find a classic crisp white to complement the citrus flavours – try a minerally Muscadet or a lively Sancerre.

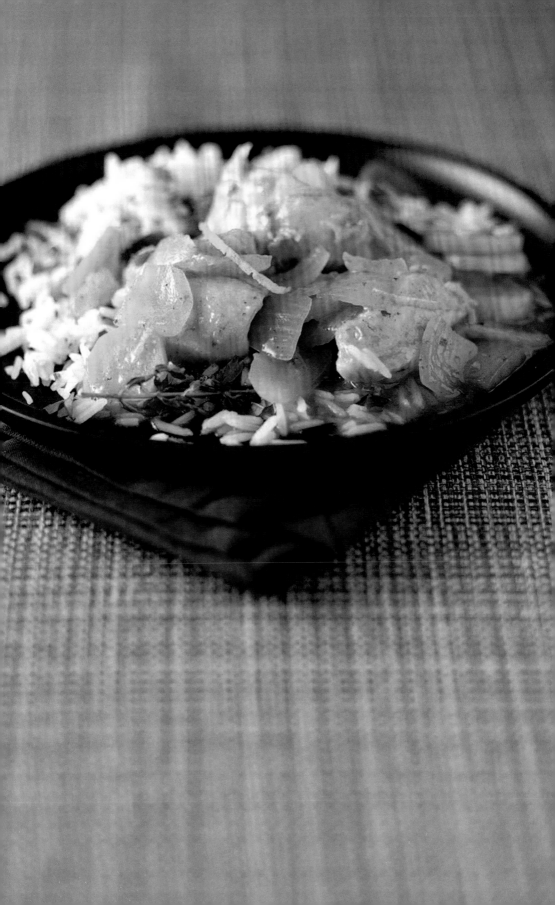

Jambalaya

So good they wrote a song about it! Just perfect for keeping out the cold.

Serves 2
Preparation time 4 minutes
Cooking time 16 minutes

✔ 410 Kcal per serving
✔ Reduced sugar

2 chicken thighs, skinless, cut into strips
2 tbsp olive oil

50g chorizo, sliced
1 tsp paprika
1 tsp turmeric
1 tsp ground ginger
1 tsp chilli flakes
100g long grain rice
55ml white wine
500ml vegetable stock
100g peas

■ Heat the oil in a large saucepan. Add the chicken and cook for 2 minutes.
■ Add the chorizo and spices and cook for 2 minutes.
■ Add the rice and stir well to coat the rice in the spices.
■ Pour in the wine and stock. Next, add the peas. Cover and leave to simmer for 10-12 minutes, or until the rice is cooked.
■ Serve immediately.

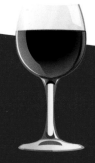

The intensity of flavours in this dish demand a big, bold fruity red, such as a Shiraz from Australia. Strong spicy peppery flavours, loads of dark fruit and a big oaky finish all add up to lots of flavour.

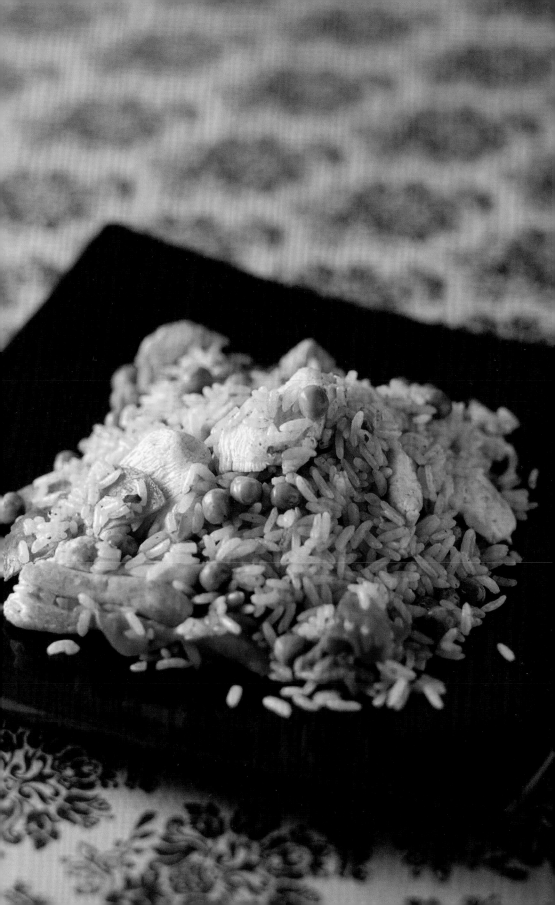

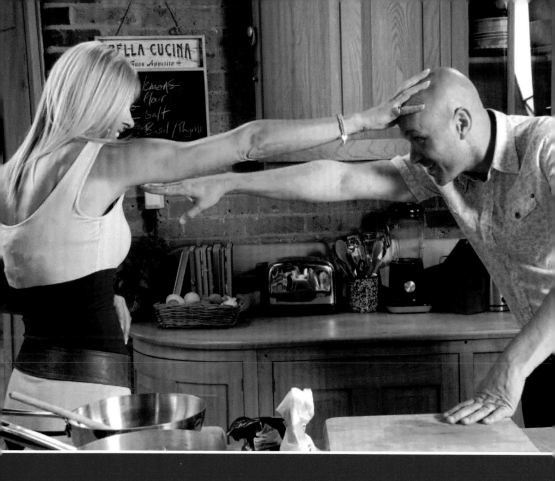

"I was brought up in the West County and so I love fish. I'm a supper person and like to make dinner for the 5000."

Sharron Davies

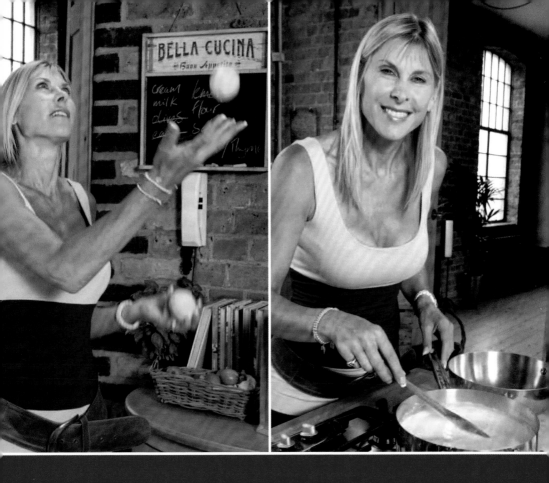

Sharron is Britain's most successful all round swimmer. At 13, she was the youngest member of the 1976 Olympic team in Montreal, and in 1992 the oldest member of the squad at the Barcelona Games.

Simon had a theory that men make better swimmers than women because men have longer arms and stronger chests, but Sharron soon put him right. Not only are her arms longer than his, but she assured him that good swimming is all in the leg work!

As for whether women make better cooks, all we can say is that you never forget your mum's cooking. Sharron's is a hearty, homely, tasty recipe adaptable to whatever fish or veg you might have at home, and you can also make it in advance and freeze it. Her kids love it. 'There are never any leftovers, so I must be doing something right,' she says.

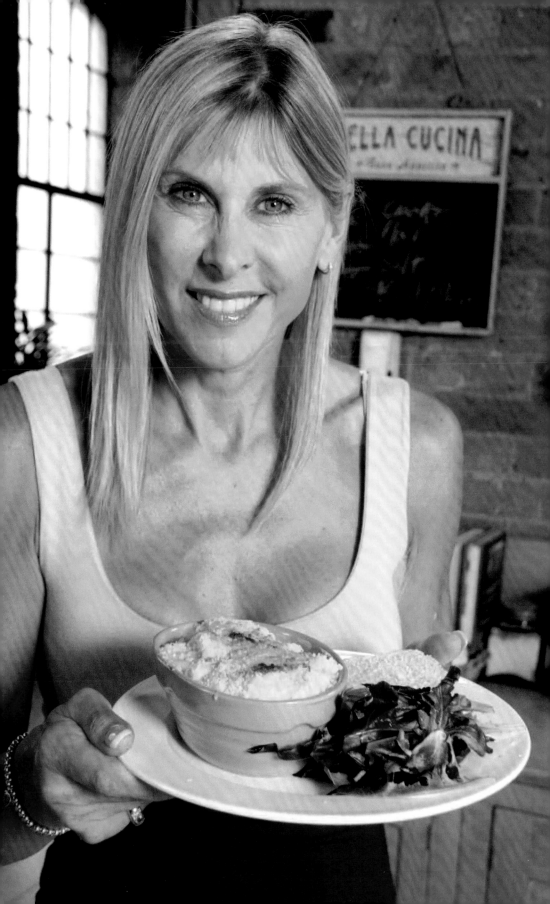

Sharron Davies – Fish Pie

This fish pie is one of Sharron's family's favourites, and she finds that it is a good way to get her three children eating more vegetables.

Serves 6
Preparation time 10 minutes
Cooking time 30 minutes

✔ 493 Kcal per serving

500g firm white fish such as cod or haddock (or a mixture) skin removed
500ml milk
75g butter
3 bay leaves

250g prawns, shelled and deveined
6 scallops, sliced (optional)
A handful of peas and sweetcorn (frozen is fine)
50g plain flour
100g cheddar cheese, grated
50g breadcrumbs
1 clove of garlic, crushed
1kg floury potatoes
Sea salt and freshly ground black pepper

■ Peel and quarter the potatoes, boil in salted water for 10 minutes or until cooked, then drain and keep warm.

■ Meanwhile preheat the oven to 200°C/400°F/Gas Mark 6. Pour the milk into a wide-bottomed pan, add a third of the butter and the bay leaves, bring to a gentle boil, then carefully lower in the fish. Simmer for 5 minutes or until the fish is just cooked through. Lift the fish onto a plate and strain the milk.

■ Melt half of the remaining butter in a pan, stir in the flour and cook for 1 min over moderate heat. Take off the heat, pour in a little of the warm poaching milk, then stir until blended. Continue to add the milk gradually, mixing well until you have a smooth sauce. Return to the heat, bring to a slow boil and cook for a further few minutes, stirring continually – if too thick add a little more milk. Remove from the heat, stir in the fish, prawns and scallops, corn and peas then season to taste with salt and pepper, spoon this mixture either into individual dishes or one large dish.

■ Mash the potatoes with the remaining butter and the grated garlic, season well. Top the pie with a layer of cheese then the potato mixture, finally add a little more cheese and sprinkle over the breadcrumbs. Bake for 15-20 minutes at 200c or until golden and bubbling on top.

■ Serve with a garden salad and crusty bread.

Mediterranean Tuna

This dish has all the flavours we associate with Italy and it looks as good as it tastes.

Serves 4
Preparation time 8 minutes
Cooking time 26 minutes

✔ 283 Kcal per serving

2 tbsp olive oil
1 onion, finely chopped
2 garlic cloves, finely chopped
1 stick of celery, chopped

450g fresh tomatoes, chopped
1 tbsp tomato purée
Pinch of sugar
4 tuna steaks
50g black olives, pitted and sliced
1 tbsp pine nuts
1 tbsp sultanas
4 tbsp capers, drained
Salt and black pepper
Parsley, to garnish

■ Heat half the oil in a saucepan, add the onion, garlic and celery and cook until just beginning to soften.
■ Add the tomatoes, tomato puree, sugar, salt and black pepper, mix well then partially cover and simmer for about 20 minutes, stirring from time to time.
■ Heat the remaining oil in a large frying pan, add the fish and pan fry for 4-5 minutes on each side until lightly browned.
■ Meanwhile, add the capers, olives, sultanas and pine nuts and simmer for 2 minutes, stirring.
■ Spoon the tomato sauce in to four bowls and top with the tuna.
■ Garnish with the parsley and serve.

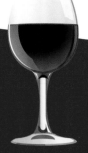

Pair with a ripe, raspberry flavoured Tempranillo from Spain, with a hint of spice and a touch of oak to complement the black olives.

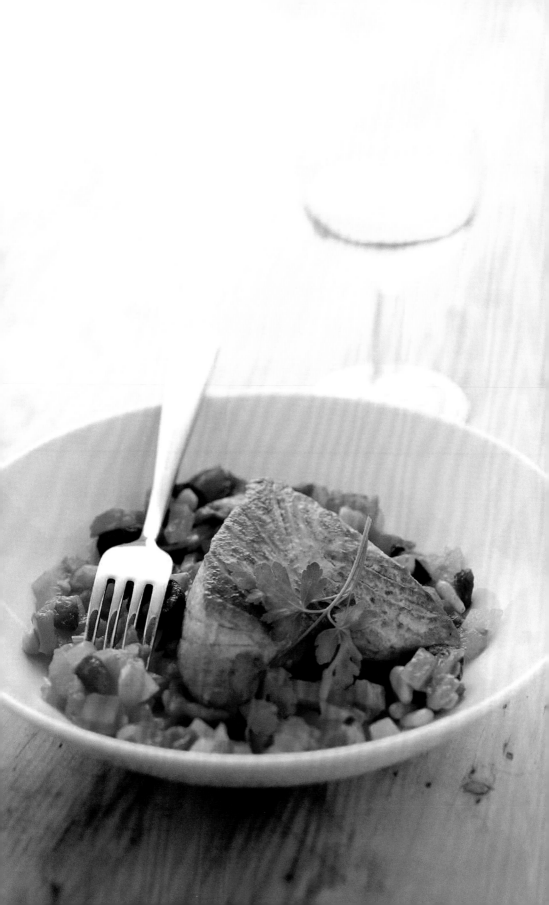

All-in-One Fish Bake

A fabulous advert for one-pot cooking with some real substance on the plate.

Serves 4
Preparation time 6 minutes
Cooking time 36 minutes

✔ 219 Kcal per serving
✔ Low in fat
✔ Low in sugar

4 x 175g thick portions cod or haddock
2 courgettes, sliced
2 tbsp olive oil
12 cherry tomatoes
125g green beans, topped and tailed
8 black olives, pitted
Salt and black pepper

- Preheat the oven to 200°C/400°F/Gas Mark 6.
- Place the fish and courgettes into a large roasting tray and drizzle with half the oil.
- Roast for 5 minutes.
- Add the cherry tomatoes, green beans and olives. Season and drizzle with the remaining oil.
- Roast for a further 15 minutes or until the fish is cooked and vegetables slightly softened. Serve immediately.

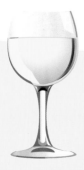

This demands the crisp perfection of a Chablis. Remarkably elegant citrus flavours with a lingering finish, from a small town in northern France.

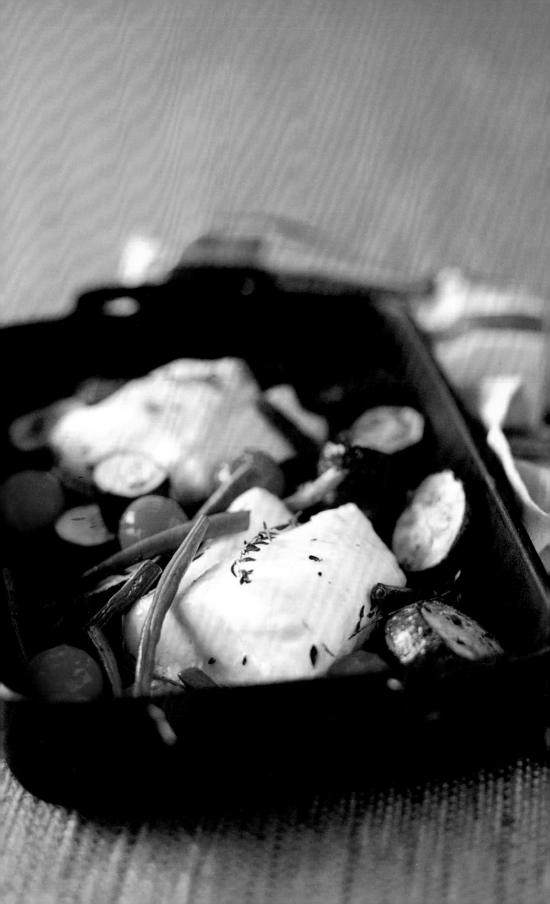

Roasted Vegetable Pizza

If time is short use ready-roasted peppers and blanch the courgettes before adding to the pizza.

Serves 4
Preparation time 10 minutes
Cooking time 35 minutes

✔ 212 Kcal per serving

1 red pepper, deseeded and cut into chunks
1 green pepper, deseeded and cut into chunks

1 yellow pepper, deseeded and cut into chunks
1 courgette, sliced
1 tbsp olive oil
1 ready-made pizza base
5 tbsp ready-made tomato pasta sauce
5 black olives, stoned and sliced
50g mozzarella cheese

■ Preheat the oven to 220˚C/425˚F/Gas Mark 7.
■ Place the vegetables on a baking tray, drizzle with the oil and toss until evenly covered. Bake in the oven for 20 minutes.
■ Spread the pizza base with the tomato sauce.
■ Top with the roasted vegetables and olives.
■ Rip the mozzarella into pieces and place over the vegetables. Bake the pizza in the oven for 10-15 minutes or until the cheese is just melted.

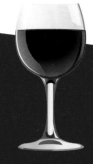

Try with a big, plummy Carmenere from Chile. This grape produces intense colour, green pepper and spice flavours rounded off with a touch of cocoa.

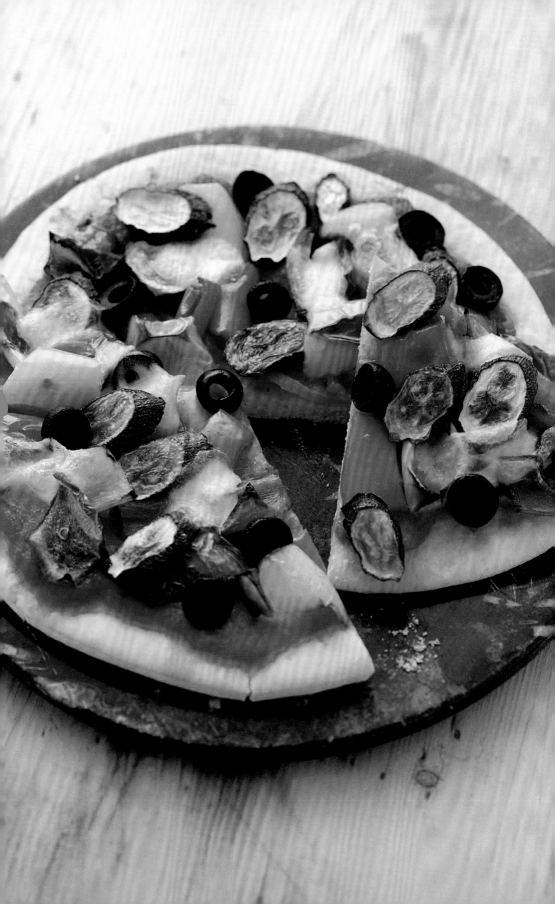

Moroccan Vegetable Stew with Couscous

A taste of the Medina brought to a stove near you – tantalising and guilt-free.

Serves 4
Preparation time 8 minutes
Cooking time 32 minutes

✔ 401 Kcal per serving
✔ Low in fat

1 small cauliflower, divided into florets
1 tbsp olive oil
1 medium onion, chopped
3 cloves garlic, crushed
1 tsp turmeric
1 tsp ground ginger
1 tsp paprika

½ tsp ground cinnamon
½ tsp chilli powder
2 x 400g cans chopped tomatoes
1 red pepper, deseeded and thinly sliced
1 carrot, sliced
50g stoned prunes, halved
150ml vegetable stock
1 cinnamon stick
175g runner beans, cut diagonally
1 × 410g can chickpeas, drained
Salt and freshly ground black pepper
250g couscous
2 tbsp fresh parsley, chopped

■ Heat the oil in a pan, add the onion and garlic and cook for 5 minutes.
■ Stir in the spices and add in the tomatoes, red pepper, carrots, prunes and stock. Cover and cook for 15 minutes.
■ Place the cauliflower florets to blanch in boiling water for 3 minutes and drain.
■ Stir in cauliflower florets, beans, chick peas and seasoning into the tomato mix and cook for a further 5 minutes.
■ Make the couscous as per the pack instructions. Stir in the parsley and serve with the stew.

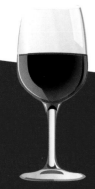

Pair this spicy stew with a young Beaujolais, made from the Gamay grape. Bright and jammy, with redcurrant fruit and a soft mellow finish.

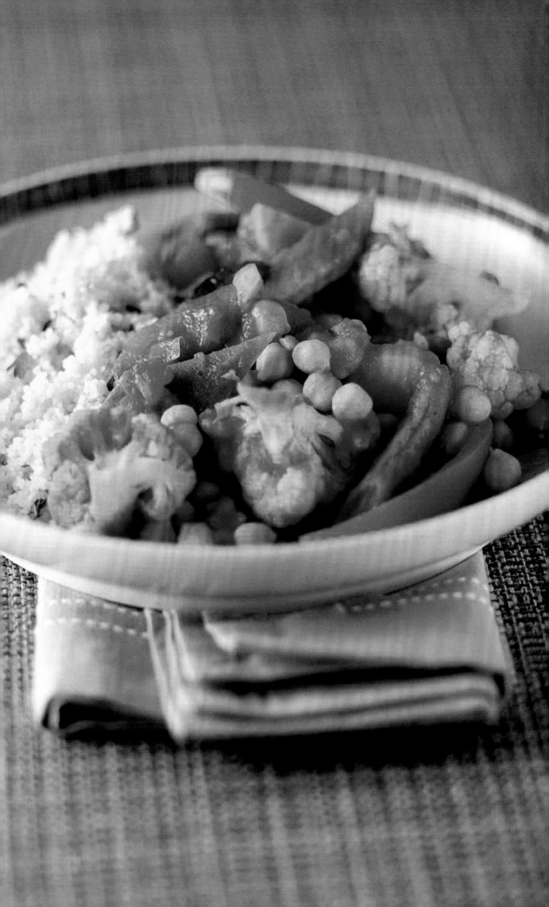

Pancetta-Topped Crushed New Potatoes

A simply flavoured and tasty dish. New potatoes are best bought as fresh as possible to make the most of their flavour.

Serves 2
Preparation time 5 minutes
Cooking time 22 minutes

✔ 398 Kcal per serving
✔ Low in sugar

500g baby new potatoes, washed and scrubbed but not peeled

1 tsp olive oil
2 cloves garlic, crushed
140g pancetta
4 spring onions, finely sliced
1 tbsp fresh flat-leaf parsley, chopped
1 tbsp fresh thyme, chopped
Plenty of freshly ground black pepper

■ Place the potatoes in a large saucepan and cover with cold water. Bring them to the boil and cook for 15 minutes. Drain, return to the pan and keep warm.
■ Heat the olive oil in a large frying pan and cook the garlic and pancetta for 6-7 minutes until they are golden.
■ Using a potato masher, lightly crush the potatoes to give them a coarse texture.
■ Stir the pancetta and parsley into the potatoes and top with the thyme and spring onion and plenty of black pepper.

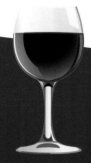

Try a classic Chianti Classico from Tuscany to complement the pancetta, full of smoky, cherry flavours with a smooth, lingering taste.

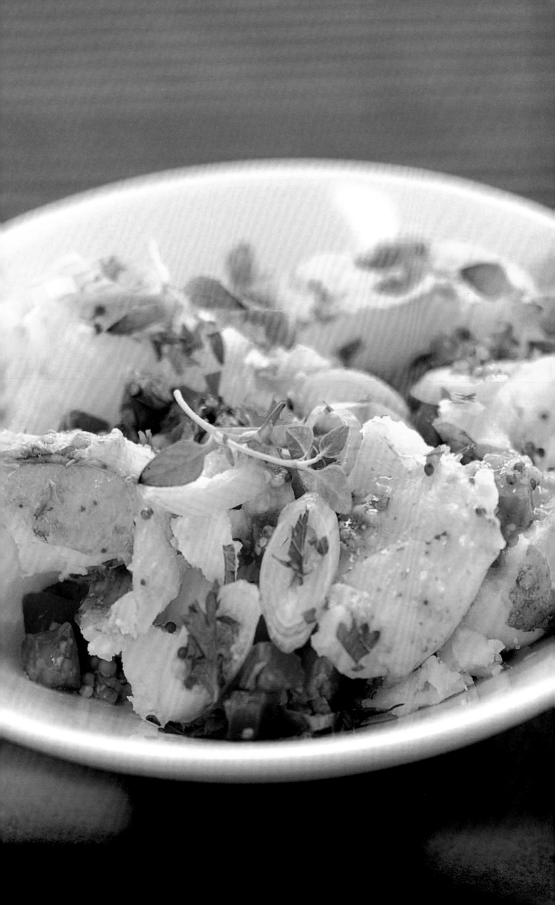

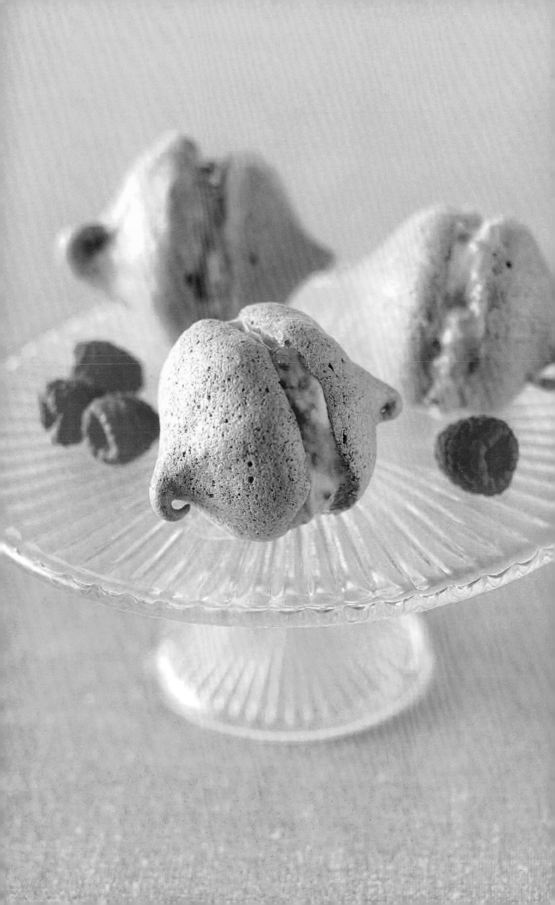

Puddings

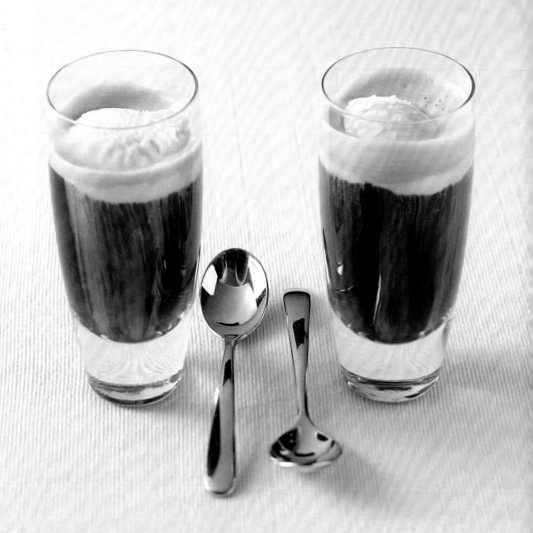

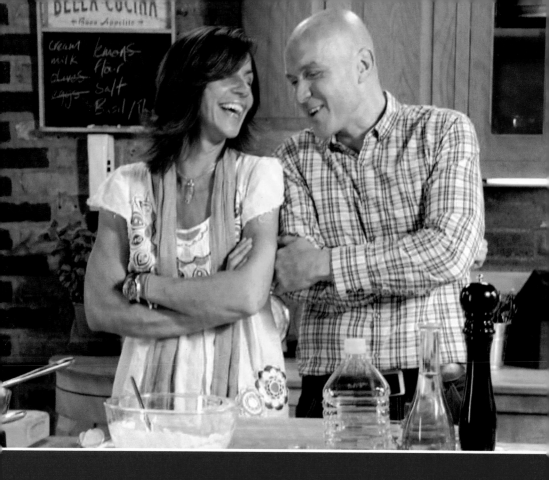

"Loukoumades are Greek honey doughnuts. I used to make them with my Yaya (grandmother) every time I stayed with her for the summer holidays."

Julia Bradbury

146

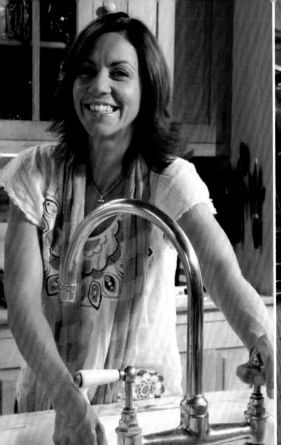
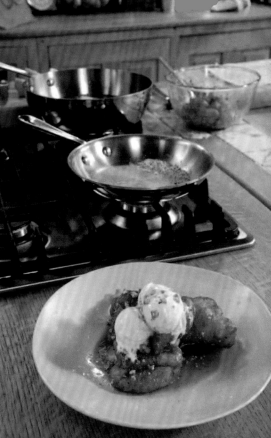

Reporting rural issues every Sunday on the BBC programme Countryfile, or striding over the Lakeland Fells in the BBC4 series Wainwright Walks, Julia seems as English as summer pudding. But while her Dad's British, her mum is Greek, and both are really good cooks. It's a good job Julia does all that energetic country walking, because this family recipe for Greek doughnuts is not low in calories!

Loukoumades have always been a popular sweet in Greece, especially as a mid-morning snack in cafes and pastry shops. They are the oldest recorded European pastry and were awarded to the victors in the ancient Olympic games. Award them to your guests, served with a scoop of ice cream, and you'll be a winner too!

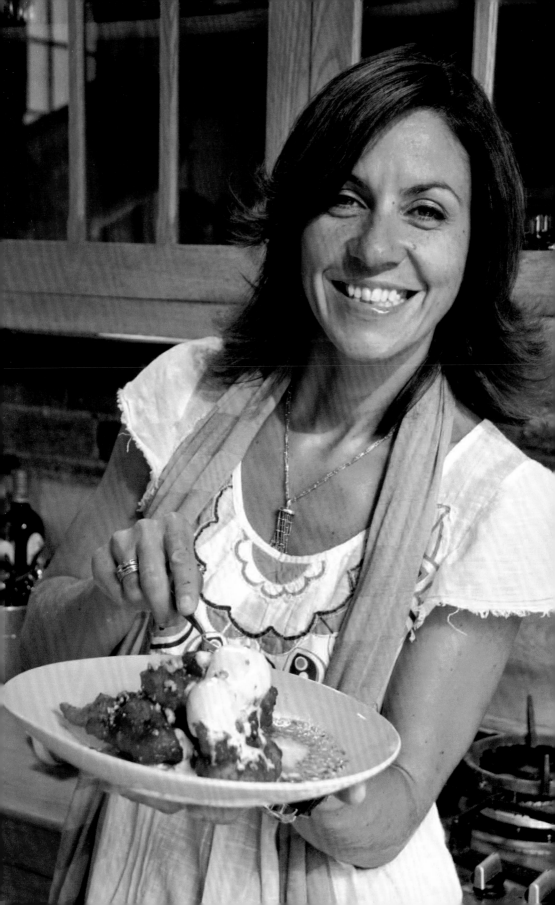

Julia Bradbury – Loukoumades (Greek Honey Balls or Puffs)

These doughnuts are sometimes also sprinkled with chopped nuts, especially walnuts, or sesame seeds, and are best eaten on the same day as they are made.

Makes 15 doughnuts
Preparation time 30-45 minutes
Cooking time 6 minutes

✔ 148 Kcal per doughnut

250g plain flour
1 level tsp salt
140ml clear Greek honey
140ml lukewarm water

1 level tsp dried yeast
70ml lukewarm water
Deep fat for frying
Strained juice of ½ lemon
¼ level tsp cinnamon
or more to taste
1 tbsp water
A handful of pistachios, crushed
and toasted
Vanilla ice cream to serve

■ Sift flour and salt into a warmed bowl. Stir 1 teaspoon honey into ¼ pint lukewarm water, sprinkle on dry yeast. Leave in a warm place for 10 minutes until frothy.
■ Stir yeast mixture into sifted ingredients, mix to a soft dough with ⅛ pint water. Cover and leave in a warm place until doubled in size. Heat the fat till a slight haze appears. Drop teaspoons of the mixture in to the hot fat and cook for 4-5 minutes till well puffed and golden brown. Drain well on soft, kitchen paper, keep hot.
■ Pour remaining honey into a small saucepan, stir in lemon juice, cinnamon and water. Bring to the boil, boil for approximately 5 minutes till thick and syrupy. Sprinkle the honey balls with extra cinnamon, pour honey sauce over and serve with the pistachios and ice cream.

Truffles

An utter indulgence for the most special of seasons, but keep a couple back for later...

Serves 10-12
Preparation time 10 minutes
Cooking time 10 minutes (30 to chill)

✔ 277 Kcal per serving
✔ Low in salt

200g good quality dark chocolate, chopped

¼ tsp cardamom seeds, taken from pods
280ml double cream
2 tbsp instant coffee
4 tbsp caster sugar
Cocoa powder
Grated white chocolate

■ Put the chocolate in a large bowl and set over a pan of just-boiled water to melt. Crush the cardamom seeds as finely as possible in a pestle and mortar.
■ Heat the cream, coffee and sugar in a pan, stirring, until the cream is just boiling. Add to the chocolate bowl. Add the cardamom and stir until all the ingredients are evenly blended.
■ Remove the bowl from the pan. Cover the surface of the chocolate mix directly with plastic wrap. Leave to cool at room temperature for about an hour.
■ When firm enough to handle line a baking tray with greaseproof paper.
■ Take a heaped teaspoon of truffle mixture and with cold hands roll into a ball. Place on the baking tray. Chill the truffles for 30 minutes.
■ Roll some truffles in the grated white chocolate and some in the cocoa powder.

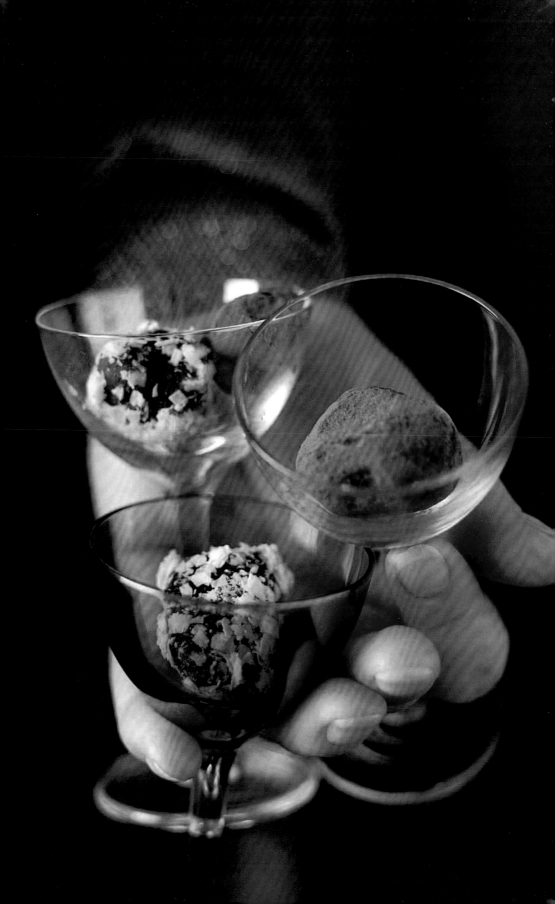

Berry Syllabub Trifle

The classic British dessert, boosted and laden with fruit, cream and custard.

Makes 6
Preparation time 14 minutes
Cooking time 6 minutes

✔ 730 Kcal per serving
✔ Low in salt

For the custard
4 medium-sized egg yolks
1 tbsp cornflour
1 tsp vanilla extract
75g caster sugar
568ml full-cream milk

For the trifle
12 ratafia biscuits
4-6 tbsp Grand Marnier or orange juice
200g fresh or defrosted raspberries and or blueberries

For the syllabub
284ml double cream
200ml crème fraiche
50g caster sugar
100ml dry white wine, chilled
Finely grated zest of 1 lemon
Additional berries, to decorate

■ To make the custard whisk the egg yolks in a bowl with the cornflour, vanilla, sugar and 2 tablespoons milk. Bring the remaining milk to the boil in a pan, then pour over the egg mixture slowly, whisking all the time. Return to the pan and cook gently, stirring, until thick enough to coat the back of a wooden spoon.
■ Cover the surface of the custard with clingfilm to prevent a skin forming. Leave to cool.
■ Place the ratafia biscuits in the bottom of 6 tall glasses and soak with the Grand Marnier or orange juice. Top with berries.
■ Make the syllabub by whisking the cream and crème fraiche, sugar, wine and lemon zest together until the mix just holds its shape. Spoon the cold custard over the ratafia, then top with the remaining berries and then spoon over the syllabub. Chill for 3-4 hours. Decorate with some remaining berries.

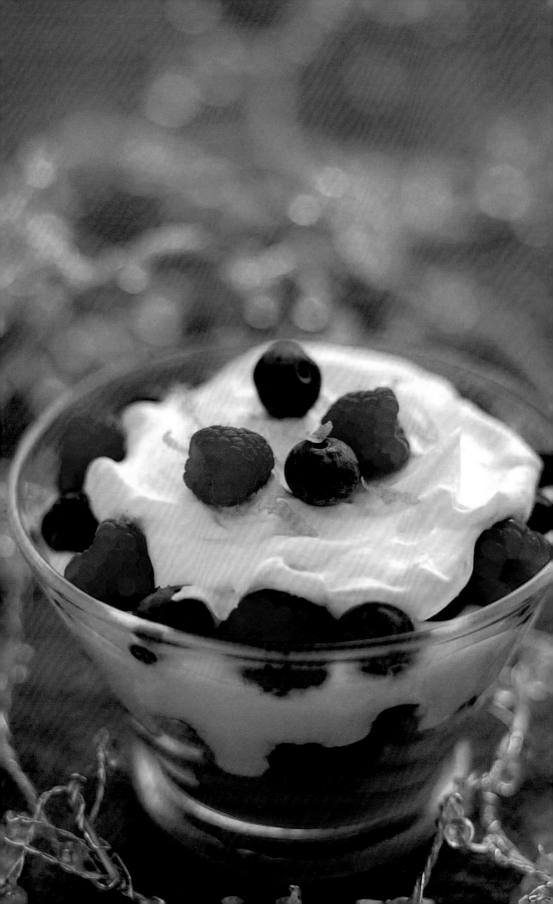

Chocolate Log

No yuletide season is complete without a slab of chocolatey indulgence.

Serves 6
Preparation time 14 minutes
Cooking time 6 minutes

✔ 675 Kcal per serving

6 large eggs, separated
150g golden caster sugar

50g cocoa powder

For the filling
225g 70% cocoa plain chocolate
2 eggs, separated
225ml thick brandy or
Cointreau cream
1 Cadbury's Flake, crumbled

■ Preheat the oven to 180 °C/350 °F/Gas Mark 4. Line the base and sides of a tin 29 x 18 cm with baking parchment.
■ For the filling, break the chocolate into a bowl with 2 tablespoons water. Melt the chocolate slowly is a bowl over a pan of water. When melted, remove from the heat and beat until smooth. Beat the egg yolks and add to the chocolate. Leave to cool.
■ In a clean dry bowl, whisk the egg whites, until stiff and fold into the chocolate mixture. Leave to cool. If the mixture becomes too hard – just heat gently for 30 seconds.
■ For the cake, place the yolks in a bowl and whisk until they thicken. Add the sugar and continue to whisk until the mixture is slightly thicker and lighten in colour. Don't let it get too thick. Stir in the cocoa powder.
■ In a clean dry bowl, whisk the egg whites to a soft peak and fold into the chocolate mixture. Pour the mixture into the prepared tin and bake for 20-25 minutes until springy. Leave the cake in the tin to cool.
■ Dust a sheet of baking parchment with icing sugar and carefully turn the cake out onto the paper – the lining paper will be facing upwards. Peel away the paper. Spread the chocolate filling over the cake. Fold the crumbled Flake into the cream and spread over the filling. Roll the cake into a log shape. Dust with icing sugar, cocoa powder and serve.

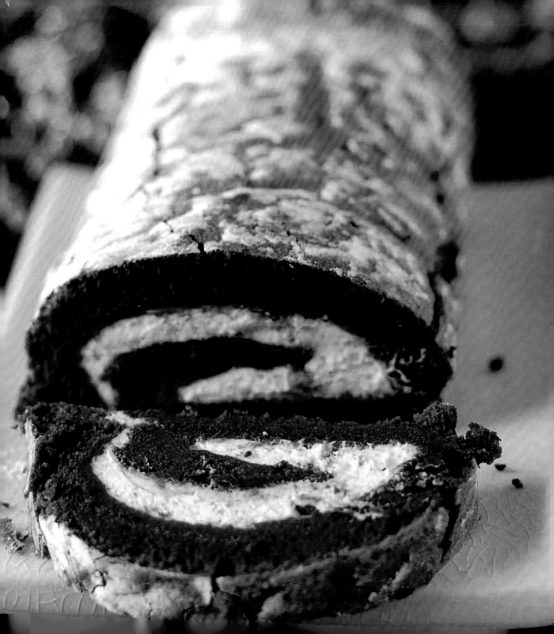

Sparkling Blueberry Jellies

These refreshing jelly puddings look impressive and can be made in advance – so they are ideal for serving to guests at a dinner party.

Makes 4
Preparation time 5 minutes
Cooking time 22 minutes

✔ 77 Kcal per serving
✔ Reduced salt

150ml sparkling white wine
200ml water
150ml strawberry and blueberry squash
1 sachet (approx 11g) powdered gelatine
55g blueberries, washed
Strawberries, to garnish

■ Take 5 tablespoons out of the 200ml water and pour into a small saucepan. Sprinkle the gelatine over the top, taking care that it is completely absorbed by the liquid and that there are no dry patches – it should look sponge-like. Avoid stirring if possible and set aside for at least 5 minutes.

■ Put the pan over a low heat, allow the gelatine to melt without boiling, the liquid should be clear.

■ Place the remaining water, wine and squash into a pan and heat for 1 minute or until hot, but not boiling. Stir the dissolved gelatine into the mixture and leave to stand for 15 minutes to cool.

■ Place a few blueberries into four glasses. Pour the jelly into the glasses and chill. Serve topped with half a strawberry.

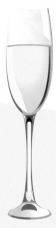

What better than a lightly sparkling orange blossom and lemon Asti from Italy to lift the bubbles in this dessert?

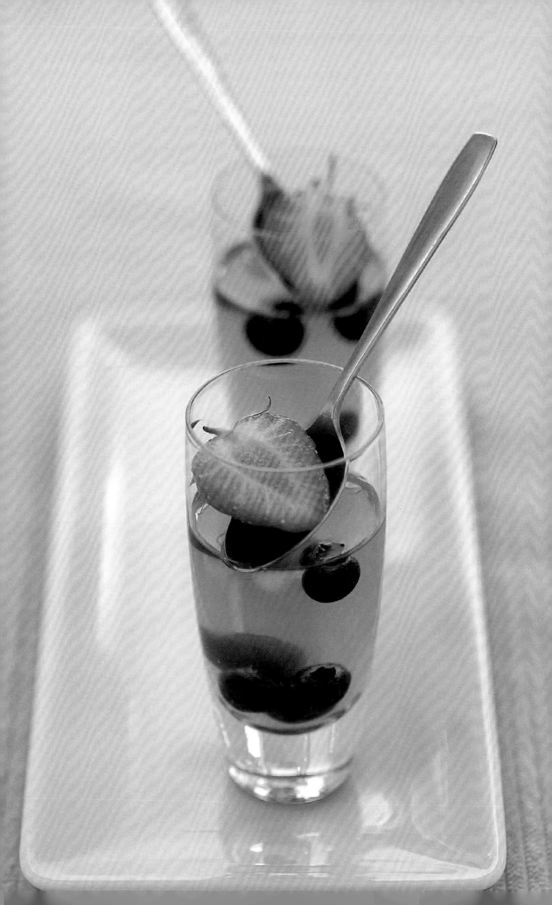

Chocolate Meringues

These fluffy meringues will give you the sweet fix you're after, but you won't feel so guilty.

Makes 8
Preparation time 10 minutes
Cooking time 20 minutes

✔ 137 Kcal per serving
✔ Reduced salt
✔ Low in fat

4 egg whites
200g caster sugar
20g cocoa powder, sieved
2 tsp white wine vinegar
1 tsp cornflour
5 tbsp low-fat natural fromage frais
200g raspberries, crushed

■ Preheat the oven to 140 °C/275 °F/Gas Mark 1. Line a baking sheet with non-stick baking parchment.
■ Make sure the bowl and whisk are completely clean and dry. Whisk the egg whites until stiff but not dry.
■ Mix together the caster sugar and cocoa powder, then whisk a tablespoon of the powdery mixture at a time, into the egg whites.
■ Whisk until the mixture is thick and glossy, then fold in the vinegar and cornflour.
■ Pipe or spoon the mixture into 16 mounds onto the baking sheet. Bake for about 1½ hours or until the meringue is firm and crisp.
■ When ready to serve. Mix together the fromage frais and raspberries and spoon between two meringues.

See picture on page 144

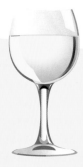

Chocolate is always a challenge for wine, but a rich, sticky Muscat from the south of France will be up to the task.

Affogate al caffe

This bitter sweet dessert is so quick to make, but should also be eaten immediately.

Serves 2
Preparation time 5 minutes
Cooking time 3 minutes

✔ 193 Kcal per serving

✔ Reduced salt
✔ Low in fat

2 freshly made espresso coffee
4 scoops low-fat light vanilla ice cream

■ Make the coffee, using an espresso maker if you have one. It must be really strong and hot.
■ Scoop 2 neat balls of ice-cold vanilla ice cream into each of 2 bowls.
■ Pour the espresso over and around the ice cream and serve and eat at once – do not delay or the ice cream will melt into the coffee.

See picture on page 145

Index